JACK THE RIPPER

PAUL BEGG & JOHN BENNETT

JACK THE RIPPER
THE FORGOTTEN VICTIMS

YALE UNIVERSITY PRESS
NEW HAVEN AND LONDON

For information about this and other Yale University Press publications, please contact:
U.S. Office: sales.press@yale.edu   www.yalebooks.com
Europe Office: sales @yaleup.co.uk   www.yalebooks.co.uk

Set in Adobe Caslon Pro by IDSUK (DataConnection) Ltd
Printed in Great Britain by TJ International Ltd, Padstow, Cornwall

Library of Congress Cataloging-in-Publication Data

Begg, Paul.
   Jack the Ripper : the forgotten victims / by Paul Begg and John Bennett.
      pages cm
   Includes bibliographical references and index.
   ISBN 978-0-300-11720-2 (alk. paper)
   1. Jack, the Ripper. 2. Serial murders—England—London—History—19th century.
3. Whitechapel (London, England)—History. 4. Victims of crimes—England—London—
History—19th century. I. Bennett, John, 1968– II. Title.
   HV6535.G6L6173 2014
   364.152'32092—dc23   2013041140

A catalogue record for this book is available from the British Library.

10 9 8 7 6 5 4 3 2 1

For
Adam Wood
for his true friendship and help beyond the call of duty
and for
Judy, Siobán and Cameron
and
Laura

Contents

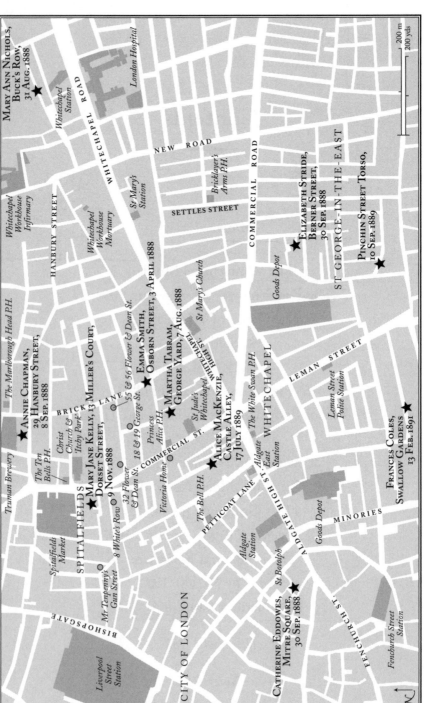

Whitechapel, c. 1888.

Introduction

———

THE SERIES OF GRISLY MURDERS THAT CONVULSED LONDON'S East End in 1888 and 1889 was in many ways a product of the extraordinary times. By the 1880s, writers, such as Charles Dickens and Guy de Maupassant, journalists and social commentators had all revealed conditions in Whitechapel, Spitalfields and Bethnal Green to be as far removed from London's perceived wealth and splendour as it was possible to imagine. The East End was a byword for poverty, squalor, hardship, dirt, decay, danger and vice. Its filthy denizens seemed to lack both morals and decency.

The advent of the popular pastime of 'slumming', when privileged young men ventured into the East End to experience the thrill of the music hall, the beer-shop and the common prostitute, meant that it also became something of a sideshow attraction – to be sampled cautiously and not for too long.

But the wary regard for the East End extended further than just the taboo experiences on offer in its alleyways: with unionism and left-wing ideology on the rise, it became a threat politically. It was home to the angry unemployed, the unpredictable anarchist, the mysterious foreigner and the socialist agitator – all the elements that threatened to rise up and shatter London's smug complacency. The East End embodied the fears of the late-nineteenth-century Londoner as no other place on earth could.

In a sense, the Whitechapel murders punctured what was effectively a growing abscess, revealing the pus and poison within to an appalled world. As one woman after another was murdered and horribly mutilated, the details that emerged of the grim lives they had led shocked many at home and abroad.

A murder has more than one victim. Of course the dead person's family, friends and acquaintances are affected by it; but the ripples extend further, to touch the lives of people who had never met the person, or even heard of them. A murder in the neighbourhood makes people uncomfortable and, more to the point, scared. They look at strangers differently. It can make them mistrustful – uncertain whether a smile is genuine or masks a killer. It can play on their deepest fears.

In 1888, Mary Burridge was 50 years old. As far as anyone knows, she had led a quiet, uneventful life selling mops from her home at 132 Blackfriars Road in Southwark. Perhaps her one pleasure in life was each day to purchase a copy of *The Star* newspaper. She bought one as usual on the afternoon of 8 September. As she stood in her doorway, her eyes scanned the columns of dense print before settling on a report of a gruesome murder in Hanbury Street, Spitalfields. It was a particularly lurid piece of prose, which claimed that a ghoul-like figure – half beast, half man – was relentlessly stalking victims in the East End. The police were helpless, claimed the report, and despaired of catching the monster – or even of obtaining a single clue as to his identity. Mrs Burridge returned indoors much affected by her reading. In her kitchen, she had a fit and slipped into unconsciousness. She rallied briefly a day or two later, but then had a relapse and died.[1]

Another woman who was greatly affected by reports of the murders then being committed in the East End was Mrs Elizabeth Sodo.[2] Also aged 50, she was the wife of a Spitalfields silk weaver and lived at 65 Hanbury Street. She had suffered from a form of depression for some time and was very distressed by the regular coverage of the Whitechapel murders. It all became too much for her on 11 October: under the pretence of leaving the house on an errand, Mrs Sodo hanged herself in the stairwell. She left behind an 8-year-old daughter and a widower, John, who was to die almost a year to the day later.

Further afield, Fanny Hill lived at 123 Pacific Street, Brooklyn, New York. She received regular visits from both her father and her daughter's former boyfriend – notwithstanding that both of those gentlemen were dead. But Mrs Hill had the support of a loving family, and appears to have enjoyed an otherwise normal and contented life. That is, until she became increasingly convinced that Jack the Ripper had crossed the Atlantic and was now chasing her. Her family had managed to cope with the delusional visits from the dead, but Jack the Ripper was a step too far. In June 1889, they brought the 45-year-old Fanny before the Charities Department and had her confined to the county asylum.[3]

Perhaps Mary Burridge would have had a fit anyway, and news of the Jack the Ripper murder had nothing to do with bringing it on. Perhaps Elizabeth Sodo's suicide was inevitable, and maybe Fanny Hill's precarious mental state would eventually have proved too much for her family, even without Jack the Ripper entering her delusions. Perhaps.

Jack the Ripper murdered a number of women in 1888 (the exact figure is not known), but Mary Burridge, Elizabeth Sodo and Fanny Hill were also his victims. Not prey to his knife, but his victims nevertheless.

This book is about several women who were murdered before, during and after 1888. Some are confidently counted among Jack the Ripper's victims; others are not generally thought to have been killed by him (though they could have been); and a third group were assuredly not his victims at all, but their killers may have been inspired by him. However, the media and street gossip certainly ensured that, at the time of their murder, the name 'Jack the Ripper' was used in connection with them.

It is often asserted that Mary Ann Nichols, Annie Chapman, Elizabeth Stride, Catherine Eddowes and Mary Kelly were the 'true' or 'official' victims of Jack the Ripper. Their names are well known and register in the collective consciousness. But the names of some of the other unfortunate women – victims all – are often forgotten. In recent years, though, other murders of the time have attracted growing and deserved interest from researchers and historians, forcing a reappraisal of which crimes the Ripper may actually have committed. As a result, the definition of a 'Ripper victim' is now, like a 'Ripper suspect', fluid. In the words of Charles Fort, that noted chronicler of the unusual, 'one measures a circle, starting anywhere'.[4]

The fact that these other murders were linked to the Whitechapel fiend – even if sometimes only briefly – is evidence of the fear that gripped the East End streets (and beyond) and of the 'knee-jerk' reactions inspired by that fear whenever a fresh outrage was reported. The various accusations against escaped lunatics and insane doctors reveal to us a simple dread of the unknown, of the outsider. The fingers pointed at Jewish immigrants or foreign sailors on shore leave indicate an innate xenophobia that simmered only just below the surface. A combination of newspaper reporting and the rumour mill ensured that any suggestion of another Ripper atrocity would spread like wildfire. As the Annie Farmer case (Chapter 8) illustrates, the ensuing panic could be real enough, even if there was no substance to the rumours.

The Whitechapel murders present us with a challenging enigma. Theories about what happened, how and to whom are constantly changing, as people and events are established, forgotten, remembered and re-established. This is what makes the mystery so endlessly engaging. We hope this book will encourage people to look closely at the events. In doing so, they may recall the people, the many forgotten victims; not just how they died, but also – and perhaps more importantly – how they lived.

CHAPTER 1

The Whitechapel Murders

THE 1880S WERE A CRUCIAL DECADE OF THE LATE NINETEENTH century – a time of change, and perhaps an early indicator of what the following century would offer. In 1906 Winston Churchill wrote that the 1880s were 'the end of an epoch'.[1] The socialist poet, philosopher and early gay activist Edward Carpenter observed:

> It was a fascinating and enthusiastic period – preparatory, as we see now, to even greater developments in the twentieth century. The Socialist and Anarchist propaganda, the Feminist and Suffragist upheaval, the huge Trade-union growth, the Theosophic movement, the new currents in the theatrical, musical, and artistic worlds, the torrent even of change in the Religious world – all constituted so many streams and headwaters converging, as it were, to a great river.[2]

The decade followed hot on the heels of what became known as the 'Long Depression', a global recession that lasted from 1873 to 1879 and which hit Europe and North America particularly hard. This coincided with a 'Second Industrial Revolution', essentially a technical revolution, which saw rapid growth in industrial development in Western Europe, the United States and Japan, mainly centered upon scientific discoveries and new technologies (whereas its earlier incarnation had produced great leaps forward in mechanization). By the beginning of the 1880s, the United States had recovered, entering its 'Gilded Age',[3] and the ensuing decade promised great confidence and growth.[4]

The United Kingdom is often regarded as the country that was worst hit by the apparent economic downturn, and it has been said that the 'Long Depression' lasted well into the 1890s; though it can also be argued that this recession was not all it seemed, and was merely a myth generated by articulate landowners, farmers and members of the upper classes who were affected by a fall in profits and interest rates. Some contend that, statistically, there was no overall decline.[5]

At the time of Queen Victoria's accession in 1837, the national economy was largely based on agriculture. By the mid-nineteenth century, however, that had changed, as new developments in mechanized production placed an emphasis on output from the cities, rather than from rural communities. With the British Empire reigning supreme over the four corners of the globe, London, at its epicentre, had become the most influential city on earth. By the 1880s, it had also become the world's largest city, with a population that had effectively quadrupled since the beginning of the nineteenth century, when it stood at just over 1 million. This expansion was the result of a number of factors: the coming of the railways from the 1830s onward facilitated greater migration into the city, while improved sanitation led to a reduction in disease and thus in the overall mortality rate.[6] London was seen as a city where the 'streets were paved with gold', and it offered great opportunities for those who found life in the rural districts of south-east England difficult after the problems of agricultural productivity had begun to take hold. The first Industrial Revolution had shown many people that their future lay in the cities; London, with its links to world trade, its factories and its docks, was a lure to those seeking security in an uncertain age.

London thus became a city of opposites: a metropolis where the undeniably wealthy and influential held sway throughout much of the Victorian era, alongside a growing working class of industrious citizens who were by no means wealthy, and in many instances were mired in poverty. The physical growth of London in the latter half of the nineteenth century, and the improvement of transport systems, saw the development of new suburbs, such as Islington, Hampstead and Stoke Newington to the north, and Brixton, New Cross and Clapham (to name but a few) to the south, as the wealthy moved out to leafier environs, effectively abandoning the central, increasingly urbanized and ultimately industrial areas to the poorer working classes.[7]

By the 1880s, the differences within the demographics of London were becoming all too apparent, and Edward Carpenter's 'many streams and headwaters' began to manifest themselves. Winston Churchill was to write that it was a time when:

> The long dominion of the middle classes, which had begun in 1832, had come to its close and with it the almost equal reign of Liberalism. All sorts of lumbering tyrannies had been toppled over. Authority was everywhere broken. Slaves were free. Conscience was free. Trade was free. But hunger and squalor and cold were also free and the people demanded something more than liberty.[8]

Society generally was undergoing fundamental and radical changes that threatened the status quo. Predictably, the ruling classes, which had for so long enjoyed a complacent existence, blinkered to the real issues that affected the common man, became frightened. And it was in London – the 'Great Wen'[9] – that the threat was most in evidence.

On Monday, 8 February 1886, the Fair Trade League held a meeting in Trafalgar Square to advocate its policy of higher customs

tariffs as a cure for unemployment. A counter-demonstration by the
unemployed was called by the Social Democratic Federation (SDF),
an essentially Marxist organization. The SDF leaders treated their
audience to a series of inflammatory anti-capitalist speeches, declaring
that 'there must be a revolution to alter the state of things' and claiming
that at the next meeting they would 'sack the bakers' shops in the west
of London. They had better die fighting than die starving'.[10] The
crowd, well and truly whipped up into an anti-capitalist frenzy, was
then led by the SDF on a march along Pall Mall, which encouraged
jeering from the occupants of the wealthy gentlemen's clubs in the
area. Provoked, the crowd began throwing stones at club windows
and, in a marked escalation, turned into Piccadilly and South Audley
Street, where shopfronts were smashed and premises looted. The
rioting reached Oxford Street before the police regained control of the
situation. The handling of the riots exposed the longstanding inade-
quacy of Metropolitan Police Chief Commissioner Sir Edmund
Henderson, who resigned in consequence.[11]

After these disturbances, known by some as 'Black Monday',
Trafalgar Square became the venue of choice for political protest.
Making their presence felt were the destitute unemployed who
camped, symbolically, in the square, further reinforcing associations
with the downtrodden. By 1887, there were great concerns about
public order in the square and Home Secretary Henry Matthews was
moved to consider the possibility of banning such demonstrations,
owing to the problems they caused and the cost to ratepayers.[12] But
this was not only Matthews' problem: it was also of concern to
Charles Warren, Henderson's successor as chief commissioner of the
Metropolitan Police. Warren's appointment in 1886 had originally
been met with considerable approval: *The Times* described him as
'precisely the man whom sensible Londoners would have chosen to
preside over the policing of the Metropolis'.[13] The *Pall Mall Gazette*,
while expressing its delight at the appointment, prophetically warned
that the then home secretary, Hugh Childers, should 'allow his chief

commissioner a free hand, and back him up like a man . . .'[14] Childers did so, but when Gladstone's government fell in June 1886, his successor, Henry Matthews, did not. This would become a source of constant friction between the two men. On 17 October 1887, Warren, who felt that the growing use of Trafalgar Square as a place of protest was potentially dangerous, declared a temporary ban on demonstrations there. Two days later, Matthews, concerned about the legality of such a ban, revoked it, unwittingly causing the situation to get worse.

The optimism over Charles Warren's appointment soon waned in the light of his dealings with such instances of civil unrest, the most significant being the events surrounding the Trafalgar Square demonstrations of 13 November 1887, the notorious 'Bloody Sunday'. Two days previously, the Metropolitan Radical Association had announced plans to stage a demonstration. Word quickly spread, ensuring the involvement of the Home Rule Union, assorted socialist and anarchist groups, and a strong representation of the unemployed and the SDF. Among the marchers were Annie Besant and William Morris, prime movers in the SDF, and George Bernard Shaw. In the face of such a mass protest, Charles Warren elected to put 5,000 constables on duty, with a battalion of Grenadier Guards and a regiment of Life Guards on standby. It was estimated that up to 50,000 marchers converged on Trafalgar Square, and the authorities responded with a heavy hand. This inflamed the angry mob, and considerable violence ensued. By the time order was restored, a hundred people had been sent to hospital with injuries, seventy-seven police officers were hurt and forty rioters had been arrested. Two men died and there were seventy-five complaints of police brutality. In the words of one commentator, 'much odium fell on Warren, who was indeed largely to blame; and much on the home secretary, Matthews, who was already unpopular in parliament'.[15]

It was a catastrophe as far as Warren's reputation was concerned – one from which he never really recovered. It was also to taint his tenure as chief commissioner throughout the sensational events of the following year.

It is significant that 5,000 of the protestors had marched from the East End of London. It was this downtrodden district of the gigantic, powerful, but fractious metropolis that came to embody all the fears and terrible realities that the liberal middle classes had managed for so long to sweep under the carpet. In the words of John Henry Mackay, the East End was:

> the hell of poverty. Like an enormous, black, motionless, giant kraken, the poverty of London lies there in lurking silence and encircles with its mighty tentacles the life and the wealth of the city and of the West End . . . a world in itself, separated from the West as the servant is separated from his master. Now and then one hears about it, but only as of something far off, somewhat as one hears about a foreign land inhabited by other people with other manners and customs.[16]

Even before the 1880s, the character of the East End of London had been well defined by imaginative writers such as Charles Dickens and observers like Henry Mayhew,[17] as well as through the evocative engravings of Gustave Doré.[18] To say that life was hard for some was putting it mildly.

The problems of the East End were legion. Throughout the Industrial Revolution of the early nineteenth century, it had been a magnet for migrant workers from the shires and provinces, seeking to earn a living in the factories and workshops located there by a City wary of 'noxious trades'. The economic downturn of the 1870s and beyond affected agricultural labour opportunities and helped to swell London's population. Breweries, slaughterhouses, tanneries and smithies flourished. Some, disposed to working at home or in less industrial surroundings, would settle into smaller industries like cigar manufacturing or cabinet making, matchbox assembly or tailoring – trades which had long been a feature of East End working life. The creation and subsequent growth of London's docks had seen to it that areas close to the river grew particularly quickly, as London became a hub of world trade.

It was the coming of the railways that geographically compounded the problems of inner-city life in this part of London. Warehouse walls came to tower over once-open streets, casting alleyways and small lanes in a forbidding gloom, while railway lines, perched on seemingly endless arches, cut a swathe through tight-knit neighbourhoods:

> East Londoners showed a tendency to become decivilised when their back streets were cut off from main roads by railway embankments. The police found that by experience! Savage communities in which drunken men and women fought daily in the streets were far harder to clear up if walls or water surrounded the area on three sides, leaving only one entrance.[19]

It was evident that the East End could not cope comfortably with the rapidly growing population. Fields, orchards, gardens and tenter grounds (where newly manufactured cloth was stretched and dried) had long since disappeared under new housing, crammed dangerously into the limited space available and often only accessible through small alleyways and dark passages. The average population density in London in 1888 was 50 people per acre, but in Whitechapel it was 176 – and in the Bell Lane district of Spitalfields it was 600 people per acre.[20] With so many people in one place, it was practically impossible for everyone to find work. The sheer number of people, coupled with the ravages of the long-standing recession, led to 'unemployment' (a word coined in the 1880s) becoming a condition that touched many. It is estimated that by 1888, of the

456,877 people in Tower Hamlets, over one-third were living below subsistence level and 13 per cent faced chronic want.[21]

The neighbourhoods of Whitechapel and Spitalfields became particularly notorious, especially those streets around Commercial Street, a road that had been built in the 1850s with the intention of clearing slums, as well as of extending trade routes from the London Docks. It cut through decaying, overcrowded courts and alleys, but the population thus displaced continued to cause problems by resettling close by. Thus Flower and Dean Street, Thrawl Street and Dorset Street became synonymous with the worst of London poverty, consisting of overcrowded common lodging houses which were home to the flotsam and jetsam of the transient poor.

Philanthropy was in considerable evidence: Commercial Street was home to Toynbee Hall, set up in 1884 by Canon Samuel Barnett of St Jude's, Whitechapel, to bring help, education and culture to the poor East Londoners. His wife, Henrietta, wrote thirty years later of her perception of the conditions faced by many of her husband's flock:

> Each chamber was the home of a family who sometimes owned their indescribable furniture, but in most cases the rooms were let out furnished for 8d a night. In many instances, broken windows had been repaired with paper and rags, the banisters had been used for firewood, and the paper hung from the walls which were the residence of countless vermin . . .[22]

The Salvation Army, formed by William Booth in 1865, had its genesis on the streets of Whitechapel, and Thomas Barnardo, a former medical student at the London Hospital, was moved to provide care and shelter for the destitute children of the East End in the 1880s, after seeing so much poverty. But the East End proved a resilient adversary and the problems persisted, while many of the attempted solutions either failed or were too slow in bringing about obvious change. One such attempt was the passing of the Artisans' and Labourers' Dwellings Improvement Act back in 1875:[23] the neighbourhoods around Flower and Dean Street, Goulston Street, George Yard and Wentworth Street were targeted for redevelopment. While certain areas were demolished and new construction began reasonably quickly,[24] some people suffered when (as in the Flower and Dean Street area) demolition was a long time coming and delays in rebuilding on the vacant lots allowed over-crowding and transience to continue unchecked:[25]

> Thieves, loose women, and bad characters abound, and, although the police are not subject, perhaps, to quite the same dangers as they were a few years ago, there is still reason to believe that a constable will avoid, as far as he can, this part of his beat, unless accompanied by a brother officer.[26]

One further ingredient that impacted significantly on the life of the East End during those turbulent years was mass immigration. The French Huguenots had made Spitalfields their home in the seventeenth and eighteenth centuries, and then Irish travellers fleeing the potato famine of 1845–52 had made their mark on Whitechapel. But from 1881 onwards, Jews from Eastern Europe settled in huge numbers, and it was this wave of immigrants that many felt exacerbated the existing problems.[27] London was an ideal choice for many, especially the East End, with its small, already established Jewish communities. And Whitechapel, because of its proximity to the docks and the River Thames, became the point of entry to the United Kingdom for those who disembarked at St Katharine Dock, near the Tower of London. In 1887, Charles Booth[28] put the number of Eastern European Jews in Tower Hamlets at around 45,000.[29] In 1888, he said: 'They fill whole blocks of model dwellings; they have introduced new trades as well as new habits and they live and crowd together and work and meet their fate independent of the great stream of London life surging around them.'[30]

With the unemployed barely scratching a living, these newcomers, who needed work as much as anybody else, were blamed for making an already difficult situation worse. Large numbers of unskilled and semi-skilled Jewish workers were prepared to labour long hours for low wages, effectively undercutting the indigenous workers. As these new immigrants began to descend upon specific areas of Whitechapel and Spitalfields, further resentment came from those who believed that they were responsible 'for pushing up rents by accepting overcrowded conditions, therefore forcing native East Enders to move out'.[31]

They also brought with them radical ideas about labour and politics. As we have seen, the rising tide of socialism in the wake of great social divisions had already led to the East End being labelled a place that should be feared, as though at any moment the 'great unwashed' could rise up from their slums and factories and threaten all that the comfortable middle classes held dear. Now Eastern European socialists and anarchists were adding to the volatile mixture, and for many the hub of such potential unrest was the International Working Men's Educational Club at 40 Berner Street, St George-in-the-East. Set up in 1885, it was attended by both social democrats and anarchists and was a venue for lectures on politics, economics and literature, as well as for plays, concerts and dances. Significantly, strikes, rallies and marches were also planned here, and William Morris, one of the few prominent Englishmen to sympathize with the socialists, was a regular speaker. Although largely attended by Jews, it was open to all. However it was frowned upon by more orthodox Jews, who felt that the members were unruly and showed the local Jewry in a poor light.[32]

In 1886, the club took over publication of the Yiddish newspaper *Der Arbeter Fraint* ('Worker's Friend') and set up a printing office at the rear of the building. The newspaper became a sounding board for diverse immigrant radicals and trade unionists, and at one point its popularity became a cause for concern in parliament.[33] Revolution seemed to be in the air, and this particular publication, with its strong-willed contributors and bristling editorials, appeared to be sowing the seeds of some great uprising, declaring that 'the workers must once and for all realize that they alone can free themselves from all burdens, this is through the social revolution that will eliminate all parasites who sucked their blood for centuries and saddled their yoke'.[34]

By 1888, the 'Great Wen' of London clearly had its most purulent region: the East End, a pus-filled sore, angry and fit to burst. It had attracted the attention and scrutiny of a veritable army of mostly well-to-do philanthropists, determined to rescue and even convert the fallen. They were duly accompanied by journalists, novelists, social investigators, artists and photographers intent on satisfying the curiosity of a sensation-seeking public. In the eyes of that public, unfamiliar with the general realities of a fractious locale,[35] the East End was a putrid, foul-smelling warren of slums, populated by bullies and petty thieves, wretched, bootless children and dirty, amoral women. It was a district that inspired revulsion and (at times) sympathy, yet with all its taboos, this 'alien' land was alluring and captivating.[36]

And then, on top of everything, came the Whitechapel murders – that series of unsolved East End crimes which has become associated with the almost mythical figure of Jack the Ripper.

It need scarcely be emphasized that these murders, in terms of their impact and ability to fascinate, are unparalleled in the history of crime. Over 120 years have passed since they were committed, during which time the enigmatic figure of Jack the Ripper has become the subject of innumerable books and television programmes. His development as a figure of London folklore, as the stalker in the fog, with his top hat, cloak and black bag, has seen him become the subject of musicals and operas, Hollywood horror movies, video games, novels, comic books and pop records. Every year millions of people visit Ripper-themed exhibits at the London Dungeon[37] or Madame

Tussauds, and go on guided walks of the East End streets made famous by the grisly crimes.[38] It is truly a phenomenon. But why?

There are a number of reasons, but timing must surely be high on the list. As we have just seen, the political and economic development of the East End of London meant the area was very much on people's minds at exactly the time that it became the killing ground of Jack the Ripper. One essential element in the fascination was the targeting of prostitutes: according to an official police report from October 1888, there were some 1,200 prostitutes and 62 brothels in the Whitechapel (or 'H') Division of the Metropolitan Police.[39] However, with casual, irregular prostitution a necessity for some, the number of women willing to sell themselves to make ends meet was likely to have been much higher even than that.

* * *

Developments in media and communications technologies meant that news of the crimes spread rapidly and in a multitude of ways.[40] Perhaps the most important medium was the popular press. For the avid reader in late-Victorian Britain, there were countless publications by way of which the (literate) citizen could keep up with the daily or weekly events of the time. They catered for every requirement, locality and political tendency and, helped by an increase in literacy levels, were assured of a growing readership. Some, like *The Times*, the *Daily Telegraph* and others, took a sober view of events, offering in-depth and (one would hope) reliable reporting. Others such as the *Illustrated Police News* and the *Penny Illustrated Paper* offered their readerships handsome engravings depicting often sensational events. A small number of newspapers, however, chose to use their popularity to further social and often political causes. By the autumn of 1888, two papers in particular, the *Pall Mall Gazette*[41] and *The Star*[42] had become the firebrands of what would soon be called the 'new journalism'. They helped to inflate the Whitechapel murders into an often extravagant narrative of shock and horror.

They shook their fists at the perceived inadequacies of public figures like Charles Warren and Henry Matthews, and effectively used the murders as a stick with which to beat the authorities, or as a lever to instigate change. For the 'new journalism', the Whitechapel horrors were as much to do with politics as with crime, and newspapers around the world quickly sat up and took notice.

Although criticism of the police methods of the time was (and still is) commonplace, such accusations of incompetence cannot go unchallenged. In the twenty-first century, crime investigators have reaped the benefits of a century of forensic development. But in 1888, the absence of such scientific methods meant that the police would have had to use fundamental and basic detection methods – methods which, by today's standards, seem simplistic and almost naïve. The absence of fingerprinting, blood grouping, DNA testing, electronic surveillance and psychological profiling conspired against the investigators, allowing the perpetrator (or perpetrators) to remain uncaught.[43]

It may be reasonable to argue that had the Whitechapel murders taken place in any other decade of the nineteenth century, they would not have gained the profile they did – a profile that remains high to this day. They happened at precisely the time that the East End had come to embody London's fears – of the unemployed, the socialist, the anarchist, the homeless, the foreigner, the violent criminal – and Jack the Ripper rolled all these anxieties into a unique, terrifying and unignorable bundle: the 'Nemesis of Neglect'.[44]

Viewing the murders from 'alternative universes', with events dictated by alternative timelines, we could say that if they had occurred much earlier, the media sensation would have been considerably muted, and perhaps the murders of Jack the Ripper would be a mere footnote in the annals of crime; and if they had been committed much later, advances in communication or detection might well have seen the murderer apprehended. There would then be fewer books, television documentaries or movies, and certainly no souvenirs or ephemera (although 'Jack the Ripper' would still probably have a place in the 'Chamber of Horrors' waxworks, albeit under his real name). The permutations are numerous; but what happened happened in a certain way, and the legacy is a powerful one.

The political zeitgeist of the late 1880s therefore goes a long way to explaining why the Whitechapel murders exerted such a strong hold over the world at the time. They not only embodied the elements of a true-crime mystery, but also touched on politics, sociology, popular psychology and the mass media in a way that no other series of murders had done before. But it is the prevailing mystery that explains the *continual* fascination – the big question: 'Who was Jack the Ripper?' And it is a question that many have attempted to answer over the years, creating a self-perpetuating 'industry' of sorts. Because that mystery has never been solved to the satisfaction of all concerned, Jack the Ripper has been left open to manipulation; because the identity is unknown, it can be moulded, reconstructed and even deconstructed to fit whatever one wants it to be. Thus innumerable mythologies and legends prevail, whereby the Ripper transcends time, space and perceptions of taste. Often even the mood of a specific era can influence theories about the murderer's identity and motive. Jack the Ripper has been the foreign lunatic, the mad doctor or the syphilis-crazed gentleman; he has been part of a tsarist plot to discredit the London police, a vengeful midwife and a religious fanatic bent on ridding the streets of prostitutes. At the extreme he has been the product of a royal conspiracy, a satanist or a creature of the popular imagination such as a ghoul or vampire. He is somebody both unknown and known, the latter evident in the number of theories which point to noted individuals being the Ripper.[45] Significantly – and frustratingly – even those well placed to point us in the right direction, the leading detectives of Scotland Yard and the City Police, appeared to differ in their opinions of who was the most likely candidate.

The popular image of Jack the Ripper is now the tall gentleman with the top hat, long cloak, glinting knife and Gladstone bag, walking through the narrow foggy alleyways of Whitechapel. This is the image that was seized upon by the movie industry of the late twentieth century and which appears on so much Ripper ephemera, from souvenirs bought at London tourist attractions to the mural on the interior of the Whitechapel High Street branch of Burger King. And this is what also makes him endure. He has become a super-villain, whose very silhouette is as immediately recognizable as those of Sherlock Holmes, Batman or James Bond. Over the years, this has even led some to believe that Jack the Ripper did not exist, but was merely the product of a Victorian gothic novelist like Edgar Allan Poe or Sheridan Le Fanu.

But did Jack the Ripper exist? Can we prove that each of the infamous Whitechapel murders was committed by the same hand? The name 'Jack the Ripper' was first seen on a letter purporting to come from the killer which was sent to the Central News Agency in September 1888.[46] The authenticity of this letter has long been debated, with many (not least the investigators of the day) believing that it was a journalistic hoax. But from the moment the soubriquet was published, the unknown killer was given a name, a lasting and convenient label with which to define the indefinite, to give it shape and perhaps meaning. To reach any conclusion as to the common authorship of these crimes, we must look to the victims themselves, women of whom we would never have heard had it not been for the fact that they were murdered by some person or persons whose name or names we shall probably never know. And therein lies a conundrum – who exactly was murdered by the serial killer that we call Jack the Ripper?

If one is honest, it is difficult to say. For those less conversant with the events we call 'the Whitechapel murders', there were only five victims, sometimes known as the 'canonical five':[47] Mary Ann Nichols, Annie Chapman, Elizabeth Stride, Catherine Eddowes and Mary Jane Kelly. Around 1891, Chief Inspector Donald Swanson wrote a list defining the Whitechapel murders thus:

Emma E. Smith
Martha Tabram
Mary Ann Nichols
Annie Chapman
Elizabeth Stride
Catherine Eddowes
Mary Janet [*sic*] Kelly
Alice McKenzie
Frances Coles

Alleged attempted murder: Annie Farmer
Alleged murder: Rose Mylett alias Catherine Milett alias Davies.[48]

Considering that Swanson had, at one time, overall responsibility for overseeing the Whitechapel murders investigation in the absence of Assistant Commissioner Robert Anderson, the list is unsurprisingly a full one. These are the Whitechapel murders as they were perceived at a time when Mary Ann Nichols was considered to be the *third* in a series; however, Swanson here makes no distinction as to which murders he feels were by a common hand.

The origins of a 'canon' of five can be seen early on in a report written by Dr Thomas Bond on 10 November 1888.[49] Bond had just completed the post-mortem of victim Mary Jane Kelly and had also been furnished with notes from the autopsies of the previous victims. His report outlines the killer's *modus operandi* and significantly puts forward a hypothesis about the type of person the killer was.[50] But in doing so, he referred to only five murders – Nichols, Chapman, Stride, Eddowes and the recently deceased Kelly – adding that 'all five murders were no doubt committed by the same hand'. By ignoring Emma Smith and Martha Tabram, Bond *appears* to discount them. But that may not necessarily be the case: perhaps he was not acquainted with the notes regarding those particular crimes; or perhaps he felt that those five warranted special attention, on account of the similarities he perceived.

However, following the murder of Alice McKenzie on 17 July 1889, Bond stated, 'I am of opinion that the murder was performed by the same person who committed the former series of Whitechapel murders.'[51] However, he appeared to stand alone in his judgement, at least at the time.

In May 1892, Chief Inspector Frederick Abberline gave a press interview stating his belief that Mary Kelly was the final Ripper victim: '. . . that the Miller's Court atrocity was the last of the real series, the others having been imitations, and that in Miller's Court the murderer reached the culminating point of the gratification of his morbid ideas'.[52] He thus effectively eliminated the murders of Alice McKenzie and Frances Coles. The following month, in the same publication, Sir Robert Anderson stated that 'the morning of the day I took up my position here the first Whitechapel murder occurred'.[53] Anderson had begun as assistant commissioner (CID) of the Metropolitan Police on 1 September 1888, the day of the Nichols murder, and thus he appears to promote her as the first in the series. Some years later, though, in his autobiography, Anderson seems to have changed his mind, describing the Nichols killing as 'the second of the crimes known as the Whitechapel murders'.[54]

Superintendent Thomas Arnold, speaking in 1893,[55] appeared to discount Mary Kelly as a true Ripper victim, confidently asserting that the deaths of Nichols, Chapman, Stride and Eddowes brought the death-count to a mere four.

But it was Melville Macnaghten, appointed assistant chief constable of the Metropolitan Police CID in 1889, who put some form of 'official stamp' on the number of murders when he wrote a memorandum in February 1894[56] naming three individuals who were more likely to be the murderer than the recently accused Thomas Cutbush.[57] Macnaghten also delivered the subsequently influential judgement that 'the Whitechapel Murderer had 5 victims

& 5 victims only', before naming the victims from Nichols to Kelly. Tabram, McKenzie, Coles and an unidentified torso found under a railway arch in Pinchin Street in September 1889 were given short shrift, and Smith was not mentioned at all. Bearing in mind that Macnaghten's notes were not for public consumption, until they were discovered it was common for studies of the Ripper crimes to include Martha Tabram. So influential was the memorandum upon its release that some researchers have chosen to call the 'canonical five' the 'Macnaghten five' instead.

Our final example of early 'victimology' among those who were in a position to be well informed comes from Detective Inspector Edmund Reid, who at the beginning of the crimes was the divisional inspector for 'H' Division (Whitechapel), being joined by Frederick Abberline after the Buck's Row murder. In 1910, he stated that there were 'nine murders said to have been committed by "Jack the Ripper" '. Commenting on the opinions of the early Ripper theorist Dr Lyttleton Forbes Winslow, who believed that McKenzie was the last victim, Reid unequivocally stated that 'the last murder was Frances Coles in Swallow Gardens on 13th February 1891. Much has been said and written which is not true about certain mutilations having characterised these murders, and if Dr Baxter [sic] Phillips, who held the post-mortems in conjunction with Dr Percy Clark, was still alive,[58] he would confirm my statement.'[59]

If, in the twenty-first century, we are to accept Melville Macnaghten's creed of '5 victims & 5 victims only' then we are surely ignoring the modern developments in criminal profiling which today feature so prominently in any serial murder investigation and which are being increasingly used in 'cold case' approaches regarding the original Ripper murders. It is frequently the case with serial murderers that their methods are not fully formed, and they often begin with less violent crimes. Furthermore, not all their attempts at murder are necessarily successful: they may be affected or thwarted by any number of outside influences.[60] With this in mind, in the chapters which follow we also examine those women who fall outside the 'canonical five'. Some of their deaths exhibit the characteristics of a Ripper-style crime, but whether they were all murdered by that one malign individual is open to scrutiny. And were some of the other violent attacks carried out in the Whitechapel district at the time bungled attempts at another atrocity?

The questions are there to be answered; the 'forgotten victims' are there to be reassessed. But are the answers that straightforward?

CHAPTER 2

The East End was a Dangerous Place

Annie Millwood (25 February 1888)

THE WINTER OF 1887–88 WAS HARSH AND UNRELENTING RIGHT across Europe. In some parts of Britain snow had reached a record depth of 20–24 inches. Meanwhile in the United States snowstorms had paralysed the East Coast and claimed 400 lives in what became known as the 'Great Blizzard'.

Saturday, 25 February 1888 was another cold day. Dark skies and dirty rain made the streets even greyer and gloomier, dulling the mind and depressing the spirit. Just before 5 p.m., Annie Millwood turned up at the imposing and forbidding Whitechapel Infirmary in Baker's Row. It is not clear whether she was brought there or reached it of her own accord, but she had been stabbed several times. Her heavy breathing fogged the air as she battled against pain and exhaustion.

According to the admissions register at the infirmary, Annie was about 38 years old and was the widow of a soldier named Richard Millwood.[1] The *Eastern Post and City Chronicle* reported that she had been stabbed with a clasp knife in the legs and lower part of the body by a man she did not know. The admissions register shows that she was admitted from 8 White's Row, a common lodging house also known as Spitalfields Chambers, but we do not know if that was where the attack took place, if it was where Annie lived, or if it was just a sanctuary, from where she was taken to receive medical aid. In fact, we know very little about the attack, except that nobody witnessed it. And no newspaper at the time is known to have carried a report of it. All we do know comes from a few details given in a couple of East End newspapers a month later, when Annie died – from medical problems apparently unrelated to the attack – and an inquest was held.

It is generally accepted that serial killers like Jack the Ripper do not begin their careers with a full-blown murder and mutilation, and so researchers have trawled the newspapers for stories of assaults and injuries that could have been the work of an 'embryonic' Ripper. It will never be known if Annie Millwood was an early victim of a nascent Jack the Ripper, but a knife attack focused on the lower torso has strong Ripper-like characteristics. Whatever the actual facts, Annies story does serve to illustrate the sort of casual violence that was common in the East End of London.

The East End was rife with common lodging houses like Spitalfields Chambers, and all the victims of Jack the Ripper lived (or had lived) in them. These were the poor man's home or hotel, where 4d (equivalent to £1 in today's money) could buy a bed for the night (a double would cost 8d), use of the cooking facilities and the warmth of a communal kitchen, an outhouse with the usual facilities, and somewhere to get washed and to launder one's clothes. Many lodging houses also supplied a few basic necessities, such as soap, and sometimes food could be purchased. They were governed by various parliamentary Acts, among them the Common Lodging Houses Acts of 1851 and 1853, the Sanitary Act 1866, and the Sanitary Law Amendment Act 1874. Among other things, these specified that the walls and ceilings had to be limewashed in April and October, that the rooms had to be adequately ventilated (every window in the house had to be thrown open at 10 a.m.) and that there had to be a proper water supply. In many ways this made them preferable to rented rooms, which provided a degree of privacy and were cheaper for a family, but which were frequently insanitary and lacked washing and toilet facilities. The authorities were also greatly concerned with ensuring that good moral standards were maintained in these establishments, so that most catered for one sex only (or in a few cases, for married couples). But there was a widespread belief, somewhat supported by the facts, that a blind eye was turned to prostitutes arriving with their clients, and such lodging houses were consequently viewed as hotbeds of vice, immorality and criminality. All was overseen by the lodging house deputy or manager, who often had an office by the front door to keep an eye on the people entering the house.

In Metropolitan London, responsibility for ensuring that common lodging houses conformed to the rules laid down in the Acts rested with the commissioner of the Metropolitan Police,[2] and the police had a legal right to enter and inspect any common lodging house at any time. Some were well run – *Dickens's Dictionary of London* (1888) refers to St George's Chambers in St George's Street, near the London Docks, as 'about the best sample of this kind of establishment extant' – but lodging houses generally had an evil reputation for dirt, squalor, disease and violence.

Montagu Williams, the presiding magistrate at Worship Street Police Court (and widely regarded as a 'friend of the poor', who was as likely as not to take the side of a working-class complainant against a wealthy or influential opponent), would often denounce the evils of the common lodging house. In 1888 'a powerfully built young woman' named Mary McCarthy, a notorious character in the area, was up before him for stabbing Ann Neason,[3] the deputy of a Spitalfields lodging house, in the face and neck with a skewer. But the disgusting attack was all but forgotten in the courtroom when Williams discovered that no effort had been made to establish whether couples staying in the lodging house were married or not. 'Precisely what I thought,' he said. 'And the sooner these lodging houses are put down the better. They are the haunt of the burglar, the home of the pickpocket, and the hotbed of prostitution. I do not think I can put it stronger than that. It is time the owners of these places, who reap large profits from them, were looked after.' Later he fumed:

> As a magistrate I have made it my business to go over some of these places, and I say that the sooner they are put down the better. In my humble judgement they are about as unwholesome and unhealthy, as well as dangerous to the community, as can well be. There are places among them where the police dare not enter, and where the criminal hides all day long.[4]

Williams' remarks were quoted in parliament and the home secretary, Henry Matthews, responded:

> In the opinion of the police it cannot be said that crime is due to common lodging-houses. There is no doubt that a certain number of the criminal class do live in common lodging-houses; but the owners of those houses are ready, as a rule, to assist the police with information, and the inmates are under police supervision to a greater extent than they would be if they were driven to live elsewhere.[5]

Spitalfields Chambers, which was licensed to provide fifty-one double beds, was owned by a well-known lodging house keeper named William Crossingham.[6] He also had properties in neighbouring Dorset Street and Paternoster Row, and he evidently profited from his businesses, leaving an estate valued at over £11,000. White's Row itself does not seem to have had a particularly bad reputation, unlike Dorset Street. In October 1888, John Henry Stevenson, a rescue officer for an organization known as the Reformatory and Refuge Union, brought a court case concerning three children who had been found living there with prostitutes. He said he knew the women to be prostitutes because he had seen them soliciting, but he described the lodging house itself as usually a quiet house and indicated that he did not consider it to be a brothel, but rather a place 'where cohabitation was . . . the normal condition between the inhabitants'.

However, White's Row may have been troubled by one of the many street gangs in the area. A labourer named John Hall was stabbed in the neck, leaving his left arm permanently paralysed, in a street attack there in November 1888. The young man named George Birmingham who was charged with the crime was described as a member of the White's Row gang.[7] White's Row also had a number of connections with the Whitechapel murders themselves: leaving aside Annie Millwood, both Alice McKenzie and Frances Coles stayed there, and Annie Chapman was staying at one of Crossingham's properties in Dorset Street when she was murdered.

Ada Wilson (28 March 1888)

Almost a month to the day after the knife attack on Annie Millwood, a similar assault was made on a 39-year-old dressmaker named Ada Wilson. She lived in Maidman Street, an area that had once been described as semi-rural but that by 1888 was a typical East End urban jungle. It ran off a relatively new thoroughfare called Burdett Road, built to connect Mile End Road with the East India Dock Road. Maidman Street would receive a direct hit from a bomb during the Blitz in the Second World War and the bomb site survived into the 1960s, receiving a little publicity in 1959 when it was used by thieves to dump a safe they had stolen.

Ada Wilson lived at 19 Maidman Street. At 12.30 a.m. on Wednesday, 28 March 1888, she answered a knock at the front door. Outside stood a man aged about 30, 5ft 6in tall, with a fair moustache and a sunburnt face, as if he had been abroad (like a soldier, or more likely a sailor). He was wearing a dark coat, light trousers and a type of hat known as a wideawake. The man immediately pushed Ada backwards into the small hallway and threatened to kill her unless she handed over all the money she had. Ada refused. The man took a clasp knife from his pocket and stabbed her twice in the throat, then ran. Ada screamed loudly and collapsed.

That, at least, was the story she managed to tell the police.

A young woman named Rose Bierman, who shared two upstairs rooms with her mother, gave a slightly different version of events to a journalist from the *Eastern Post and City Chronicle*.[8] Ada, she said, was married (although she had never seen the husband) and she often had visitors (although she had rarely seen them in person). Bierman knew that Ada had returned home that evening with a man, but all had been quiet in the house until she heard 'the most terrible screams one can imagine', went to the top of the stairs and looked down. There she saw Ada partially dressed, wringing her hands and crying. 'Stop that man for cutting my throat! He has stabbed me!' she shouted, before collapsing. A young man then rushed to the front door, opened it and fled into the street.

A couple of young women had also heard the screams and had gone into the house, where they found Ada Wilson lying in the hallway covered in blood. They rushed off to find a policeman. The two constables they tracked down – Ronald Saw and Thomas Longhurst – were on duty outside a pub called the Royal Hotel on the corner of Mile End Road and Burdett Road. They went to the house and found Ada Wilson bleeding profusely from the wound in her throat. The policemen sent for Dr Richard Wheeler, an Irish-born doctor with a practice in Mile End Road. He could do little but attend to her immediate needs, which he did, and then arranged for her to be taken to the London Hospital, where she was treated by Dr William Rawes, and afterwards by Dr John Couper. Her condition was critical, but she was able to recount what had happened to her. Fortunately she survived and was discharged on 27 April.

There were many theories, one being that Wilson had been stabbed by her husband, with whom she had argued.[9] The testimony of Rose Bierman also makes one wonder whether Ada's story was true. According to Rose, Ada had been partially dressed: would she have answered the door in such a state to a stranger late at night? Bierman's account also suggests that the man was not visible to her from the top of the stairs, but was well inside the house, with Ada positioned between him and the door, as if she had been letting him out, not letting him in. Overall, Ada Wilson's story sounds like a concocted tale to explain why she was alone in her rooms in a state of partial undress with a man; in that case the true cause of the attack is and will forever remain unknown. It is possible that the attacker was her husband, or he may have been one of her many visitors, which could put a different complexion on her profession. Although two detectives, Inspectors Richard Wildey and William Dillworth, were sent to find her attacker, they never did so.

While Ada was recovering in hospital, Annie Millwood was discharged to the Whitechapel Union Workhouse, Mile End. At about 11.40 a.m. on 31 March 1888, she was talking to a workhouse messenger named Richard Sage. He was distracted from their conversation for a few minutes, and when he turned back he found that Annie had collapsed. The master of the workhouse, Thomas Badcock, telephoned the infirmary and summoned Dr Wheeler from his surgery. When the doctor arrived, he found Annie already dead, from a 'sudden effusion into the pericardium from the rupture of the left pulmonary artery through ulceration'.

The Coroner – Wynne Baxter

An inquest into the death of Annie Millwood was held at the infirmary in Baker's Row on Thursday, 5 April 1888, the coroner for East Middlesex, Wynne Baxter, presiding. The jury recorded a verdict of death from natural causes. Apart from a couple of short reports of the inquest in the newspapers,[10] the attack on Annie Millwood was forgotten. Wynne Baxter would go on to become one of the most important figures in the history of the Whitechapel murders, presiding over the inquests into the deaths of Annie Millwood, Emma Smith, Martha Tabram, Mary Ann Nichols, Annie Chapman, Elizabeth Stride, Rose Mylett, Alice McKenzie, the Pinchin Street Torso and Frances Coles. However, Baxter has not been remembered kindly, the late Tom Cullen typifying how he was long perceived. Cullen wrote that Baxter 'conceived it as his mission in life to expose the stupidities of the law guardians. Indeed, the police became so incensed at his carping criticisms and insinuations that the inquest into one of the Ripper murders was wrested from Baxter's hands, even though the murder had occurred inside his bailiwick as coroner.'[11]

But that is unfair. It is difficult to assess a man's personality from limited biographical information, especially when the main source is obituaries (which tend to smooth the rough edges of a man's character and emphasize his personal qualities and achievements); however, the perception of Baxter as a fussy, pedantic man who was a thorn in the side of the police is almost certainly wrong.

* * *

Wynne Baxter was born in 1844 in the town of Lewes, Sussex, the son of the proprietor and editor of the *Sussex Express*. Educated at Lewes Old Grammar School, he was called to the Bar in 1867 and practised as a solicitor in Lewes, where he was appointed coroner for Sussex in 1876. By 1885, he was deputy coroner for the City of London and the Borough of Southwark. Then in December 1886, he was elected coroner for East Middlesex.

The election was an extraordinary affair. Snow fell on Friday, 10 December, briefly settling to give London a wintry Christmas-card appearance, until the sun managed to melt it. The election proceedings at the Vestry Hall, Bethnal Green, were, as *The Times* reported, 'of a very disorderly character, owing to a mob of roughs having by some means gained admission to the hall. Several fights took place among them, and they hissed and hooted indiscriminately.'[12] One incident even ended up in court, William Upton claiming that an estate agent named Ephraim Brooks had grabbed him by the throat, almost throttling him, in an effort to prevent him from getting in to vote. According to Upton, the roughs trying to gain entry were known as 'Baxter's Lambs'.[13]

Any 'freeholder' was entitled to vote, but all that was required was the word of the voter that he owned property. And since there was no proper definition of 'freeholder' anyway, many of those who voted did so on the basis of owning something as small as a burial plot.

Eventually Mr George Hay Young was elected on a show of hands – a huge surprise, since a tight contest had been expected between Baxter and Dr Roderick MacDonald. Finally it was decided that the disorder had been so great that the precise number of votes cast could not be properly ascertained, and a fresh election was called for the following Monday. Again a large number of roughs managed to gain entry to the Vestry Hall and got into fights. The police had great difficulty in keeping order.[14]

At the conclusion of the election, one of the candidates, Mr Beard, 'hinted . . . very broadly that no small amount of bribery and corruption had been used'.[15] All in all the election was almost a farce, giving 'opportunity for the greatest abuses'.[16] Eventually, however, the votes were counted: Baxter polled 1,401 votes, McDonald 1,069, Young 696, Beard 254 and one Dr Porter a mere 55 votes.

* * *

The following year, 1887, Baxter presided over the inquest into the death of Miriam Angel. She was murdered at 16 Batty Street in the East End by an immigrant Jew named Israel Lipski. The case has remained a minor *cause célèbre* because it was widely believed at the time that Lipski was innocent. There was a great campaign both inside and outside parliament for his reprieve, and Home Secretary Henry Matthews came under considerable pressure. He declared, however, that he entertained not a shadow of a doubt about Lipski's guilt and he greeted Lipski's eventual confession with considerable relief. Lipski was hanged at Newgate Prison on 29 June 1887, though his motive for confessing has been questioned and his guilt is still debated to this day.

In 1888, Elizabeth Stride, generally considered to have been murdered by Jack the Ripper, was killed in a street close to Batty Street. A man named Israel Schwartz claimed to have witnessed a woman, whom he identified as Stride, being assaulted just outside the gates leading to a passage where, fifteen minutes later, her body was found. According to Schwartz, the man committing the assault had cried out 'Lipski!' but what he meant was unclear. Inspector Frederick Abberline volunteered an answer, stating in an official report that 'since a Jew named Lipski was hanged for the murder of a Jewess in 1887 the name has very frequently been used by persons as a mere ejaculation by way of endeavouring to insult the Jew to whom it has been addressed'.[17]

Most of the Whitechapel murder cases fell to Baxter, and he gained undeserved notoriety for advancing the theory that the murders were committed in order to obtain the victims' internal organs. In fact this was not his theory at all. It came about because the day after the medical evidence had been given about the murder of Annie Chapman, during which it was revealed that the killer had extracted and taken away the uterus, Baxter received a message from the sub-curator of the pathological museum at what he described as 'one of our great medical schools', to the effect that several months earlier an American doctor had been offering to pay £20 for a uterus. (Seemingly he had planned to give away one with every copy of a publication he was writing.) Baxter did not say that he believed this extraordinary story, and nor did he suggest that the American doctor was murdering women for their internal organs. But he did wonder if the story, no matter how absurd it was, had reached and had 'incited some abandoned wretch to possess himself of a specimen'.

This was by no means an outrageous suggestion. Furthermore, as Baxter pointed out, if he had not got the doctor giving evidence to divulge the medical facts (for which he, Baxter, had come in for criticism), he would not have heard from the sub-curator. This was a valid point, given that one reason for the inquest was to elicit further important information that would aid the police investigation.

The London correspondent of the *Chicago Tribune* reported:

I learned today from a Scotland Yard man working on the case that the mysterious American who was here a few months ago offering money for specimens of the parts taken from the bodies of the victims has been discovered. He is a reputable physician in Philadelphia with a large medical practice, who was over here preparing a medical work on specific diseases. He went to King's College and Middlesex Hospital and asked for specimens, and merely said he was willing to pay well if he could not get them otherwise. The statement that he offered £20 each or named any other large sum seems to be a delusion of the coroner. These facts were given the police by an eminent London physician, who saw a great deal of the Philadelphian when he was here, but would only divulge the information on a written guarantee from Sir Charles Warren that neither his name nor the name of the physician in question should be given to the public. He said the doctor had gone back to America and his mission here was purely legitimate.[18]

The identity of the Philadelphia physician has never been established.[19]

Interestingly, the theory in which Wynne Baxter may have placed the greatest credence was revealed in an obituary of him published in the *Evening News*. This stated that he attributed the Whitechapel murders to the Fenians and had 'advanced his theory to the Home Office, who told him he was not alone in his opinion'.

The possibility that there was a Fenian involvement in the Ripper murders lends the crimes a completely new historical dimension. The Fenian Brotherhood was an American organization that had the avowed aim of overthrowing British rule in Ireland. We know from other sources that the theory may indeed have had a solid factual foundation. In 1956, Douglas G. Browne published *The Rise of Scotland Yard*. It is clear that he had accessed (at the time closed) official files relating to the Whitechapel murders and had found therein a possible reference to Fenian involvement. As Browne wrote, 'A third head of the CID, Sir Melville Macnaghten, appears to identify the Ripper with the leader of a plot to assassinate Mr Balfour at the Irish Office.'[20]

This claim is unsupported by any of Macnaghten's extant writings, and Macnaghten himself seems to have considered a barrister and teacher named Montague John Druitt as the prime candidate for being the Ripper, but Browne's claim cannot be casually dismissed. A large number of documents have gone missing from the files, so Browne could have got the information from documents that are no longer extant. Furthermore, it is now known that there *were* Fenians aspiring to assassinate Balfour. However, how the Jack the Ripper murders could have furthered Fenian ambitions is unclear.

* * *

On the eve of Baxter's inquest into the death of Annie Millwood, at about 4 a.m., a woman named Emma Smith staggered into her lodgings with severe internal injuries. Today she is not generally regarded as having been a victim of Jack the Ripper. But one detective at the time, Walter Dew, believed otherwise.

CHAPTER 3

The Gangs of Whitechapel

Emma Elizabeth Smith (3 April 1888)

THE DAY BEFORE WYNNE BAXTER SAT DOWN TO CONDUCT the inquest into the death of Annie Millwood, the authorities at the London Hospital informed him, as a matter of routine, that a woman had died at the hospital from injuries sustained in a street assault. Her name was Emma Elizabeth Smith and, according to the story she told a doctor who attended her, she had been set upon by three men, all unknown to her, one of whom had thrust a hard and blunt object into her vagina. Emma's injuries were so severe that she died from them, and the police file was included in the Whitechapel murders file along with those committed by Jack the Ripper.

Easter Monday, 2 April 1888, continued miserable. The temperature in London had not risen above 6.6 degrees Celsius (44 degrees Fahrenheit) all day, and as darkness fell it dropped to just above freezing. There were occasional flurries of sleet or snow to add to the misery of walking the streets.

Emma Smith needed money. Aged around 45, standing about 5ft 2in, with light brown hair and a scar on her right temple, she was a prostitute. She was almost certainly also an alcoholic, and was belligerent when drunk. She often appeared bruised from a brawl or sporting a black eye after being hit by a man, and once someone had even thrown her through a window.[1] But by some accounts, she had once enjoyed a more prosperous and settled life, with a husband and two children. Detective Walter Dew would later write about her character and previous life:

Emma, a woman of more than forty, was something of a mystery. Her past was a closed book even to her most intimate friends. All that she had ever told anyone about herself was that she was a widow who more than ten years before had left her husband and broken away from all her early associations.

There was something about Emma Smith which suggested that there had been a time when the comforts of life had not been denied her. There was a touch of culture in her speech unusual in her class.

Once when Emma was asked why she had broken away so completely from her old life she replied, a little wistfully: 'They would not understand now any more than they understood then. I must live somehow.'[2]

By the time he wrote these lines, Dew had acquired the sort of celebrity status later reserved for movie stars. He was the policeman who had arrested the murderer Dr Crippen, after a thrilling race across the Atlantic. But at the time of the Whitechapel murders, he was just a young policeman recently transferred to 'H' Division CID. This information about Emma Smith's previous life, unknown from any other source, suggests that he was actively involved in investigating her murder. It may be significant, therefore, that Dew believed she had been murdered by Jack the Ripper:

The silence, the suddenness, the complete elimination of clues, the baffling disappearance all go to support the view which I have always held that Emma Smith was the first to meet her death at the hands of Jack the Ripper.[3]

Dew was writing half a century after the murder, and he cannot have anticipated that people would one day scrutinize his every word for the slightest nuance. He was relying on his memory, and occasionally it let him down. For example, he wrote that Emma Smith was found lying unconscious in the street;[4] in fact, after the attack she managed to get back to her lodgings and went from there to the hospital. But such details may have been unimportant to Dew, who probably considered it of far more significance that she had been assaulted in an open and well-frequented thoroughfare, unlike the 'dark alleys and sinister courts' chosen by the Ripper. But, wrote Dew, 'it must be remembered that if this was a Ripper murder it was the first. The need for caution was not so great.'

As Dew intimated, little is known about Emma Smith. She had been married, but most of the newspaper reports stated that she was a widow.[5] Her husband has been tentatively identified as John Smith, born in Margate, Kent, and a pensioner of the 35th (Royal Sussex) Regiment of Foot.[6] He appears in the 1881 Census living at 118 Central Street, St Luke's, together with his wife Emma, born in Plymouth, and two children. Emma's age is given as 37, which matches fairly well with the estimated age of Emma Smith in 1888. She was also said to have been the mother of two children, a boy and a girl, who at the time of her death were living near Finsbury Park in North London, presumably with a relative.

For the final eighteen months of her life, Emma had been living in a common lodging house at 18 George Street, one of a row of mean, three-storey tenements connecting the notorious Flower and Dean Street with Wentworth Street. It was a street with many connections to the Whitechapel murders. She usually left the lodging house between 6 and 7 p.m. to find money and alcohol, and this inclement Easter Monday evening was no different.

According to Mary Russell, the deputy keeper of the lodging house, who claimed to have known her for two years, Emma usually returned drunk, and when in drink she could behave like a madwoman. Violence against women was common in the East End; it is possible that Emma's drunken belligerence could have upset or angered someone so much that just giving her a black eye was not enough.

Easter Monday slipped away for another year. Margaret Hayes, who also lived at 18 George Street, saw Emma Smith in Farrant Street, one of the many roads that led off Burdett Road. Hayes was getting out of the area. She had been badly assaulted just before Christmas 1887, and only minutes earlier had been stopped by two men who had asked her the time, before one of them hit her across the mouth. Both had then run away. 'There had been some rough work' going on, she stated mysteriously, without explaining what she meant by 'rough work'. As she hurried home, she saw Emma talking to a man dressed in dark clothes and a white scarf. It was 12.15 a.m. on Tuesday, 3 April.

Around 1.30 a.m., Emma Smith was making her way down Whitechapel Road. Near Whitechapel Church (destroyed in the Second World War) she saw two or three men, one of them a youth aged about 19. They so alarmed her that she apparently crossed the road to avoid them and turned into Osborn Street, which after a short distance merges into Brick Lane.

We do not know what it was about the men that so frightened Emma – she did not say. Indeed Mary Russell was reported as suggesting that she seemed unwilling to go into details, did not describe the men and did not say what had happened. However, later, while being helped to hospital, she did point out where the assault had taken place – opposite 10 Brick Lane, near Taylor Bros. Mustard and Cocoa Mill, on the corner of Brick Lane and Wentworth Street. She also seems to have been reluctant to go to the police and report the assault – as Inspector Edmund Reid noted in his report: 'She would have passed a number of PC's en route but none was informed of the incident or asked to render assistance.'[7]

How clearly Emma saw who attacked her is uncertain, but the assault was brutal. Obviously knocked to the ground, she then had something rammed into her, causing severe injuries.

Though the attack took place just 300 yards from her lodgings, reports suggest that she did not get back until 4 or 5 a.m. If the time of the assault was even remotely accurate (and it probably was, since Emma would almost certainly have glanced at the large clock of Whitechapel Church), then it took her two hours or more to get home. There are several possible explanations: the timings could be way out; she may have been in so much pain that she could only walk extremely slowly; she could have been left unconscious in the street, and assumed to be drunk or sleeping rough by anyone who saw her. The newspapers and Dew, the policeman, believed that a man had found her and taken her home; Emma seems to have been so reluctant to discuss what had happened that she may not have mentioned him, or perhaps never thought to do so.

When Emma Smith did finally reach 18 George Street, she was met by Mary Russell, the deputy keeper, Margaret Hayes and several lodgers, one of whom we know by name, Annie Lee. Her face was bleeding, her ear was cut, and she was obviously in distress and in need of hospital treatment. The women decided to take her to the London Hospital in Whitechapel Road, half a mile or so away. Emma was unwilling to go – perhaps because she was in so much agony that she didn't want to walk there, or maybe because she knew she would be asked questions, or possibly because she simply did not want to go to the hospital at all.

The hospital was indeed a frightening place. Dr Frederick Treves was surgical registrar and assistant surgeon at the London Hospital, and later became surgeon and head of the school of anatomy. He is perhaps best known today for his association with the tragically deformed Joseph Carey Merrick (1862–90), the so-called 'Elephant Man', to whom he gave a home in the London Hospital. As Treves explained:

The hospital in the days of which I speak was anathema. The poor people hated it. They dreaded it. They looked upon it primarily as a place where people died. It was a matter of difficulty to induce a patient to enter the wards. They feared an operation and with good cause, for an operation then was a dubious matter. There were stories afloat of things that happened in the hospital, and it could not be gainsaid that certain of these stories were true.[8]

Despite Emma's misgivings, two of the women – Mary Russell and Annie Lee – struggled to get her to the hospital (incidentally, on the way passing a waxworks that would soon boast models of Jack the Ripper's victims). There she was attended by one Dr Haslip,[9] but nothing could be done for her and she died of peritonitis at 9 a.m. on 4 April. An inquest was held at the hospital by Wynne Baxter, and the jury returned a verdict of 'wilful murder'.

Only Walter Dew seems to have believed that Emma Elizabeth Smith was murdered by Jack the Ripper. The general opinion was that she had been attacked 'by one or more of a gang of men who are in the habit of frequenting the streets at late hours of the night and levying blackmail on women'.[10]

* * *

Street gangs are an almost forgotten feature of the violent landscape of Victorian society. Yet throughout the 1880s, gangs terrorized the streets, violently attacking and robbing people, creating no-go areas, and generally flouting the law. They became a major problem in the big cities of Victorian Britain. Manchester had the 'scuttling gangs', like Buffalo Bill's Gang, the Bengal Tigers, the Bungall Boys, and the Forty Row. Birmingham had the Peaky Blinders, so named for their caps, worn low over the face both as a fashion statement and to prevent recognition, but also allegedly with razor blades sewn into the peaks to make the caps weapons. And London had the Hooligans, the Regent's Park Gang, the curiously named Monkey's

Parade Gang in Bow[11] and the Plaid Cap Brigade in Plaistow.[12] Various books also mention the so-called Hoxton High Rips, the Hoxton Market Gang and the Limehouse Forty Thieves.

The gang most often named in books about Jack the Ripper – and even in some East End histories – as being responsible for killing Emma Smith was the Old Nichol Gang. The Old Nichol was a notorious area of the East End that was mired in criminality. It is almost inconceivable that the area did *not* have a gang at the time, but the earliest reference to one would appear to be by a later gang leader named Arthur Harding, who wrote that a gang member named William (Billy) Newman 'was one of the Old Nichol mob – they were a crooked family'.[13]

Whether or not such a gang existed in 1888, there appear to be no contemporary newspaper references attributing the murder of Emma Smith to the Old Nichol Gang, and the idea would seem to originate with a 1959 book by Donald McCormick.[14]

At the time of Annie Chapman's murder (in September 1888), the newspapers reported that 'the police have no theory with respect to the matter, except that *a sort of "High Rip" gang* exists in the neighbourhood which, "blackmailing" women who frequent the streets, takes vengeance on those who do not find money for them'.[15]

The High Rip theory made it into a remarkable fictional penny-dreadful serial entitled *The Whitechapel Murders, or The Mysteries of the East End*.[16] This was published in weekly instalments at the very time that the Whitechapel murders were actually being committed. In the serial, a detective named Richard Ryder is taken to a low pub in the East End to meet Red Rip, the leader of a 'High Rip' gang. After infiltrating the gang, he concludes that they have no connection with the murders.

The original High Rip Gang was a street gang of infamous reputation that terrorized Liverpool between 1884 and 1886. To this day, however, it is disputed whether there was ever a large, unified gang called the High Rip, or whether the name, whatever its origins, was applied to (and perhaps adopted by) diverse and unrelated gangs.

The High Rip Gang is sometimes linked with the brutal murder of Richard Morgan in Liverpool's Tithebarn Street on Bank Holiday Monday, 3 August 1874; but in fact that murder is more correctly attributed to what were known as 'Cornermen' – groups of criminals who loafed around street corners, begging and intimidating passers-by to get money for drink, and occasionally running prostitutes for the same purpose.[17] In reality, the High Rip first came to public attention with the infamous Blackstone Street murder of 5 January 1884.

Liverpool's Blackstone Street Gang was a notorious group of young men who terrorized their neighbourhood. It came to city-wide and national prominence when it set upon Exequiel Rodriguez Nuniez, a 34-year-old Spanish sailor who was returning to his vessel in Huskisson Dock. At the corner of Blackstone Street stood a gang of youths, one of whom punched Nuniez's companion in the mouth as they passed. The shocked man made for the docks, but Nuniez turned and ran in the opposite direction, pursued by the gang. He slipped and fell, and the gang descended on him, beating him mercilessly with their belts. Nuniez twice managed to escape the gang, but was eventually cornered and knifed several times.

The police eventually caught the gang members, but conflicting evidence from assorted witnesses, many of whom were relatives of the accused, led to the acquittal of all but two – Patrick Duggan and Michael McLean – who were found guilty of murder and sentenced to death. Duggan's sentence was later commuted to life imprisonment, but McLean went to the gallows on the morning of 11 March 1884.

The Blackstone Street Gang was not originally identified as the High Rip – it was simply called the Blackstone Street Gang. But a year or so later, Patrick Mannion appeared in the magistrates' court, charged with having broken into the home of one Thomas Doyle and having struck him on the head with his belt buckle. Mannion was described as a member of the High Rip Gang which hung around Blackstone Street. The stipendiary magistrate, Mr Raffles, a man of considerable experience, asked the meaning of the term 'High Rip', which suggests that it was relatively new, and a policeman explained that that was what the gang shouted whenever a policeman approached.[18]

As late as 1897 the High Rip Gang was making the national newspapers, *The Times* in December of that year reporting that Richard Owens, a 20-year-old labourer, had been found guilty of wounding one Peter Montgomery. Owens was said to be a member of the High Rip Gang.[19] Yet to this day, it is disputed whether any such gang really existed. The chief constable of Liverpool, Sir John William Nott-Bower, claimed it did not:

This condition of affairs caused much concern and anxiety and unfortunately some genius invented an absolutely unfounded cause for it, an invention which seemed to take the fancy of the Press, who exploited it to an extent which caused considerable alarm and comment. It was suggested that the large number of crimes of violence in the Scotland Division was due to the work of an organised gang, banded together for purposes of plunder and violence and exacting vengeance on all who ventured to give evidence against them or interfere with their nefarious work. And not content, with inventing the Organisation, a most euphonious name for it was also invented and it was stated that the organisation was known as the 'High Rip Gang'. Of course all this created considerable, and entirely unjustifiable, alarm, though there was never the very faintest shadow of foundation for the suggestions made. But letters from all sorts of irresponsible persons, Press comment and a certain sort of public opinion assumed the impossible and accepted the fact of a 'High Rip Gang'. It was impossible, for such a gang could not have existed without the Police ever hearing of it and the circumstances of the various crimes were such as to render it impossible to assign them to such a cause. But for long the ridiculous scare continued to be boomed until Mr Justice Day, in a charge to the Grand Jury at the Assizes, scotched it, and gradually the discussion of it ceased.[20]

On the other hand, the reputation of Judge Sir John Charles Day was built largely on the claim that he was responsible for suppression of the gang in the 1880s through the imposition of stiff prison sentences with flogging.[21]

What really distinguished 'High Rippery', and what was so terrifying about it, was the gang's willingness to engage in random and often completely unprovoked acts of vicious violence and murder. This is what the police meant when they attributed the early Whitechapel murders to 'a sort of "High Rip" gang' – namely a gang that engaged in motiveless savagery. It is quite possible that this early theory was the inspiration for the name 'Jack the Ripper', which was first used in a letter sent to the Central News Agency and was popularly attributed to a journalist.

CHAPTER 4

Soldiers

Martha Tabram (7 August 1888)

Aᴜɢᴜꜱᴛ Bᴀɴᴋ Hᴏʟɪᴅᴀʏ Mᴏɴᴅᴀʏ 1888 ᴡᴀꜱ ᴜɴꜱᴇᴀꜱᴏɴᴀʙʟʏ cold. The organizers of entertainments across London eyed the leaden skies with concern. But fortunately the rain held off and a brief appearance by the sun encouraged the crowds to descend on the various venues offering holiday attractions: 21,000 people went to the Zoological Gardens in Regent's Park, 14,000 to the Tower of London, over 12,000 to the South Kensington Museums, nearly 8,000 to the Natural History Museum, and 7,000 people visited the State Apartments in Windsor Castle. In the East End, 26,000 people gathered to see the Duchess of Albany open an art exhibition at the People's Palace. But the biggest draws that day were the spectacular entertainments at Crystal Palace and Alexandra Palace.

Over 56,000 people went to Crystal Palace, 'that monstrous greenhouse'[1] originally built for the Great Exhibition of 1851, and in 1888 the centrepiece of a sort of theme park providing a popular mixture of indoor and outdoor entertainments. That day the events included organ recitals, a promenade concert, a performance of the ballet *Midsummer Night's Dream*, and in the evening a balloon ascent by 'Captain' William Duncan Dale. Watching people go up in a balloon was a big attraction in the 1880s and Dale regularly appeared at Crystal Palace. He made 200 ascents and was a huge crowd-puller, but his career ended tragically on 30 June 1892, when his balloon, having reached 600 feet, was seen to deflate suddenly, a large rent having developed near the top part of the silk. It 'fell like a rag', and the four occupants of the basket frantically threw anything of weight over the side, even ripping the metal buttons from their jackets. Their efforts made no difference and the basket hit the ground with a sickening thud, killing Dale and his passengers.[2]

But on this August Bank Holiday nothing went wrong, and Captain Dale safely made his ascent to the great awe of the assembled public. Afterwards there was a firework display by Brock's, the oldest fireworks company in Britain, the centrepiece depicting the destruction of the Spanish Armada. Established in the early eighteenth century by John Brock in Islington, Brock's became so closely associated with Crystal Palace that for a while the company called its products C. T. Brock & Co.'s 'Crystal Palace Fireworks'.

The other big draw that day was Alexandra Palace, where 50,000 people passed through the turnstiles to enjoy a similar programme that included organ recitals by a Mr Henderson and flying trapeze feats by some Russian gymnasts called the Cleo Troupe, a dramatic farce called *Current Cash* and three performances of a military tournament featuring over thirty men and horses of the Royal Horse Artillery. In the evening, the crowd watched mesmerized as 'Professor Baldwin'[3] went a step further than Captain Dale, by going up in his balloon and parachuting to the ground. The firework display afterwards was described as a 'scenic and pyrotechnic' extravaganza that depicted 'The Last Days of Pompeii'.

The evening also offered special performances, including by the Mohawk Minstrels at the 3,000-seat St Mary's Hall, attached to the Agricultural Hall in Islington. The Mohawks, renowned for their sentimental songs and high level of humour, were hugely popular and performed to capacity audiences well into the twentieth century (subsequently going into decline in the face of slicker entertainment). But in 1888 they were at the peak of their popularity, and the crowd that queued in the street to get in far exceeded the hall's capacity. Those who managed to get seats had a great evening and were especially appreciative of a comic song called 'Troubles at the Picnic'.

By contrast, the audience that turned out to see the opening night of *Dr Jekyll and Mr Hyde* at the Opera Comique off the Strand went home less than happy (though apparently they laughed as loudly and as heartily as those watching the Mohawks, albeit for different reasons). Two actor-managers, Daniel Bandmann and Richard Mansfield, had recently come to London with rival productions of *Jekyll and Hyde*. Mansfield had pipped Bandmann to the post by opening on the Saturday night, when he won acclaim for his transformation from Jekyll into Hyde. It was Bandmann's turn to open on the Monday Bank Holiday night, but his production was a flop. His transformation into Hyde consisted of little more than putting in false teeth and slipping on a wig while the house lights were dimmed. Then, as *The Times* put it, he hopped 'about the stage after the manner of a kangaroo, omitting a wheezing sound like a broken-winded horse'. The *Daily News* preferred to liken Bandmann's hopping to that of 'a galvanised frog'. The audience laughed out loud, it said, and 'unseemly tittering' even accompanied a murder.

It was at about 6 p.m., a couple of hours before the curtain went up on Bandmann's disaster, that the rain started to come down. A drizzle at first, it grew harder, before turning into a downpour that continued for several hours. People scurried home (if they had one to scurry to) or made their way to the theatres and music halls, or took shelter in a pub for a sing-song around a battered piano. Many people braved the cold and the wet that night, and one of them was Martha Tabram.

Martha had been born on 10 May 1849 at 17 Marshall Street, London Road, Southwark, the youngest of five children born to warehouseman Charles Samuel White and his wife Elizabeth (née Dowsett). Her eldest brother, Henry, was 12 when she was born;

then came Esther (10), Stephen (8) and Mary Ann (3). Her parents separated around the year 1865 and Martha, who was 5ft 3in, with dark hair and a dark complexion,[4] took up with a man called Henry Samuel Tabram, who at the time of Martha's death was described as a short, well-dressed man with steel-grey hair, a moustache and 'imperial' beard, and who was employed as a foreman packer at a furniture warehouse in Deptford. They married at Trinity Church in St Mary's Parish, Newington, on Christmas Day 1869, and in February 1871 their son Frederick John was born, followed in December the following year by Charles Henry. But the marriage soon ran into trouble, apparently because Martha was a drunk. By 1875, her husband had had enough of her behaviour and left her.

Martha sounds like a bit of a fighter: she took out a warrant for Henry Tabram's arrest for desertion, and he was brought up before the magistrate, a Mr Benson. Henry explained that his wife's 'intemperate habits' were the cause of the desertion,[5] but nevertheless agreed to allow her 12 shillings a week (very nearly £50 in today's money),[6] which he appears to have paid regularly for three years. But Martha was not satisfied with this princely sum and began accosting Henry in the street, demanding more money from him. He finally responded by reducing the payment to 2s 6d (about £10). Martha retaliated by having a warrant taken out against him, so that Henry was again arrested and locked up and was forced to resume paying the full amount. Eventually, though, he learned that Martha had taken up with another man, whereupon he flatly refused to support her any longer. It does not seem that Martha took any further action against him, and she apparently had no further contact with him. He saw her in the street occasionally, the last time being in Whitechapel Road about eighteen months before she died. Perhaps not to his surprise, she was drunk.

It was Martha's belief that her widowed sister-in-law, Ann Morris, had encouraged Henry to leave her. Accordingly she embarked on a campaign against Mrs Morris, which escalated to the point where, on one occasion, she broke all that woman's windows. Ann Morris, who was described as a 'very respectable woman'[7] living at 23 Lisbon Street, Cambridge Heath Road, brought charges against Martha, who was sentenced to seven days' hard labour. Martha abandoned her campaign.

About 1879, she had begun living with William Turner, a some-time carpenter who, at the time of the murder, was hawking cheap trinkets such as menthol cones and needles and pins. Described as short, dirty and dressed in a slovenly manner, he had a pale face and a fair 'imperial' moustache. Despite his unkempt appearance, Turner was very good to Tabram and had helped to support her two children; but he told the inquest that his relationship with her was troubled by her excessive drinking and that they frequently separated. 'If I give her money she generally spent it in drink', he said. 'In fact, it was always drink.'[8]

They lived together at various addresses until about April or May 1888,[9] when they rented a room in the house of Mary Bousfield, the wife of a woodcutter named William Bousfield, at 4 Star Place, a narrow, grimy cul-de-sac off Star Street,[10] Commercial Road, which was pitted with potholes half full of murky water. At one end of Star Street was a thriving corner pub, while squalid shops that had been converted from front living rooms ran its length, selling fruit, coal, cats' meat, and assorted other goods.

It is usual for people to play down the frailties of the dead, of whom one generally speaks no ill. Accordingly, it is common to find witnesses playing down the faults of Jack the Ripper's victims. And so we must read between the lines: Henry Tabram left his wife because of her drinking; William Turner was of the opinion that Martha was a troublesome drunk, whose drinking caused several separations during their relationship; and Mary Bousfield, who at the inquest 'was nervous and very indistinct and rambling in her remarks',[11] said she had never seen Tabram drunk, but she was certainly a woman who 'would rather have a glass of ale than a cup of tea'. She was, said Bousfield, a very retiring woman and probably did not know two people in the street. As far as she knew, Tabram had never brought home any men and earned her living by selling matches and other trinkets in the street.

The late Tom Cullen, author of *Autumn of Terror*, spoke to 83-year-old James W. Bousfield, the son of Martha Tabram's one-time landlady, who showed him a key chain – one of the trinkets that Tabram had hawked – which he had retained as a souvenir after the murder.[12] About three weeks before her death, Turner had left Martha and taken lodgings at the Victoria Working Men's Home on Commercial Street. He last saw her alive on 4 August in Leadenhall Street, when he had given her 1s 6d to buy trinkets to trade. Martha had briefly stayed on at 4 Star Place, but she absconded, owing Mrs Bousfield money. A while later she had returned, forced the window, and occupied the room for one night without Bousfield knowing she was there, leaving the key behind the next morning.[13]

Martha moved into a common lodging house at 19 George Street, Spitalfields, using the name 'Emma' and trying to earn a living by selling her trinkets in the streets – and by selling herself up dark alleys or anywhere else that offered a modicum of privacy.

Another prostitute, known by the nicknames 'Pearly Poll' and 'Mogg', Mary Ann Connelly was described rather unflatteringly in the press as a big, masculine-looking woman with a husky voice and a face raddled by drink.[14] The admissions records of the Whitechapel Infirmary contain several entries for a Mary Ann Connelly, who was successively admitted between April and August 1888 for laryngitis, bronchitis and myalgia. She had been discharged after her last treatment on 4 August, three days prior to the murder. She was aged 35 and told police her address was 19 George Street (where Tabram also lived). The ailments from which she suffered may have accounted for her deep, husky voice.[15]

Connelly told the police that she met Martha Tabram at about 10 p.m. on that Bank Holiday night, 6 August. According to a report in the *East London Observer*,[16] two soldiers, a private and a corporal, had accosted them in Whitechapel Road and asked them to go for a drink in a nearby pub, a request to which the women readily acceded. Connelly initially claimed that she and Tabram had stayed in that pub drinking with the soldiers until about 11.45 p.m., but at the inquest she said they had gone on a bit of a pub crawl. It is difficult to know which story is true, but at about 11 p.m. Tabram was seen by her sister-in-law, Mrs Ann Morris, standing alone on the kerb[17] outside the White Swan pub at 20 Whitechapel High Street. That Tabram was alone at that time may cast some doubt on Connelly's story, although it is possible that Connelly and the soldiers had already gone inside (or that Tabram was waiting outside for them to emerge). If so, it is likely that Connelly's claim that they went on a pub crawl is true and that the foursome ended up at, or went on from, the White Swan.

Connelly said that at some point she had had an argument with the corporal and he had hit her with a stick; but the row did not stop the evening progressing towards its probably inevitable conclusion, when one of the soldiers suggested that the couples pair off. They duly left the pub at about 11.45 p.m. and Connelly watched Tabram turn into a narrow passage called George Yard before she headed off with the corporal towards a secluded spot a few doors along called Angel Alley.

She would never see Martha Tabram alive again.

* * *

George Yard was entered from Whitechapel High Street, through a covered archway next to a pub called The White Hart. It was not a yard, but a narrow street that ran to Wentworth Street. About 1875, a significant clearance of slums in the street had led to the construction of George Yard Buildings by a local philanthropist named Crowther, and they were sufficiently impressive to have been visited soon after by Princess Alice, the second daughter of Queen Victoria. Located in the north-west corner of George Yard, backing onto Toynbee Hall,[18] by 1888 the buildings were 'inhabited by people of the poorest description',[19] two of them being Joseph and Elizabeth Mahoney.

Joseph was employed as a carman (delivery driver), and his wife Elizabeth, a young woman of 25 or 26, worked in a match factory at Stratford from 9 a.m. until 7 p.m. They had been out all day with friends and got home at about 1.40 a.m. One of the rules of the building was that all lights illuminating the stairways were extinguished promptly at 11 p.m., so as they wearily picked their way to their room, the stairs had been in pitch blackness for some time. They reached their lodgings and Elizabeth removed her hat and cloak and returned down the stairs to the street to fetch some provisions for supper from a chandler's shop in Thrawl Street. She was gone about five minutes. Returning without seeing anything suspicious, she and her husband had their meal and went to bed. They claimed not to have heard anything unusual during the night.

However, the *Eastern Post and City Chronicle*[20] reported that John Saunders Reeves, a 33-year-old dock and riverside labourer, and his wife Louisa of 37 George Yard Buildings, had heard several fights in Wentworth Street and George Street that night. The first, they said, was at about 11.30 p.m.; there had been a second around an hour later, when they heard cries of 'Police!' and 'Help!' and terrible screaming; and the third had been shortly after 1 a.m. when again there were terrible screams. The Reeves apparently went onto their balcony and saw two separate rows going on – one close to the house in George Street where Tabram and 'Pearly Poll' sometimes lodged; the other in Wentworth Street, near the entrance to Angel Alley and a house that 'Pearly Poll' was said to have visited that evening. Both rows attracted quite large crowds before they were broken up by the police. According to the newspaper, the police on the various beats in the area confirmed that there had been several disturbances and that repeated screams and cries for help were heard at midnight and during the early hours of the morning.

At 2 a.m., PC Thomas Barrett saw a Grenadier Guardsman near the Wentworth Street entrance to George Yard. The soldier was aged between 22 and 26, was about 5ft 6in in height and had a fair complexion with dark hair and a small brown moustache turned up at the ends. He had one good-conduct badge and no medals. PC Barrett asked the man why he was loitering in the street and the soldier replied that 'he was waiting for a mate who had gone with a girl'.[21]

At 3.30 a.m., a young man in his early twenties named Alfred George Crow, who lived at 35 George Yard Buildings, went up the same stairs as Elizabeth Mahoney. A cab driver with closely cropped hair and a beardless, intelligent face, he noticed a body lying on the first-floor landing, but he did not pay too much attention, as it was not uncommon to find drunks or homeless people asleep there.[22]

It was not until 4.50 a.m., when John Saunders Reeves left his room to go to work, that the light of early dawn revealed the body to be that of a woman lying in a pool of blood. Reeves, a short man with a close-cut dark beard and moustache and wearing earrings, was naturally alarmed at the sight, particularly as his wife, Louisa, had been plagued throughout the night by a deep sense of foreboding. She had woken up several times 'under an apprehension that something was about to happen' and such was her alarm that at one point John had got up and listened at the front door for any uncommon sounds. As he looked at the body, John Reeves remembered his wife's alarm and feared to tell Louisa in case she fainted.[23] Whether Mrs Reeves did experience a premonition or whether it was a colourful piece of elaboration will never be known, but John Reeves probably would have been anxious about telling Louisa of his discovery, as she was eight months pregnant – the couple's fifth child, Harriet Elizabeth Reeves, would be born on 12 September. Reeves ran for a policeman and returned a short time later with PC Thomas Barrett, who took one look at the body and immediately sent Reeves to fetch Dr Timothy Robert Killeen from his home in Brick Lane.

Dr Killeen arrived at 5.30 a.m. and quickly examined the body, making a more thorough examination later in the day. Martha Tabram had been the victim of a frenzied attack, stabbed in the breasts, stomach, abdomen and vagina thirty-nine times, apparently with an ordinary penknife, although a wound on the chest-bone which had penetrated the sternum could have been made with a dagger or sword bayonet. Killeen thought all the wounds, with one possible exception, had been made by a right-handed man,[24] and estimated that Tabram had died at about 2.30 a.m. from haemorrhage and loss of blood. Dr Killeen was certain about one other matter of significance: although there was a lot of blood between Tabram's separated legs, there were no signs that she had recently had sex.[25] It is always possible that Killeen missed the traces, particularly if Tabram had devised a way of simulating intercourse without penetration actually taking place. Otherwise either Tabram's soldier companion had not managed to perform, or he had killed her without attempting sex – or he was not her murderer.

According to 'Pearly Poll', she and Tabram had separated a little after 11.45 p.m. Dr Killeen estimated that Tabram had died about 2.30 a.m. If these times are even remotely accurate, then Tabram almost certainly was not murdered by her soldier companion. That means she may possibly have been murdered by the companion of the soldier PC Barrett spoke to at 2 a.m. (although as far as we know, the soldier never specified that his mate had gone down George Yard). Also, assuming that George Yard Buildings was not where Tabram habitually took her customers, would she have hung around in that area for two and a half hours? The timings raise questions: if Killeen was in the least bit correct, Connelly's timings must be way out; or taking the timings together with Killeen's belief that Tabram had not had sex, one must wonder if Connelly's story was true.

It seems that Martha Tabram had been taken completely by surprise. She was given no time or opportunity to call for help or otherwise cry out. Francis Hewitt, the superintendent of George Yard Buildings, and his wife occupied a room close to where Martha's body was found. He measured the distance for a journalist. It was exactly 12 feet from the murder scene – 'And we never heard a cry.' Mrs Hewitt added that, early in the evening, a single cry of 'Murder!' had echoed through the building, but she did not think it had come from within it. Cries of 'Murder!' were quite frequent.[26]

In due course, Martha Tabram's mortal remains were placed on a police ambulance and taken to the mortuary, where on 8 August they were photographed. Her description was circulated in 116 infirmaries.[27]

* * *

There is a popular image of late-Victorian society as ordered and secure, prim and proper, well-mannered and graceful. It was and is an image fostered by many; but it was in reality a veneer that barely hid an underbelly of appalling heartlessness, vice and brutality. The nastiness was shoved into corners such as the East End and kept at a distance, hidden and largely ignored, its existence barely recognized. Victorian society was a room that looked tidy, but had all the clutter shoved in a cupboard. The fear was that it would all fall out once the door was opened.

The policemen of 'J' and 'H' Divisions, which covered much of the East End, were hardened by exposure to the poverty, misery, crime and immorality of the East End; yet even they were shocked and horrified by the frenzied attack on Martha Tabram. One remarked to a journalist: 'No crime more brutal has ever been committed in the East End, than the one at George-yard-buildings.'[28] The crime generated more press interest than the assault on Emma Smith, and the police investigation, led by Detective Inspector Edmund Reid, head of the local CID, was widely followed.

Inspector Reid faced an almost impossible task. He was hampered at the outset by problems in identifying Tabram: she was thought to be no fewer than four different people. According to the *East London Observer*, 'The difficulty of identification arose out of the brutal treatment to which the deceased was manifestly subjected, she being throttled while held down, and the face and head so swollen and distorted in consequence that her real features are not discernible.'[29] This is interesting, because the mortuary photograph of Tabram, the only photograph we possess, shows her in repose, as if asleep.

Inspector Reid's main hope of cracking the case initially lay in his belief that one of the wounds had been inflicted by a bayonet. Numerous soldiers had been seen drinking around the East End that night, one group in the nearby Princess Alice pub; but the *East London Advertiser* reported that George Street and some other streets in the immediate vicinity had 'for years been a regular rendezvous and hiding place for deserters'. Rusty bayonets could also be bought from the old-iron stalls in Petticoat Lane for about a penny each and had often been seen as playthings in the hands of children.[30]

Nevertheless, hope was kept alive by the possibility of locating the Grenadier Guardsman seen loitering in Wentworth Street by PC Barrett. As Barrett had provided a reasonable description of the man, Reid probably anticipated that he would be easily recognized in an identity parade. But any such hopes were soon dashed. On 7 August, Reid and Barrett went to the Tower of London Barracks, where the Grenadier Guards were stationed. Reid explained their business to the sergeant major, who at once took PC Barrett to the guardroom, where he was shown several prisoners. However, he did not recognize anyone because, he said, they were not in uniform. Reid arranged that the next day all the privates and corporals who were on leave on the night of 6 August would be put on parade, and at 11 a.m. on 8 August he and Barrett duly arrived again. Barrett remained out of sight by the sergeants' mess until the men had been lined up. Reid then told him to be careful because, as Reid would later write, 'many eyes were watching him and a great deal depended on his picking out the right man and no other'.

Instructed to walk along the line of men and to touch the man he saw in George Yard, if he was there, PC Barrett began his scrutiny, while Reid and the officers walked some distance away. When he got about halfway along the rank he stopped and touched a private wearing some medals. Then he turned and set off back towards Reid, who went to meet the constable. Barrett told Reid that he had picked out the man. The inspector asked him to make certain by going back and having another look. Barrett returned to the rank, walked along it, and this time picked out a soldier six or seven men away from the first. He explained to Reid that the first man he had picked out had medals, whereas the man he had seen near George Yard did not. Both soldiers were taken to the orderly room, where the man with medals was dismissed. The other man, whose name was John Leary, said that he had been drinking in Brixton with a private named Law, and that when the pub closed he had gone to relieve himself while Law had wandered off. Both had headed back into central London, meeting up again in Billingsgate at about 4.30 a.m. and going for another drink in one of the pubs that opened early for the market workers. They had arrived back at their barracks at 6 a.m. Private Law was then sent for, and, without speaking to Leary, corroborated this story. As Inspector Reid would later write in a report: 'They were unable to give me the name of any person to whom I could refer. I felt certain in my own mind that P.C. had made a great mistake and I allowed the men to leave the orderly room.'[31]

On the face of it, no effort seems to have been made to substantiate the story told by Leary and Law, who could have concocted their tale beforehand. It would appear that Reid simply accepted Law's corroboration and that was that. Neither man was able to produce anyone who had seen the two of them in any of the pubs they had visited, and nobody appears to have been sought out by the police. Leary and Law were either transparently truthful, or PC

Barrett was manifestly uncertain, or Reid's investigation was a mundane and pedestrian effort that makes one wonder if the criticism of the police was justified. Unfortunately, the surviving police papers relating to the murder of Martha Tabram are very few in number, and it is possible that the police investigation of Leary and Law was more thorough than it appears.

Reid also questioned Corporal John Henry Benjamin, who had returned to the barracks after being absent without leave since 6 August. He was asked about his whereabouts – he had been staying with his father, John Benjamin, who was the landlord of the Canbury Arms in Kingston-on-Thames[32] – and his clothing and bayonet were examined, but no marks of blood were found on them.

Two other witnesses, Jane Gillbank and her daughter, who lived at 23 Catherine Wheel Alley, Aldgate, claimed to have seen Tabram with a private of the Guards on the Sunday before her murder. They were taken to the barracks by Detective Sergeants Leach and Caunter (who rejoiced under the nickname 'Tommy Roundhead'),[33] but they failed to pick out the soldier they had seen. It was subsequently realized that the woman they thought had been murdered and had seen was a Mrs Withers, who was subsequently discovered to be alive.[34]

On 9 August, Mary Ann Connelly turned up at Commercial Street police station and told her story. Inspector Reid immediately arranged for her to attend an identity parade at the Tower of London the following day, but she did not show up. It was three days before Sergeant Eli Caunter tracked her down at the home of her cousin, Mrs Shean of Drury Lane. At the inquest Connelly would claim she had been unaware that she was twice wanted for an identity parade, but it was Inspector Reid's opinion that, after learning of Tabram's murder, Connelly 'kept out of the way purposely'. His report does not explain why she would have done that. It was also claimed that, on hearing that Tabram had been murdered, she had threatened to drown herself. While she admitted to having claimed this, she claimed it was just 'a lark'.

The identity parade was scheduled for 11 a.m. on 13 August, and several newspapers reported Mary Ann Connelly's confident and amusing performance. With the men paraded before her, she 'in no way embarrassed, placed her arms akimbo, glanced at the men with the air of an inspecting officer, and shook her head ...' She was patiently asked again if she could identify anyone. With a good deal of feminine emphasis, she exclaimed: 'He ain't here.'[35] She then explained that the soldiers who had been with her had white bands around their caps. This identified them as Coldstream Guards! They were stationed at Wellington Barracks, about 300 yards from Buckingham Palace, and on 15 August those who had been on leave on the night of the murder were paraded before Connelly. This time she unhesitatingly identified two men. One, Private George, had two good-conduct stripes and could have been mistaken for a corporal; however, he was able to prove that he had been at home at 120 Hammersmith Road with his wife, or a woman supposed to be his wife. The other, Private Henry Skipper, had returned to barracks early.[36]

Mary Ann Connelly's behaviour was odd. Her friend had been murdered, but she apparently did not hear of the murder for a day; she told her story to the police, but disappeared when required to attend an identity parade; then she identified two men so casually that Walter Dew was moved to say that she behaved 'in a fit of pique' and 'picked out the first two soldiers she saw'.[37] At the inquest, Inspector Reid also made sure that Connelly was properly cautioned and understood that what she said could be used in evidence against her. The police were evidently fed up with her antics, but why was 'Pearly Poll' so evasive? Dew was to say that: 'People from whom information was sought refused to talk. Their silence was imposed by terror. They were frightened of the Ripper's vengeance.' But this is unlikely to have applied in Connelly's case, because there was no reason to suppose at the time that there would be more murders. Overall, one feels that Mary Ann Connelly's evidence is not to be relied upon.

Whereas the attack on Emma Smith passed almost unnoticed, the murder of Martha Tabram – perhaps because of the frenzy of the attack – attracted far more press attention and public interest. Many people visited George Yard Buildings, going to the first-floor landing where the stone flags were still stained crimson by Martha's blood.[38]

* * *

The inquest had opened on the afternoon of 9 August 1888, in the Alexandra Room, the lecture room and library of the Working Lads' Institute in Whitechapel Road, near the present Whitechapel underground station. It was described in one newspaper as a 'well and prettily furnished' room, the walls displaying portraits of the Royal Family and landscapes; one particularly magnificent portrait of the Princess of Wales by Louis Fleischmann hung above the seat occupied by the coroner, who on this occasion was George Collier, the deputy coroner of the south-eastern division of Middlesex (Wynne Baxter was on a well-deserved holiday at that time). The jury, whose elected foreman was a Mr Geary, sat on Collier's left, and on his right were Dr Killeen and Inspector Reid, the latter smartly dressed in a blue serge suit (Reid always took great pains over his appearance) and giving the impression that he was 'absorbing all the material points without taking so much as a note'.[39] Perhaps the notes were being taken by one Sergeant Green, who was accompanying him.

In front of the coroner sat Ann Morris. Also present was a young woman wearing a blue dress and black hat, with a white and blue check kerchief around her neck, and a baby in her arms. She was accompanied by a woman who was apparently her mother.[40] This young woman had been taken to view the body at the mortuary by Mr Banks, the coroner's officer, and had identified it as Martha Turner. As two other women had also identified the body and had supplied different names, the inquest that day only heard evidence concerning the discovery of the body. It was then adjourned in the hope that the police would confirm the woman's identity. Collier was unusually animated. He also lacked Wynne Baxter's cool detachment, observing that the murder was 'one of the most terrible cases that anyone can possibly imagine. The man must have been a perfect savage to have attacked the woman in that way.'

Two weeks later, on Thursday, 23 August, the inquest was reopened, but interest in the crime had dwindled and only a small group of people gathered outside the Working Lads' Institute to watch the functionaries and witnesses arrive.[41] The hearing did not last long. The testimony of a few witnesses was heard, and after some excited discussion the jury returned the inevitable verdict of 'wilful murder against some person or persons unknown'. It asked that the stairs in George Yard Buildings and similar properties be lit after 11 p.m.

Inspector Reid informed the court that many people had come forward with information, but that none of it had led anywhere. He assured the court that inquiries were still being made. The failure of the police to make any headway in their investigation was quickly criticized by the press, the *Eastern Post and City Chronicle* remarking:

> A considerable amount of mystery surrounds the whole affair, which the police have entirely failed to unravel, and the evidence they have been able to obtain has been very meagre indeed. No arrest has been made, and it would seem that as usual the 'clever' detective officers have been relying upon some of the same miserable class of the wretched victim to 'give them the clue'.[42]

Walter Dew thought this criticism 'grossly unfair':

> It would be impossible to recount here all that was done, the hundreds of inquiries that were made, the scores of statements taken and the long, long hours put in by us all. No clue was turned down as too trivial for investigation.

We all had heartbreaking experiences, several times I got on to something which looked like a clue, followed it up day and night, only to find in the end it led nowhere.[43]

That was all very well, but the failure on the part of the press and public alike to appreciate the efforts made by the police and the seriousness they attached to their investigation was largely the fault of the police themselves. Their policy appears to have been not to talk to the press, and the *East London Advertiser* observed that the police were 'very reticent upon the matter generally, and are not disposed to assist in the publication of details'.[44] Walter Dew confirmed that the police kept 'the Press at arm's length' and regarded this policy – 'the policy of those in high places' – as a mistake, insofar as it 'flouted a great potential ally, and indeed might have turned that ally into an enemy'.[45]

The police investigation did not get anywhere. The only clue to Martha's murderer was Connelly's story about the soldiers. In September, *The Echo* commented that Connelly had given the police 'a slight clue' which 'was not thought much of at the time', but which, following a subsequent murder, had received support from two additional witnesses, Eliza Cooper and Elizabeth Allen. This pointed the finger of suspicion at 'a man actually living not far from Buck's Row'. It is not known what the clue was or who the man was.[46]

Was Martha Tabram murdered by her soldier companion? Was she murdered by the 'mate' of the soldier spoken to by PC Barrett? Or was she murdered by someone else entirely? The theory that she was an early victim of Jack the Ripper has gone in and out of fashion over the years. Sir Melville Macnaghten discounted the idea because her throat was not cut and she had not been disembowelled or muti-lated; but she had been the victim of a frenzied attack, and the cuts in the abdomen – one of them three inches long and the other an inch deep – may have been an attempt at 'ripping'. In later years,

Inspector Abberline told a journalist that 'the first murder was committed' in George Yard. Sir Robert Anderson stated in his auto-biography that he took office on the eve of the murder of Mary Ann Nichols, which he described as 'the second of the crimes known as the Whitechapel murders'. Walter Dew wrote: 'Whatever may be said about the death of Emma Smith there can be no doubt that the August Bank Holiday murder, which took place in George Yard Buildings, less than a hundred yards from the spot where the first victim died, was the handiwork of the dread Ripper.'[47]

CHAPTER 5

Jack Strikes

Mary Ann Nichols (31 August 1888)

THE METROPOLITAN POLICE FILE ON THE MURDERS IS KNOWN as the Whitechapel Murders file and it covers those murders committed in the East End between that of Emma Smith in April 1888 and Frances Coles in February 1891. Writing in 1894, however, the then chief constable (CID), Sir Melville Macnaghten, stated that Jack the Ripper had committed five murders and five murders only.[1] These five are popularly known as the 'canonical five'. That all five were indeed committed by the same person was disputed by some contemporary policemen, and it is fiercely debated today; also, as we have seen, other policemen attributed to the Ripper's murderous hands some of the victims who were discounted by Macnaghten.

The 'canonical five' are certainly not forgotten. Their prominence as the widely accepted victims of the world's most famous serial murderer has meant that these five women, who would otherwise be unknown to history, have taken on an almost iconic status. Their lives, family history and even their descendants have been meticulously researched; they have been played by innumerable actresses in countless television documentaries, stage productions and mainstream films. Their graves, in various East London cemeteries,[2] are regularly visited, and floral tributes (sometimes even gifts) are left by those paying their respects. They are not dead – they live on in the hearts and minds of some, and in the collective consciousness of those for whom the Jack the Ripper story is a popular legend. The other victims of the Whitechapel murders have yet to attain such 'celebrity' status, and it can be argued that, as historical 'popularism' continues to triumph over wider consideration of the events, they never will.

When Charles Cross,[3] a carman employed at Pickfords in Broad Street, found the prostrate body of Mary Ann Nichols lying on the pavement of Buck's Row, Whitechapel, at about 3.40 a.m. on 31 August 1888, he undoubtedly had no idea of the significance of his discovery. Neither, perhaps, did Robert Paul, who was passing down the street at the same time and whose attention Cross drew to the woman. The men had other concerns – they were both keen not to be late for work. Unable to agree on whether she was dead or drunk, they went on their way, looking out for a policeman. A little later, PC John Neil came upon the body, having missed the two men by perhaps just minutes. By the light of his bull's eye lantern, he could see two terrible cuts in the woman's throat, which imme-diately confirmed to him that she was dead. But PC Neil could have had no inkling of what was soon to unfold: in the mortuary, it was discovered that her abdomen had been ripped open from the groin to the breastbone, this large wound being accompanied by some other smaller cuts and stabs.

At the time of her death, Mary Ann Nichols was an 'unfortunate'; born Mary Ann Walker in the City of London in 1845, she had married printer's machinist William Nichols in 1864. She separated from her husband and their five children around 1880, after a trou-bled marriage. According to her husband, Mary Ann's drinking was the cause; but her father let it be known that William's involve-ment with the midwife who had seen Mary Ann through her last confinement was as much to blame.[4] By 1888, she had gravitated towards the easily found lodging houses of Spitalfields via the workhouse, the infirmary and a brief spell in domestic service which ended unhappily when she absconded from her employers, taking with her clothing of some value.[5] On the last night of her life, her dependency on alcohol had soaked up any money she had and she was refused admission to her Thrawl Street lodging house. Her reliance on prostitution as a convenient way of getting money to pay for a bed led to her death in the quiet, poorly lit Buck's Row.

Her murder was swiftly and widely reported in the press. It gained significantly more coverage than the deaths of Emma Smith and Martha Tabram – simply because, with those two outrages in mind, the murder of Mary Ann Nichols was considered part of a now expanding series. That evening, *The Star* went so far as to say 'such horrible work could only be the deed of a maniac',[6] and the next day, the paper nailed its colours well and truly to the mast, talking of 'the third crime of a man who must be a maniac'.[7] The concept of 'the Whitechapel murders' as the work of a lone, crazed killer was born.

With very little hard evidence to go on, the police had no luck in apprehending Mary Ann's killer. Many in the area suspected a local miscreant who went by the name of 'Leather Apron'. This man was believed to be Jewish – significant in that, even at this early stage, the innumerable Eastern European Jews in the area were seen as responsible for many of its problems, and so it was felt that one of their number was likely to have committed the murders. A Jew would be the ideal scapegoat. The police began to look for a man named John Pizer[8] in connection with the rumours, but he proved hard to locate. There was a growing unease about the Jewish community, allied with a mounting fear of 'Leather Apron'.

Annie Chapman (8 September 1888)

The horrific murder of Annie Chapman on 8 September took everybody by surprise. Her life was not dissimilar to that of the previous victim. She was the widow of John Chapman,[9] a Windsor coachman. Originally separated from her family around 1882 owing to her overindulgence in alcohol and resultant behaviour, she left her husband with their two children[10] and fell to a life of tramping the area around Clewer, near Windsor, before settling in Spitalfields. The oldest of the Whitechapel victims, she was 47 and was apparently suffering from a disease of the lungs (probably tuberculosis), which had spread to the membranes of her brain. It seems her life would have been short even if she had not been murdered in the backyard of 29 Hanbury Street, Spitalfields.

Discovered by John Davis, a resident of that house, her body bore the most shocking injuries: the neck had been cut twice, with both wounds going all the way round and deep enough to reach the vertebrae; she had been disembowelled and her intestines thrown over her shoulder; several internal organs had been removed, specifically the uterus, other portions of the sexual organs and a large piece of her bladder. Dr George Bagster Phillips, on conducting a postmortem, his first in the series, declared that 'obviously the work was that of an expert – of one, at least, who had such knowledge of anatomical or pathological examinations as to be enabled to secure [sic] the pelvic organs with one sweep of a knife'.[11] The observation was one that was of lasting significance, suggesting to some that the murderer may have had medical training or else be a butcher or slaughterman.

The Hanbury Street murder caused a remarkable reaction in the area, generating a palpable mixture of fear, anger and helplessness. Great crowds assembled at the murder sites and followed rumours of arrests with considerable rowdiness. The police were very much aware of the growing prejudice and physical threats against the Jews, and with the heady mix of sporadic unrest, mob mentality and hairtrigger responses to even the slightest rumours, this latest murder was deemed to have 'driven the inhabitants of Whitechapel nearly crazy'.[12]

Two days after Annie Chapman's death, Sergeant William Thick arrested John Pizer at his home in Mulberry Street, Whitechapel. Under questioning, the accused was able to furnish the police with cast-iron alibis that accounted for his movements at the times of the murders. The authorities had no choice but to release him. It was a disappointing development and did little to quell the panic.

Local businessmen were reporting a steep decline in business on account of the reluctance of many to venture out after dark. This led to the formation of various vigilance committees, the most prominent being the Mile End Vigilance Committee, whose president was George Lusk. As well as providing extra intelligence to the police, they were active in lobbying for the offer of rewards (not considered appropriate by the Home Office, in light of the problems that the promise of ready cash often presented).[13]

On 27 September 1888, the Central News Agency, a direct competitor to the Press Association, received a letter addressed to 'The Boss'. Written in red ink and using language that was both arrogant and threatening, the author signed himself off as 'Jack the Ripper'.[14] Originally believed to be a joke, the letter was held back at the author's request, until the murderer did 'a bit more work'. There was not long to wait.

Elizabeth Stride and Catherine Eddowes (30 September 1888)

Elizabeth Stride was born Elisabeth Gustafsdottir in Sweden in 1843. Following her mother's death in 1866, she came into enough money to enable her to emigrate to London. She married John Stride in 1869, and for a while they held onto a decent life running a coffee shop in Poplar. But their marriage failed and they separated, John dying of heart disease in 1884.

Elizabeth had been registered as a prostitute in her native country many years before.[15] Although she had taken up with a new man, Michael Kidney, it is likely that she turned to prostitution frequently towards the end of her life. Her dead body was found in Dutfield's Yard, Berner Street, at 1 a.m. on 30 September, by Louis Diemschitz, a market trader who had been returning home after a long day at the markets in Sydenham, South London. Elizabeth's throat had been cut and was still bleeding, but her body displayed none of the mutilations present in the previous victims, suggesting to many that not only was the murder a recent one, but also that the approach of Diemschitz on his cart had disturbed the murderer before he could complete his grisly task.

At 1.45 a.m. that same day, PC Edward Watkins passed into Mitre Square in the City of London and found the night's second victim, 46-year-old Catherine Eddowes. Hailing originally from Wolverhampton in the Midlands, she had for many years lived with a man named Thomas Conway, by whom she had three children. But they had gone their separate ways, and by 1888 Catherine had been living with a man named John Kelly in Flower and Dean Street[16] for seven years. Only forty-five minutes before her corpse was found, Catherine had been released from Bishopsgate police station after spending much of the night in the cells, having been arrested for being drunk and incapable in Aldgate High Street. The last purported sighting of her was by three men leaving a club only nine minutes before her body was found:[17] she had been standing with a man at the entrance to Church Passage, a narrow footway that ran into Mitre Square. Her injuries were the most violent yet: her throat had been cut through to the spine and her face had been mutilated by deliberate, often quite delicate, cuts. She had been disembowelled, pieces of intestine lay over her shoulder and around her on the pavement, and her uterus and left kidney had been extracted and taken away.

It was that night that the problems faced by the police were brought into sharp focus. The two murders had taken place within different police jurisdictions: Stride's was in Metropolitan Police territory, whereas Eddowes had been found in the district policed by the City of London force. What immediately brought these two constabularies[18] together was the removal of a piece of linen apron from Eddowes' clothing, and its subsequent discovery in Whitechapel. The material, found by a police officer, Alfred Long, had blood on it and was discovered in the open doorway to a block of artisans' dwellings in Goulston Street. Above the piece of rag was a message, written in white chalk: 'The Juwes are the men that will not be blamed for nothing.'[19] The City Police recognized a potential piece of evidence and wished to see the graffito photographed; however, before the arrangements could be made, Metropolitan Police Commissioner Charles Warren arrived on the scene and, worried that anti-Jewish rioting could result if the wrong sort of person saw the message, controversially ordered the writing to be washed off.

As promised, the letter signed 'Jack the Ripper' was duly released to the public, giving this mysterious and elusive killer his permanent sobriquet and, unfortunately, inspiring thousands of imitation letters. The same day, Central News received a postcard from the same writer, mentioning the 'double event'. This no doubt added to the excitement and panic. It led several senior detectives to assume that these two important communications were a journalistic hoax. One letter, addressed 'From Hell' and received by George Lusk of the Mile End Vigilance Committee on 16 October, contained half a human kidney, significant in light of the removal of one such organ from the body of Catherine Eddowes a fortnight before. In terms of sensation and public outrage, the Whitechapel murders had reached their peak.

Mary Jane Kelly (9 November 1888)

The murder of Mary Jane Kelly, considered by many to be the Ripper's final atrocity, took place the day after the resignation of Charles Warren as commissioner of the Metropolitan Police.[20]

Mary Kelly was the youngest victim – only 25 years of age – and according to Melville Macnaghten was 'said to be of considerable personal attractions'.[21] Her history is muddied by the fact that all we know about her is what she told people – none of these facts have ever been substantiated, then or now, and she is almost as mysterious as the monster who took her young life. Believed to have been born in Limerick, Ireland, she moved with her family to Wales when she was a young girl. She married young, to a collier named Davis, but was widowed a year or two later when her husband was caught in a mining accident.[22] She later stayed with a cousin in Cardiff, where she became involved in prostitution. She apparently spent some time at a high-class bordello in London's West End, and later with a 'gentleman' in France, perhaps where she acquired the name 'Marie Jeanette'.[23] She arrived in the East End around 1884, initially living in the Ratcliffe Highway district before moving to Spitalfields, where she met Joseph Barnett on Good Friday 1887. It is from him that we get most of our information about her alleged past. From this point on, the couple lived together in various lodgings until they separated in October 1888, their last address being Room 13, Miller's Court, Dorset Street.

Mary Kelly's savagely mutilated body was found in that very room, at 10.45 a.m. on 9 November, by Thomas Bowyer, sent by landlord John McCarthy to collect some overdue rent money. The privacy of such a room may have had some bearing on the sheer gratuitous nature of the mutilations, which were extensive. The face was mutilated beyond all recognition and the head had been almost severed from the body; the flesh from the torso down to the thighs had been stripped to the bone and placed on the bedside table; except for the lungs, most of the internal organs had also been put on the bedside table or strewn around the body on the bed where Kelly lay. The heart was absent.[24] In the words of John McCarthy, 'the whole scene is more than I can describe. I hope I may never see such a sight again'.[25]

In November 1888, the murder of Mary Kelly was not seen as the final act of 'Jack the Ripper' and it was feared that a new outrage could be just around the corner. Yet there were no murders in Whitechapel thereafter that reached the revolting heights of that awful affair in Miller's Court. As we shall see, though, the public outrage and fear meant that any attack on a woman in the East End – or anywhere else for that matter – was perceived as a potential Ripper crime, whether or not murder was the end result. Some incidents occurred during the Ripper scare; many happened some time afterwards. What they had in common was that, every time, the name Jack the Ripper would be uppermost in people's minds.

CHAPTER 6

'He's Gone to Gateshead'

Jane Beadmore (22 September 1888)

Towards the end of September 1888, a journalist for the *Daily News* took an autumn stroll through the backstreets of Whitechapel and was surprised to see that life appeared to be continuing as normal. Nobody seemed concerned about the possibility that the Whitechapel Murderer would kill again, and the journalist commented on this to a respectable-looking man standing outside a house in Hanbury Street. The man looked at the journalist: 'People, most of 'em, think he's gone to Gateshead.'[1]

Gateshead, in the north-east of England, on the southern bank of the Tyne and opposite Newcastle upon Tyne, is a long way from Whitechapel, but a murder that bore similarities to the atrocities committed in London's East End briefly led many people, including the police, to think that the murderer had moved north. The crime had, in fact, been committed near Birtley, a large village a few miles from Gateshead and some three miles from Chester-le-Street.

Birtley had a handsome church dedicated to St John the Evangelist, a Catholic church, various places of worship devoted to other denominations, a post office, a police station, a few shops, and several pubs and beer-houses. It was a hard-working community, with employment concentrated in the local ironworks and collieries and on the local farms. In 1888 there was little to mark it out as a village of distinction – save that one Ralph Goftan had died there on 28 June 1817, supposedly aged 102. Much later, in July 2010, it would gain unwelcome media attention when Raoul Thomas Moat shot and killed Samantha Stobbart and Chris Brown there (Moat then went on to shoot and permanently blind policeman David Rathband, who later took his own life).

But that is where 27-year-old Jane Beadmore was murdered in September 1888. She was better known locally by the name Jane Savage. She was 5ft 8in, had a fair complexion, brown hair and blue eyes. She was reportedly quiet and inoffensive, was generally liked,[2] and lived with her family in the isolated but grandly named Whitehouse Cottage. This was a low, brick and red-tile house with one or two attached outhouses, located at the top of a field. A central partition divided it into two accommodations, each having a large single lower room and a small room above described as a 'mere hole'. Jane and her family lived in the single downstairs room, the room above being used to keep a flight of pigeons. The other part of the house was occupied by a man named Walter Lowden and his family.

When she was very young, Jane's mother, Isabella, had married a ship's carpenter and had two children, Jane and her elder brother, Joseph, who by 1888 was living away from Birtley. But the marriage had not lasted. Isabella had later married a miner named Joseph Savage, and this second marriage had produced William, a young half-brother for Joseph and Jane, who in 1888 was in his early twenties. All the family worked: Joseph and William were both miners, William having been down the mines since he was 16, and possibly even before; Isabella got what work she could labouring on the local farms; and Jane, who had an unspecified cardiac condition, looked after the home. At the time of her murder, she had recently come out of Newcastle Infirmary and was receiving treatment as an out-patient at Gateshead Infirmary.

Saturday, 22 September 1888 was the day summer officially ended. In Birtley, the season of 'mists and mellow fruitfulness' began with fog. The north of England had been plagued by severe fogs, and the attendant dampness had damaged the crops (as indeed was the case across the country as a whole). Jane had traipsed through the gloom and damp to Gateshead Infirmary to collect some medicine, returning home at about 2.30 p.m. She then attended to household chores until about 7 p.m., when she went out, supposedly to meet her half-brother at a local pub called the Oxclose. He had gone to Newcastle to play bowls, a pastime of which he was extremely fond, and he usually called in at the pub on the way home.

However, Jane went instead to the Mount Moor Inn at Birtley North Side, where Mrs Elizabeth Morris, the landlord's wife, ran a small general shop. There Jane bought a pennyworth of toffee, saying that the medicine she had been given that morning had left a nasty taste in her mouth which she hoped the toffee would take away. Jane then went to see 47-year-old Mrs Dorothy Newell at nearby Hinde Farm, where she stayed for what Mrs Newell rather unhelpfully called a 'canny bit', but which appears to have been less than half an hour. Soon after she got there, a lad named William Waddell[3] turned up.

William Waddell was 22 years old. He was 5ft 9in or 5ft 10in tall, had a sallow complexion, brown hair and sunken blue eyes. He also apparently had some problem with his legs – tender feet, it was said[4] – which caused him to walk with his feet splayed outwards and leaning forward, as if battling a strong wind. Curiously, however, Waddell was very fond of boxing, and when engaged in that pursuit would straighten up, lose his heavy, slouching gait, and carry himself well. He was a neat and fairly skilful boxer. He seemed generally to be of a sullen and morose disposition (although friends said that this impression of his character was false). According to James Falloon, Waddell could sit in company for hours without raising his eyes from the floor, and even when addressed directly he usually just answered 'Yes' or 'No'. Falloon, whom the newspapers described as a man of 'considerable intelligence' and who had served in the

Afghan campaign in the 15th East Yorkshire Regiment of the Line,[5] said he had frequently tried to discuss books, theatre and such subjects with him, but generally received a half-idiotic laugh by way of reply. He considered Waddell a very illiterate man.

Another man, William Kibbens, defended Waddell, whom he described as a good mate and a hard worker. While agreeing that he displayed meagre conversational powers, Kibbens said he was fond of discussing bowling matches. Others who knew Waddell agreed, and stated that he was happy to join in the laughter when jokes were told or played. Friends also spoke of a very sharp knife that Waddell possessed. Some two weeks earlier he had bought a new knife, but almost straight away had swapped it with a lad named Thomas Falloon, the nephew of the veteran of Afghanistan. Indeed it was Thomas's uncle who had given him the knife he went on to swap with Waddell, scratching his own initials 'J. F.' on the blade before doing so. This was a working man's dinner knife, brown-hafted, with a broad blade that was three inches or so in length and of excellent steel that could be sharpened to a razor-like keenness.

Waddell had lived with his family, but some eight or nine months earlier had struck out on his own, found lodgings in Birtley with a 49-year-old widow named Jane McCormack at a house called Brickgarth, and got himself a job operating a slag-breaking machine for John McAvoy, who also ran a beer-house in Birtley called the Hanlon Hotel. He had turned up for work that Saturday morning, but colleagues said his behaviour was very strange: he would laugh for no apparent reason, and he persistently tapped the lad working beside him on the head with his knuckles. He then pushed the lad, whereupon William Kibbens remonstrated with him. At this point Waddell had said: 'I would like to kill him.' A little later he picked up a pickaxe and told Kibbens: 'I would like to kill you, you bastard.' He made further comments of a similar nature, and on one occasion produced his knife and told a lad nearby that he 'would like to stick him'. None of it was said with serious intent and it was treated by

Waddell's mates as a joke; but they were distinctly puzzled by his unusual and eccentric behaviour.[6] Furthermore, for some days he had been obsessing about how he would go about killing someone if he had to; and he was always reading about the Whitechapel murders and constantly talking about them. As one newspaper observed, it seemed as if Waddell was 'suffering from some slight mental derangement'.[7]

At 1 p.m. Waddell left work for the weekend, but he had to return later that afternoon to collect his wages of 19 shillings. He then appears to have gone drinking, because when he returned to Mrs McCormack's at about 4 p.m. he was drunk. This was unusual for Waddell, at least in Mrs McCormack's experience, she having found him to be of sober and temperate habits. At one point he vomited, but otherwise sat quietly in the house. At about 7 p.m. he changed his clothes and went out.

James Falloon said he saw Waddell around 6 p.m., very drunk. Either Falloon's timings were wrong or Mrs McCormack's were (or one or the other or both were misreported by the journalist). It seems likely that Falloon got the time wrong and that he saw Waddell at about 4 p.m.

There was one explanation for William Waddell's uncharacteristic behaviour. For two years he and Jane Beadmore had been going out together and were believed by many to be engaged to be married. However, it seems that Jane wanted to detach herself from the relationship. A few days earlier, while out walking with a friend named Isabella McGuinness, she had said that she had 'found someone nicer' and wanted to have nothing further to do with Waddell.[8] Jane, who was cheerful at Mrs Newell's house, appeared unperturbed when Waddell arrived, out of breath. He said nothing, but seemed morose, even sulky, and sat with his head down. He even refused some of Jane's toffee. This behaviour seems to have been in keeping with Waddell's personality, but it may have been a consequence of feeling unwell from the drink he had imbibed, or being upset with Jane. What is known is that Jane left Mrs Newell's house at about 8 p.m., saying that she was going home. Waddell quickly stood up and, without saying a word, left too.

* * *

About 8 p.m., Henry Brown and Newark Forster were bound for Birtley, travelling in a cart loaded with furniture up Black Road, which ran between the Newells' house and the Vale Pit. Both men saw a woman walking in the opposite direction, and both men thought she was alone, although Forster was not as certain as Brown, because the furniture on the cart partly obscured his view. An hour or two later, sometime between 9 and 10 p.m., James Gilmore, a miner who lived at Hebburn Quay, was heading for his aunt's house, the delightfully named Look-Out Cottages, when he saw a man and a woman approaching him. The man was about 5ft 9in or 5ft 10in tall. It was dark and their features were indistinct, but Gilmore thought the woman fitted Beadmore's description and the man's height matched Waddell's. Gilmore had said, 'Aye aye there, mon!', but neither had replied and they appeared to be arguing.

William Savage, Jane's half-brother, had returned from Newcastle by tramcar with James Page and Jack Cook, two friends from the nearby village of New York. They reached the Low Fell terminus sometime between 8 and 9 p.m.[9] From there, William and his companions had to walk home. He left Page and Cook near the Mount Moor Inn in Birtley and went inside, his companions continuing on home. It was now about 10.20 p.m., and he stayed at the inn until 11 p.m., drinking with Walter Lowden. Then he went home, where he ate some supper and went to bed. His mother stayed up, concerned about Jane, and eventually she and Joseph went to look for her. They concluded that she must have stayed with a friend for the night.

William Waddell had not returned to his lodgings either, and Mrs McCormack had likewise grown concerned at his absence.

At about 7.20 a.m. on Sunday, 23 September, John Fish, a boiler-smith who lived in Ouston, to the south of Birtley, was on his way to work in the village of Eighton Banks to the north. His route caused him to cross the track of a railway branch line (called a wagon-way), which was used to transport coal from Ouston Colliery to Bell Quay. It was a dismal area, and no part was more dreary-looking and desolate than Sandy Cut. There, in a ditch running alongside the railway track, he spotted what seemed to be a young woman. The body lay about three or four feet from the line, the head being in a gutter about nine or ten inches deep, with the legs pointed towards the wagon-way. It leaned partly over to the left, and on the right side of the throat, just below the ear, a frightful gash was visible. The position in which the corpse was found was such as to indicate that the woman had been seized with sudden alarm. The palms of her hands were stretched out, and were close to each other.[10]

Fish clambered into the ditch and touched her right cheek and then her arm. Finding the body cold, he realized that she was dead. He then ran to a nearby house for directions to the home of the local policeman, John Dodds. Leaving his lunchbox and tools at the house, Fish went to fetch the constable and returned with him to the scene, where Dodds recognized the woman as Jane Beadmore. He made a quick examination of the scene, but could find no evidence of a struggle or any clues such as footprints. In her pockets he found the toffees she had bought earlier, a pair of gloves, and a handkerchief with sixpence wrapped up in it, the presence of the money perhaps suggesting that robbery had not been the motive. Dodds then arranged for messages to be sent to Dr Walter Galloway in nearby Wrekenton and to the police station, where Sergeant Hutchinson was in conference with the senior officer of the Gateshead Division, Superintendent Harrison, who was paying a visit to Birtley. The three men were quickly at the scene and the body was quietly removed to Whitehouse Cottage, Jane's family being moved elsewhere.

Jane Beadmore had been struck with a knife on the right side of the head, behind the ear, with a sweeping stroke delivered with such force that it would have stunned her and probably knocked her down. A second wound, made by a downwards stroke, was on the right side of the face. Neither would have been fatal, but there was a severe gash to the lower part of the body, probably inflicted when Jane was on the ground, and there was a wound in the abdominal cavity, an inch or two in length, inflicted by a knife held with its cutting edge upwards. Another wound within the abdominal wall had been caused when the knife was withdrawn, and it was this that had undoubtedly killed her. The intestines protruded from the lower wound, but none were missing, and no attempt had been made to remove them. Medical opinion was that there would have been no time for Jane to have struggled or screamed, and that death would have occurred within a minute of the start of the attack. She had died from internal and external haemorrhage from a wound in the lower part of her body.

The newspapers were quick to identify a link between this murder and those committed in London. 'Gateshead has been the scene of a Whitechapel murder', reported *The Star*.[11] 'The methods and success of the murderer so closely resemble those of the Whitechapel fiend that the local authorities are strongly inclined to connect the two crimes. As in the last two London cases the murder was effected without any violent struggling on the part of the victim, the actual cause of death was the cutting of the throat, and the same parts of the body were mutilated in a very similar manner', said the sober *Daily Telegraph*.[12] The *Daily News* wrote that the murder 'has caused quite a panic in the district, the resemblance to the Whitechapel tragedies encouraging the idea that the maniac who had been at work in London has travelled down to the North of England to pursue his fiendish vocation'.[13] And the *Morning Advertiser* noted that 'The similarity of this crime with the recent tragedies in the East end of London has caused the wildest excitement in the neighbourhood.'[14]

It is clear that for a time the police seriously suspected that Jane Beadmore might have been killed by the Whitechapel murderer, and on the evening of 24 September Scotland Yard dispatched Inspector Roots and Dr George Bagster Phillips (who had performed the post-mortem on Annie Chapman) to Durham. The following morning, Inspector Roots and Dr Phillips were taken by Colonel White, the chief constable of Durham, to Birtley, and that afternoon Dr Phillips viewed the body and made a close examination. Afterwards he refused to make any comment to the press, but it was nevertheless reported, apparently on the authority of Inspector Roots, that a connection with the Whitechapel crimes was discounted. The reason given was that the murderer of Annie Chapman was generally believed to have displayed some anatomical knowledge, whereas the murderer of Jane Beadmore appeared clumsy, and she had been over-come by brute force.[15] Back in London, Dr Phillips, who was inter-viewed by a representative of the Press Association, confirmed what the press had been reporting, saying that Beadmore's murder had been 'a clumsy piece of butchery'.[16]

Inspector Roots and Dr Phillips stayed only the day in Durham, and by 26 September both men were back in London. Whether or not the local police had welcomed the involvement of the men from the capital is unknown, but it is certainly possible that they did not, their own thoughts about the murder by now tending to focus else-where. As *The Times* reported, the arrival of Roots and Phillips really only served to intensify the anxiety of the local population, who were taking a keen interest in the crime. As had happened back in London, thousands of people visited the scene of the murder.

While it was now generally accepted that the murder of Jane Beadmore and the Whitechapel murders had been committed by different people, *The Times* did perceptively observe that the two were probably connected, insofar as 'the perpetrator of the former had attempted an imitation of the Whitechapel murders after brooding over the cruel details of how the bodies of the women

Nichols and Chapman had been mutilated'. Although the newspapers did not make too much of the fact that the Whitechapel murders had inspired another killer (perhaps because the horror of the 'Double Event' had put everything else in the shade), *The Star* did observe that:

> As the nights grow darker and longer, the facilities for murderous action will become enormously increased, and it is only fair to the police to say that their difficulties will grow also. The question to which the citizens of London will expect an answer is, whether steps are being taken to cope with so serious a problem.[17]

Real suspicion had fallen on William Waddell as soon as it became known that he had disappeared from Birtley. The initial feeling of the police was that Waddell would have killed himself, and a search began of the disused mine shafts in the area. Then it was learned that Waddell was fond of taking long walks, and would often leave home after breakfast to walk to Sunderland, Newcastle or further afield. Once it was appreciated that he was very familiar with all the roads and by-roads round about and could probably cover a considerable distance in a relatively short time, the search was widened and the police distributed handbills describing him. These led to reported sightings in Gateshead and Newcastle, among other places. In a suburb of Newcastle, a rumour that Waddell had been captured resulted in a crowd following a police constable and a man he had arrested on some minor charge to the police station. Another rumour was that a person answering Waddell's description had been seen loitering about the remote uplands near Satley, a village a few miles south of the town of Consett, and a Superintendent Oliver and some constables went to search the countryside there.

A man named Robert Lodge believed he had seen Waddell at 7 a.m., about 14 miles from Birtley, at the Byers Green Colliery, where Lodge was a foreman coke burner. He described this man as rather melodramatically wielding a large knife and apparently using his leather boot to whet or clean it. The man is supposed to have asked Lodge the time, and then disappeared.[18] Whoever it was that Lodge saw (if he in fact saw anyone), it was not Waddell, who at that time was about 18 miles west of Newcastle upon Tyne, near the town of Corbridge. Waddell's brother lived here, but Waddell didn't know where, and it was at about 6.45 a.m. that he stopped and spoke to a man named George Taylor, asking if he knew where someone named Waddell or Tweddle lived. Taylor, who thought Waddell looked exhausted, told him that a man of that name did live in the town, but he didn't know where.

On the afternoon of 26 September, the remains of Jane Beadmore were interred in the graveyard of Birtley parish church. The coffin, which bore a plate plainly inscribed 'Jane Beetmoor [sic]. Died Sept. 22, 1888', was followed to the grave by a cortège fully half a mile long, and the ceremony, conducted by Rev. Arthur Watts, who made several touching remarks, was witnessed by an enormous crowd, many of whom had travelled considerable distances to be there.[19]

By 27 September, Waddell had reached the historic border town of Berwick-upon-Tweed, where, at about 11 a.m., he visited Elizabeth Brodie's second-hand clothes shop in Water Lane. Saying that he was hard up and in need of money, he wanted to exchange his suit for a cheaper one and some cash. This he did, leaving the shop with a different suit and five shillings, which he indicated he would use for the train fare to Edinburgh. Taking pity on the lad, Mrs Brodie also gave him some bread, coffee and sugar. He then went across the street to a shop owned by a Mr Ferguson and bought a cap for sixpence to replace his round felt hat.

Later that day, he appeared in Spittal, a small town near Berwick (which, like Spitalfields, derived its name from a medieval hospital). It was here that Waddell was approached by a suspicious police constable, John Frizzle, in answer to whose questions Waddell claimed to be William Lee from Otterburn and to be heading for the town of Ancroft. Although far from certain that he was being told the truth, the constable noted that Waddell's front teeth were missing – a fairly distinctive feature that was not mentioned in the circulated description of Waddell and which eventually led Frizzle to conclude that the man before him was not the man being sought.

Waddell crossed the border into Scotland and approached the village of Yetholm, a small community nestling in the foothills of the Cheviots, the range of rolling hills astride the border between England and Scotland.[20] It was here that William Waddell was finally caught. On Monday morning, William Stenhouse, a wool dealer in Yetholm, was heading along a lonely road leading out of Yetholm towards Halterburn, to the south-east, when he came across Waddell and engaged him in conversation. Waddell said he was looking for harvest work. Suspecting that this could be the wanted man whose description he had read, Stenhouse suggested that the man accompany him back to Yetholm, where he thought work would be available. On the journey back to the village, Waddell claimed his name was Laws, said he was from Coldstream, and mentioned some people, in particular a farmer called Jonathon Rutherford, and a hotel there, none of them known to Mr Stenhouse, who was familiar with the place.

Stenhouse took Waddell straight to the police station, but found the village policeman, PC Thompson, absent on a search for Waddell. Stenhouse managed to get the still-unresisting Waddell into a cell, and then waited for the policeman's return. When PC Thompson got back, he spent an hour talking to Waddell, questioning him and trying to get him to confirm his identity; but Waddell insisted that his name was Laws, that he did not know Birtley, had not been there, and did not know a Jane Beadmore. Finally, perhaps succumbing to disorientation, when asked if he knew a Jane Savage, Waddell claimed that she was his wife and said that he had left her dead on Birtley Fell the previous Saturday. People who saw Waddell at this time claimed that he looked and behaved like a simpleton.[21] PC Thompson contacted the police in Berwick, and Sergeant David Christie, who was stationed at nearby Blaydon, was sent to collect Waddell and take him to Berwick, where Superintendent Harrison from Gateshead would collect him.

The weather on Thursday, 29 November 1888 was awful, but the final scenes of the Birtley tragedy were about to be played out, and the elements were not going to keep a large crowd from gathering outside Durham Court House. Judge Sir Charles Edward, Baron Pollock, arrived at 10 a.m., an imposing legal figure, tall and thin, with a permanent frown that enhanced his slightly pugnacious features.

Waddell was quickly seated in the middle of the dock. He looked in better condition than he had when brought before the magistrate, and appeared calm and composed. The coroner's jury had delivered an open verdict at the inquest into Beadmore's death, and the fact that the verdict had not been one of murder may have lifted Waddell's spirits. The prosecution was headed by D. F. Steavenson and W. B. Hans Hamilton, while the unenviable job of defending Waddell rested with Mr Skidmore and Mr Petherick.

After the jury was sworn, Waddell was asked how he pleaded. In a low but firm voice he replied 'Not guilty'.

There were thirty-four witnesses for the prosecution (all of whom were told to remain outside the court until called), and no witnesses for the defence. In the main, Waddell's defence rested on the verdict reached by the inquest jury and the claim that the evidence against him was circumstantial.

Mr Steavenson opened the proceedings with a lengthy outline of the basic facts, which he followed with a succession of witnesses. Mr Skidmore made a speech in which he drew attention to the open verdict reached by the coroner's jury and pointed out that Waddell was a man of good character, with a job, who had been courting Jane Beadmore, had never treated her badly, and had no motive for killing her. He did his best to work around Waddell's disappearance from Birtley and his decidedly suspicious behaviour, claiming that it was not the responsibility of a defence counsel to 'account for the movements of a man at a particular time, unless the movements themselves coupled with other testimony formed a piece of an irresistible chain'.

The jury retired at 5.05 p.m., and it took them a mere half hour to reach their verdict: guilty. Waddell was given the opportunity to make a statement before sentence was passed, but he declined to do so. Judge Pollock then passed sentence:

> I certainly cannot hold out any hope to you that the sentence which necessarily follows upon a crime of this character will be interfered with. I say this because I ask you most earnestly not to cling to any false hope that any change in that sentence may take place, and to occupy your thoughts and such time as is still left to you here by attending to the comfort and assistance which I have no doubt will be given you in directing your mind towards God in asking for pardon from him. To me it remains only to pass a sentence which alone the law awards to crime such as yours, that is that you be taken from hence to the place from whence you came, and from thence to a place of execution, and that you be there hanged by the neck until you shall be dead, and that your body be afterwards buried within the precincts of the prison in which you were last confined after your conviction. And may the Lord have mercy on your soul.

William Waddell was removed from the court back to Durham Prison, where he would spend his remaining time in the condemned cell on 'A' Wing. This cell – really three cells knocked together – contained a toilet and washbasin, and a room where the prisoner could be readied for the gallows. Its most famous occupant was the multiple murderess Mary Ann Cotton, who was executed by the inept William Calcraft on 24 March 1873. It was from this condemned cell that Waddell wrote a letter to his siblings:

Dear Brother and Sister,

I write you a few words to let you know that I am quite well at present, hoping to find you the same, and hoping that you arrived home quite safe on Saturday. Dear brother, I have just written a letter to Robert [another brother]. I would like very much to know where father is, for I should like to write to him very much, or to see him if possible. Dear brother, you must not trouble yourself too much about me, as it may be for the best. The Lord knows what is best for us, so I will leave it all in His hands, for I am happy to tell you that I have made my peace with God, and if I die I know I am going to a better place where no sorrow ever comes, and I hope to meet you all there by-and-by, for I can trust all to the Lord now, and He will hold me up. Dear brother, I must tell you that I am very happy now since that I gave my heart to God, and found in Him a Saviour for the Lord is my Shepherd, I shall not Want. I shall not be afraid to die and leave this unhappy world, as it is nothing but a world of sin and sorrow, and there is nothing good in it. So I will now conclude, with much love to all

From your loving brother
WILLIAM WADDELL[22]

Whether or not Waddell took the advice of the judge, it seems that while in prison he did listen to the ministrations of the prison chaplain, Rev. Fletcher, and found a remarkable inner strength. Rev. Fletcher became convinced that Waddell wanted to confess and he asked the dean of Durham to attend the prison. The dean, Dr William Charles Lake, was at first refused permission to see

Waddell, but after communicating directly with the Home Office, he was allowed to do so. On his first visit Waddell confessed, with every sign of genuine emotion: 'Yes, sir, I did it.' The following day the dean spoke to him at greater length, and one newspaper reported, 'It is impossible to give the details of the confession; some of them are shocking.'[23] However, from what was published, it is questionable whether the confession differed significantly from what Waddell had previously stated. He attributed his crime to being drunk or temporarily insane, and 'He also stated that he had been reading the accounts of the murders in London.'

William Waddell's execution was scheduled for 8 a.m. on Monday, 17 December 1888. The hangman was Yorkshire-born James Berry, who dispatched 131 people in a career that lasted from 1884 to 1891. His 'customers' included two people with connections to the Ripper murders: Israel Lipski in 1887 (see Chapter 2) and William Bury in 1889 (in his memoirs,[24] Berry said he thought Bury was Jack the Ripper).

On his arrival in Durham the day before Waddell's execution, Berry reported to the gaol, got something to eat and took a stroll. He then went into a bar to hear what was being said about the execution. There he met a man who was opposed to it. The following exchange ensued:

'I don't think the law ought to commit another murder like what's going to happen tomorrow. I'd hang Berry if I had my way.'

'That would be rather a funny way of putting an end to capital punishment,' I said with a laugh.

'How do you make that out?'

'Because if you hanged Berry there would be nobody left to hang you.'

'I'd like to see Berry hang me,' he said.

'So would I! You can bet your life he would make a good job of it.'

Laughing at the incident, I slipped my card into the man's
hand, and was out of the place before he had time to read it.

As Berry enjoyed the attractions of Durham, in London parliamentary questions were being asked about the correctness of
the conduct of the police. Edward Hare Pickersgill, the Radical
Liberal MP for Bethnal Green, whose campaign for the reform
of criminal law and abolition of the death penalty made him one
of many slight thorns in the side of Home Secretary Henry
Matthews, asked about a policeman's admission that he had questioned Waddell in his cell without having first cautioned him.
Matthews said he had consulted the judge, who had concluded that
the policeman was in the cell in the proper execution of his duty, but
that he should not have questioned the prisoner as he did. The
policeman belonged to a Scottish force, and Matthews had accordingly drawn the attention of the secretary of state for Scotland to
the matter.[25]

* * *

Fellow Liberal, James Joicey, 1st Baron Joicey, the wealthy coal-
mining magnate and MP for Chester-le-Street, asked Matthews
whether any inquiry had taken place into Waddell's sanity. As the
conviction was based entirely on circumstantial evidence, he
wondered whether Matthews planned to recommend commutation
of the sentence. Matthews replied that, as he had no reason to doubt
the sanity of Waddell, he had made no inquiry into it and had no
cause to interfere with the due course of law.[26]

There was to be no commutation. William Waddell would not
see Christmas. He slept well and awoke between 5.30 and 6 a.m.
He was reportedly cheerful – by which one supposes that he was
as cheerful as it was reasonable to expect anyone to be in the
circumstances – and ate a little breakfast. He was afterwards taken
by two warders, accompanied by Berry, the hangman, to a room

where his arms were pinioned. Berry, who had risen early and tested the trapdoor to make sure it worked efficiently, assured Waddell that he would make it as quick as possible. Berry thought that Waddell seemed indifferent to his fate and claimed that this unnerved him;[27] but a journalist thought Waddell displayed 'decided signs of the mental anguish he is known to have undergone since his trial' and to his eye it seemed that the ordeal had aged him. At 7.55 a.m., a small procession formed. The sheriff's warden, W. Shadforth, took the head of the little group, followed by Rev. Fletcher, the prison chaplain, then the chief warder, the under sheriff, and Waddell, two prison guards on either side; behind him walked Berry, some more warders, and finally a small group of journalists. Waddell walked with a firm step, although at one point he placed his hand on a warder's arm as if needing support.

On the scaffold he silently suffered the final ministrations of Berry and the chaplain's quietly spoken prayers. It was a raw, cold morning and the icy air cut through to the bone; but as early as 7.30 a.m. spectators had begun gathering outside the gates of Durham Gaol. Journalists would later complain that the way in which the scaffold had been erected, combined with the darkness of the grey dawn, meant that little of the execution could be witnessed. However, according to Berry:

I gave Waddle [*sic*] a drop of five feet, because he was slightly built, and would not weigh more than 10 stone at the out-side. He submitted most patiently to the pinioning but never said a word. He walked very firmly to the scaffold, but the light was so bad inside that I had to keep close to him for fear of making a mistake. Having done all but draw the bolt, I looked for the signal, but not observing it, and seeing that Waddle [*sic*] was fainting, I pulled the lever. The only utterance he gave was a deep sigh as the minister said 'Lord have mercy on your soul.' The minister was holding out his hand as the drop fell.[28]

Death was instantaneous. The black flag was raised over the prison
gate to signify that the execution had taken place, and the hundred
or so onlookers began to drift away.

* * *

At 10 a.m., the usual formal inquest on the executed man was held
by the coroner, John Graham. The jury was sworn and taken to view
Waddell's body, the small group of journalists present being denied
entry on the orders of Under Sheriff Edward Hutchinson. One of
them, Thomas Walton, protested, saying that he wished to see the
body to confirm that the sentence had been properly carried out, but
the journalists were still not allowed sight of the body. At the
inquest proper, the prison surgeon, Dr Treadwell, stated that death
had been by strangulation. Chief Warder Proctor confirmed that
the dead man was the same man as had been held in the condemned
cell and said that the execution had been properly conducted without
a hitch.

CHAPTER 7

Bits of Body Turning Up Here and There

————————————

THE THAMES-SIDE TOWN OF RAINHAM IS ABOUT 12½ MILES from Whitechapel. For much of its long history it was a rural community, widely known for the wheat and fruit grown there. In the 1880s it was best known for the two ancient ferries across the Thames and for a pub, the former ferry house, which by then was called the Three Crowns.

It was here that there began a series of murders as baffling as those committed by Jack the Ripper. These are sometimes known as the 'torso murders', and the first two are dealt with in this chapter. Assuming that all of them were committed by the same person, it would seem that the killer may have been making a statement, dumping the remains of one of his victims in the foundations of the new Scotland Yard building, and wheeling the remains of another into the heart of the Ripper's Whitechapel (Chapter 13).

The Rainham Mystery (May–July 1887)

Edward Henry Hughes[1] was a Thames lighterman, responsible for transferring goods from ships moored in the middle of the Thames to the quayside or to riverside factories in a flat-bottomed boat called a lighter. Lightermen were extremely skilled and strong and had to have a very good knowledge of the river's tides and currents; but when the docks were built and the ships could moor alongside, the job of the lighterman was not so essential, and they later came to be more concerned with delivering goods from the quayside to riverside factories.

On Wednesday, 11 May 1887, Hughes was on his barge alongside Frederick Hempleman's fertilizer factory at Rainham Ferry. This was one of several 'obnoxious' factories that began to locate there after 1869 (termed 'obnoxious' because of the smell they produced; Hempleman's made fertilizer from blood and fish by-products, and it continued to operate until about 1917, being particularly remembered for its 185ft chimney stack).

As he glanced out at the river, Hughes spotted something floating in the water. He managed to hook it and haul it aboard his lighter. The bundle was wrapped in a common coarse canvas sacking and was secured with cord, which had been wrapped around it several times; but part of the canvas had come open, and inside was what appeared to be the remains of a body. A man was sent to fetch a policeman, and he quickly returned with PC Stock, who in turn summoned other officers. The bundle was found to contain part of a woman's torso, minus the legs, arms and head, with the internal organs missing. The remains were taken to a shed next to the Phoenix Hotel in Rainham to await further examination. The Thames River Police very quickly set about searching for other bundles, but none were found. Attempts by the police to identify the remains were largely hopeless and quickly ground to a halt.

It was Dr Edward Galloway (in some reports called Edwin Calloway) who undertook an examination of the remains of this first corpse. As the doctor was to testify at the inquest, the upper half of the bust, the head, arms, legs and thighs were all missing. What the canvas bundle contained was practically the entire lower half of the body and the last two bones and half of the lumbar vertebrae above the trunk. The trunk had been sawn through with a very fine, sharp saw, the outer layer of muscle being cut with a keen-edged knife. The thighs had been cleanly removed from the sockets of the pelvis, and the spine had been severed where it offered the least resistance. This, together with the fact that the dissection had been skilfully done, indicated to Dr Galloway that it had been the work of someone with a thorough and intimate knowledge of surgery. He had considered the possibility that the remains came from a hospital dissection room, but their general appearance suggested that the body had never been used as a hospital subject. His opinion was that the woman had been murdered.

Dr Galloway was unable to specify the cause of death, the remains betraying no signs of external injury, but the woman, who was probably aged between 27 and 29, had been dead for about two weeks.

The inquest was opened on Saturday, 14 May 1887 by Mr C. C. Lewis, the coroner for South Essex, at the Phoenix Hotel in Rainham. After hearing the medical testimony from Dr Edward Galloway, he adjourned the inquiry for three weeks to allow the police to pursue their investigations. When the inquest resumed on Friday, 3 June, Inspector Dobson for the police stated that they 'could throw no light on the matter'. The jury returned an open verdict.

Two days later, at 10 a.m. on Sunday, 5 June 1887, a pierman named J. Morris had his attention drawn to a large parcel floating near the lower side of Temple Pier. He dragged it out of the water and opened it to find a human thigh. He immediately called the Thames Police.

There was some initial confusion, as the remains appeared to be quite fresh, and it was thought that they were evidence of a new murder; but after an examination by the assistant divisional surgeon, Dr Hammerton, the remains were sent to Dr Galloway, who confirmed that the thigh came from the Rainham victim. He reiterated that in his opinion the murderer possessed anatomical skill – and, it would seem, the knowledge of how to preserve body parts from decay.

The thigh was sent to the City mortuary, but Mr Langham, the City coroner, declined to hold an inquest, since according to the law only a 'vital part' of a body could be the subject of a coroner's inquiry. And so the remains of the thigh were put into a pauper's coffin and sent to the City of London Cemetery at Little Ilford, where they were buried. This was the cause of some irritation to the police, who did not learn of this until an inspector from Scotland Yard made inquiries at the City mortuary, where an initially evasive coroner's officer finally admitted what had happened. The thigh was exhumed from Little Ilford and the other remains from Rainham churchyard, where they had by now been buried.

Meanwhile, Assistant Commissioner James Monro asked Dr Thomas Bond, the divisional surgeon, to examine all the remains. This he did, also coming to the conclusion that there was evidence that the murderer had anatomical skills.

That same Sunday the thorax and chest of a woman *sans* breasts was found off Battersea, on the south bank of the Thames.

Finally the arms and legs turned up, fished out from different parts of Regent's Canal: at about 3.30 p.m. on 30 June, a boy found Francis Thurle, lock-keeper at the St Pancras Lock, and told him that a human arm had been pulled from the canal onto the towpath. Thurle went to the scene, took possession of the arm and carried it to the mortuary. The following morning, 1 July, a labourer named Perry found another arm near the same spot, and in the afternoon George Mansfield, a labourer in the employ of the Regent's Canal Company, found two legs in the canal and handed them over to the police.

As the police set about dragging the canal, Scotland Yard requested Dr Galloway to inspect the remains. Accompanied by Inspector Hare, he went to St Pancras mortuary and undertook a minute examination, concluding that the limbs belonged to the torso discovered at Rainham.

On Saturday, 11 June, near Battersea, the police and medical men gathered together for a consultation. Among those present were Inspector John Shore, Dr Galloway and Dr Kempster, and

Athelstan Braxton Hicks, the coroner for the Battersea area. *The Times* reported that one outcome of the meeting was that Dr Galloway's theory 'that the dissection was performed by a man well versed in medical science was more than strengthened'. Braxton Hicks decided not to hold an inquiry, but he gave his officer instructions that the remains should be preserved in a hermetically sealed glass jar of spirits of wine. This was done during the afternoon.[2]

The various remains had been found within four coronial districts, those of Mr Langham, the City coroner (where the piece of thigh had been discovered), Mr Braxton Hicks (where the upper part of the torso and thorax had been found), Mr Lewis (lower part of the trunk) and Mr George Danford Thomas, coroner for Central Middlesex (where the legs and arms were found). The four men met and it was decided that the inquest would be conducted by George Danford Thomas.

The inquiry opened at the Crowndale Hall, Camden Town, on Monday, 11 July 1887. Evidence was heard from Dr Galloway to the effect that the remains came from the same person, whereupon the coroner stated that, as the home secretary had ordered a more detailed examination of the remains, the inquiry would be adjourned until 6 August.

* * *

In the meantime a small side story had unfolded: on 2, 4 and 8 July, the *Evening News* had published a series of stories about a woman who had been seen in the neighbourhood of Charing Cross Station with a canvas bag that smelled bad. In light of the recent discoveries, the implication was that it may have contained some of the body parts. The story had been given to the newspaper by 'a gentleman of unimpeachable veracity' and had apparently originated with the coroner's officer, PC Tom Ralph.[3] Doubt was cast on the story when it transpired that the 'gentleman of unimpeachable veracity' was a freelance journalist named James Greville Burns; furthermore,

PC Ralph denied ever having told him any such story. Burns was duly arrested and charged with defrauding the *Evening News*. Similar journalistic shenanigans would occasionally pepper reports into the later Whitechapel murders.

* * *

The inquiry established little beyond the known facts and the murder case faded from the headlines – not having made much of an impact in the first place. The head was never found and the woman was never identified, though a number of people did come forward in an effort to identify the remains, including a Mrs Cross of Albany Terrace, Rainham, whose 28-year-old daughter had been missing since 20 May. Apparently, shortly before she disappeared, the daughter, who was of 'weak intelligence and fond of going on the barges on the river', had been robbed by a man of sinister appearance who had threatened to kill her if she did not hand over her purse.[4]

The Whitehall Mystery (11 September–17 October 1888)

The Grosvenor Road Railway Bridge, today known simply as Victoria Bridge, was built for the London, Brighton and South Coast Railway and was the first railway bridge to span the Thames into central London. The first train crossed over it into Victoria Station in 1860. On the south side of the bridge stands the now forlorn and derelict landmark of the once-grand Battersea Power Station.

But the Whitehall Mystery (as it was to become known) began on the opposite, Pimlico side of the river, when, on 11 September 1888, a human arm was found on the foreshore.

At about 12.45 p.m. that day, Frederick Moore, a porter working at Ward's Deal Wharf at 113 Grosvenor Road, was standing outside the gates of the wharf when he noticed several workmen looking over the Embankment at something lying in the river mud near the sluices from Seager, Evans and Co.'s Millbank distillery. Whatever the object was, it was entangled in some timber that was floating on the riverside. A group of boys, thinking it was the carcass of a drowned dog, had amused themselves by pelting it with stones; but some men who had observed what was going on thought it looked like a human arm. Moore went over and joined the men. He did not share their opinion, but someone got hold of a ladder and, as the tide was going out, he climbed down. It was indeed an arm. It was not wrapped in anything, but it had a string tied tightly round the upper part. Moore fished the arm out, and put it on some timber. He also had sense enough to search the mud for further remains, but found none. He then tracked down PC William James, who was on duty on Grosvenor Embankment. The constable took charge of the arm and conveyed it to the police station in Gerald Street, and then to the mortuary. For a week or more, James would scrutinize the mud for more remains, but would find nothing.[5]

When PC James brought the arm to the station, the senior officer, Superintendent Shepherd, at once instructed Inspector Adams to call in Dr Thomas Neville, the acting divisional surgeon, who lived at 85 Pimlico Road and had a practice at 23 Sloane Street. His service as a medical officer in the Russo-Turkish War in the late 1870s meant that he had considerable experience of examining dismembered limbs. Dr Neville concluded that it was the right arm of a woman; because the muscles were not more contracted, he thought it had been cut off after death, cleanly severed from the body with a sharp implement. He reckoned it had been in the water for two or three days.

On 16 September, Dr Charles Alfred Hebbert[6] examined the limb. It was indeed a woman's right arm, 31 inches in length, 13 inches in circumference at the shoulder and 6½ inches at the wrist. The hand was 7½ inches long and the nails were small and well shaped. It had been separated from the shoulder joint after death, and it was Dr Hebbert's opinion that it had been done by someone who was not an anatomist but knew the joints and knew what he was doing. Around the upper part of the arm was a piece of string that had been tied tightly enough to leave an impression in the skin; when it was loosened, it turned out there was a great deal of blood still in the arm.

Superintendent Shepherd had immediately alerted other police divisions and the Thames Police, and they began a search of the river. Investigations were set in train by Inspector Adams, Inspector Arthur Hare, Inspector Kendrick and other officers. *The Times* reported that 'an average number of mysterious disappearances of women' had been reported during the preceding week, and that the missing persons records had been examined without furnishing a clue – although what sort of clue they might have afforded is not specified and is difficult to imagine.[7] However, a reporter for the *Irish Times* felt that 'A remarkable feature . . . is the number of missing women brought to the notice of the authorities . . . It is thus shown that very many women leave their friends without communicating with them, and pass out of sight of those nearest to them.'[8]

* * *

Among those who had gone missing was 17-year-old Emma Potter, a tall and well-formed young woman described as being of weak intelligence, who appears to have been in the habit of wandering the streets at night – a cause of no little distress to her mother. On Saturday, 8 September she had been brought home by a policeman at 2 a.m. and had eventually fallen asleep on a couch. Her mother had gone out briefly at 11 a.m., when the girl was still sleeping peacefully. But on her return, Emma had vanished. Mrs Potter had gone to all the places that Emma frequented and had checked the workhouses and infirmaries; but the only clue she could glean was from a policeman who knew the girl by sight and believed he had seen her in the area of Buckingham Gate at 5.30 p.m. Frantic, Mrs Potter had gone to see Dr Neville and described her daughter to him. From this description, the doctor thought the arm could have been Emma's and referred her mother to the magistrate at the local police court, Mr d'Eyncourt, who was unable to do more than alert the police and the press. We know that, fortunately for Mrs Potter, Emma turned up alive. According to an Inspector Webber, who appeared before the magistrate with the news, she was found by the police on Thursday night.[9]

* * *

The discovery of the arm created what one newspaper, *The Echo*, described as 'a profound sensation'. It commented:

> the wildest rumours are already afloat as to whether another hideous crime, even more mysterious than the Whitechapel murders, has or has not been perpetrated in the West-end of London. There are believed to be some startling features in connection with the case which cannot at present be revealed, as officials are now engaged in making their investigation into this, the latest London mystery.

The newspaper went on to report speculation that the arm belonged to a woman:

> killed by the same unseen hand that committed the dastardly crimes in Whitechapel, and that the arm had eventually been brought from the East-end to Pimlico, in order to throw the police off the scent. Inspector Abberline, Inspector Helson, Inspector Reid, and other officers engaged in investigating the Whitechapel crimes have been in communication with Scotland Yard with reference to the finding of the arm, but no clue has as yet been found.[10]

At about 7.30 a.m. on Friday, 28 September, a 14-year-old boy walking to work along Lambeth Road passed the Blind School, the garden of which faced the road and was surrounded by iron railings. In the garden (or, according to one report, wedged between two of the railings) was a parcel, which the boy pulled out. On opening it, he found that it contained a decomposed human arm. A bricklayer named Moore, who saw the boy retrieve the parcel and was watching as he opened it, ran and told a policeman on fixed point duty nearby what had been found. He then went into the Crown and Grapes – a pub immediately opposite the Blind School – and announced that 'some "Leather Apron" tricks' were going on across the road. One of the customers, William George Davis, went outside and saw a policeman with a bundle tied up in what looked like coarse brown paper (but was in fact material), part of which had been torn away to reveal a wrist and hand, the fingers pressed close together, with the thumb underneath. Another witness, William Allen, a licensed shoeblack who had his pitch outside the Crown and Grapes, also went to view the discovery and likewise noticed the curled fingers. He also thought the arm had been laid in lime. He reckoned that the parcel had not been there much above an hour when found, because the road sweepers who passed the spot had not seen it, and he thought they would have noticed it had it been there. The policeman borrowed a piece of billiard chalk from one of the onlookers and put two crosses on the spot where the arm had been found. The limb was then taken to the police station in Kennington Lane.

Interestingly, it was reported that when the first arm was discovered, the police had emphatically denied the fact for as long as possible.[11] They now repeated this behaviour, denying all knowledge of the find. An early news agency report was published in several newspapers, including *The Star*, but when that newspaper sent its own reporter to check the facts, he encountered denials from every quarter. The policeman on fixed point duty said that he had heard nothing of it, and an inspector at Kennington Lane police station stated that he had heard a rumour that a bone had been found, to which he attached no importance, but claimed that no arm had been brought in to the station.[12]

This second arm soon disappeared from the story, the *Daily Telegraph* reporting 'the authorities are quite positive that it was not amputated recently, and in fact they have received some assurances as to the source from which the bones in question were derived'.[13] Sadly we know no more.

These discoveries, though grisly, made little real impact, and the mystery tended to be overshadowed by the Whitechapel murders, and in particular the newspaper reports on the inquest into the death of Annie Chapman in Hanbury Street. The dominance of public interest in the Whitechapel murders was reinforced at the end of September, with the shock of two murders on the same night and then publication of the infamous letter signed 'Jack the Ripper'. But things looked set to change on Tuesday, 2 October 1888, when a human torso was found in the cellars of the new Scotland Yard building then under construction.

* * *

Today, Scotland Yard is housed in an unremarkable and architecturally nondescript office block at 10 Broadway, behind St James's Park underground station, its only memorable external feature being the revolving sign, which has featured in countless television programmes and movies, but which is rather disappointing 'in the flesh'. However, for most of its life, the headquarters of the Metropolitan Police was housed in a magnificent purpose-built structure on the Victoria Embankment.

Originally, the commissioner's office was in what had once been a private house at 4 Whitehall Place, at the back of which was a courtyard with a building that was used as a police station. The courtyard was known as Great Scotland Yard. Nobody really knows why, although one story has it that it was owned by the kings of Scotland; another argues more prosaically that it recalls an owner in the Middle Ages named Scott. Whatever its origins, Scotland Yard forever became associated with the headquarters of the Metropolitan Police.

By 1887, the police headquarters had absorbed not only 4 Whitehall Place, but also 3, 5, 21 and 22 Whitehall Place, 8 and 9 Great Scotland Yard, and 1, 2 and 3 Palace Place, plus assorted unnumbered outbuildings and stables. It was obvious that the still-expanding police needed a new building, and the site chosen was on land largely reclaimed from the Thames when the Victoria Embankment was constructed. The Embankment, which was completed in 1870, had seen the demolition of many expensive riverside properties and involved building out onto the foreshore of the Thames, thus narrowing the river.

The site selected for New Scotland Yard had originally been chosen for a national opera house, a magnificent, albeit ultimately tragic project promoted by Colonel James Henry Mapleson, a theatre impresario. Construction of the theatre was nearing completion when the money ran out and Mapleson was obliged to declare himself bankrupt. The site was finally sold to the government and Mapleson's dream was demolished, replaced by a seven-storey red-brick building which, in 1889, would become New Scotland Yard.

However, the opera house boasted a warren of corridors, bricked passages, archways and vaulted chambers in its extensive foundations. According to Mapleson's memoirs, published in 1888,[14] there was an underground passageway to the Houses of Parliament, so that MPs could listen to 'beautiful music rather than dull debates'. There was also a connection to a station on the District line, and this was incorporated into the New Scotland Yard building. The entrance (which apparently still exists but is not used) was located at the east end of the eastbound platform of the station and enabled the police to move men around without bringing them onto the streets.

It was in this maze of passages that the torso of a woman was discovered.

* * *

A lot of work had been going on in the foundation passages of New Scotland Yard, including the digging of shallow trenches for drainage. Heaps of soil and builders' debris were scattered in the labyrinth of tunnels and passageways. The few workmen familiar with the site used one particular place – a vault 30 feet long, 24 feet wide and about 12 feet deep, with loose wooden planking that cut out the sunlight above – to hide their tools when they finished work on Saturdays. Among them was Frederick Wildbore, a carpenter working for J. Grover and Sons, a building firm based in Pimlico and one of the contractors working on the building.

At 6 a.m. on Monday, 1 October, he went into the vault to pick up his tools, which had been left there by his mate the previous Saturday. As usual, the vault was very dark, but he had struck a match to look for the equipment. As it happens, his mate had already removed the tools, but in a recess Wildbore saw what he thought was an old coat. At the end of the working day, about 5.30 p.m., he returned to the vault with his mate. The object was still there and they struck a match. They could see that it was a bundle of some kind, but they paid no more attention to it. Giving the matter no further thought, they went home.

The following day, 2 October, at about 1 p.m., Wildbore noticed the object again. There was no smell about it, so far as he could recall, but he mentioned it to Charles William Brown, who in turn spoke of it to Thomas Chaney (sometimes called George Chaney), foreman of the bricklayers. Those men, together with two labourers called George Budgen and Ernest Hedge, went to inspect the parcel. They found it wrapped in old cloth and tied with three or four strings. Budgen had taken a lamp with him, but could make nothing of the parcel: 'I looked at it and found all the top of it bare, the rest being wrapped up in some old cloth. I thought it was old bacon at first, thrown away there, or something of that sort, but as I could make nothing of it I took hold of the strings round it and dragged it out into the light. I then got my pocket knife and dragged the strings off it.' What was revealed was a woman's torso, minus head, legs and arms.[15]

Charles Brown immediately ran for the police, arriving at King Street police station at 3.20 p.m. He described the discovery to the inspector there, who sent Thomas Hawkins, a detective attached to 'A' Division, to the building site, where he was shown the remains and then taken to where the parcel had been discovered. There he found two pieces of dress material. Leaving the remains in the charge of a police constable, Hawkins went back to the police station, where he communicated with the divisional surgeon, Dr Bond. Returning to the site, he directed all the witnesses to go to the police station, where their statements were taken down.

Shortly before 4 p.m., the divisional surgeon, Dr Thomas Bond, arrived at the site. After a cursory examination, he ordered the torso to be removed to the mortuary. The coroner's officer, PC Ralph, accordingly had it placed in a temporary coffin and took it there. Bond saw that the torso was put in spirits to preserve it. PC Ralph meanwhile went to fetch the Pimlico arm.

Back at the site, Detective Inspector Marshall arrived at 5 p.m. and took charge. He viewed the torso shortly before its removal, and inspected the corner of the vault from which the bundle had been pulled, noting that the wall was badly stained. On the ground he found a piece of newspaper from *The Echo* of 24 August. If associated with the body, this would indicate that death had occurred after that date.

According to the examination conducted by Dr Bond and Dr Hebbert, the torso was 17 inches long, 35½ inches around the chest and 28½ inches at the waist. The breasts were large and prominent. The appearance of the collar-bones indicated that the woman was of mature development, certainly over 24 or 25 years of age. She had fair skin and dark hair, was full fleshed and well nourished, and would have been about 5ft 8in tall (which Dr Bond considered to be of 'considerable stature'). She did not appear to have borne a child. She had died anywhere between six weeks and two months earlier, but had neither suffocated nor drowned. The body was badly decomposed, especially where the head and limbs had been removed, but a minute examination revealed no wounds that could have been the cause of death. Although the inside of the heart was pale and free from clots, Dr Bond thought death was likely to have been caused by haemorrhage or fainting.

The head had been removed from the trunk by sawing through the sixth cervical vertebra. The neck had been divided by several jagged incisions at the bottom of the larynx, which had been sawn through. The lower limbs and pelvis had been removed with a series of long, sweeping cuts with a saw through the lumbar vertebrae, and the arms had been removed at the shoulder joints by several oblique downward incisions, carried round the arms and straight through the joints.

The body appeared to have been wrapped up in a very skilful manner, the wrapping so securely tied that over the body there were clearly defined marks where the strings had been. According to the testimony of Inspector Marshall at the inquest, a mixture of string had been used: one piece was sash-cord, while the remainder was of different thicknesses, and even included a piece of black tape. The wrapping was a piece of dress made from broché satin cloth, a common material that probably cost about 6½d per yard, was of Bradford manufacture and with a pattern probably three years old. There was a six-inch-wide flounce at the bottom.[16]

An examination of the internal organs showed that the liver and stomach, kidneys and spleen were normal. The left lung was healthy, but the right lung was firmly adherent to the chest wall of the diaphragm, which showed that at some time the woman had suffered from severe pleurisy. The stomach contained about an ounce of partly digested food. Interestingly, Dr Bond stated that the uterus was absent.

The doctor had also examined the Pimlico arm and it accurately fitted the torso. The hand was long and very well shaped; the fingers were long and tapered; and the nails were in good condition. There was no indication of a wedding or other kind of ring. The woman, they thought, was not used to manual work.[17]

* * *

A journalist working for the *Daily Telegraph* saw the remains within half an hour of their discovery. He reported that the body was wrapped in a skirt and that the flesh had a dark reddish hue 'as if it had been plentifully sprinkled with antiseptic, such as Condy's fluid'.[18] This was a solution of 1 per cent compound of manganic and permanganic acids and 4 per cent sodium chloride and was widely used to remove odours. It was commonly used to pour on faeces as a disinfectant and deodorant, and it had featured a couple of years previously in what was known as the 'Pimlico Mystery' – the death in mysterious circumstances of Thomas Edwin Bartlett in Claverton Street (near the Millbank distillery and where the arm had been found a few weeks previously).[19]

This fluid had apparently masked the smell of the woman's torso in the vault, since it turned out to be in an advanced state of putre-faction. The cords had cut deep into the skin, and the legs, arms and head appeared to the journalist to have been removed in a 'brutal, bungling manner'. The remains might have weighed over 50 lbs, which, as the journalist observed, was 'no light load for even a strong man to carry any distance'.

At first there was considerable discussion in the press about how the murderer could have ferried his heavy bundle to the site, through the surrounding streets, without being seen, and then how he could physically have got it and himself into the site, which was surrounded by a hoarding seven or eight feet high. As the *Daily Telegraph* remarked: 'The difficulty and danger which the wretch must have encountered in bearing the body to the portion of the buildings where it was hidden increase the horror and mystery surrounding the whole proceeding.'[20]

There were three entrances to the site, two in Cannon Row and one from the Embankment. The Embankment was immediately dismissed as improbable because of the risk of being seen. But Cannon Row, though almost opposite the Home Office in Parliament Street, was a very dark and lonely spot. How the murderer had scaled the hoarding still exercised the speculative pens of the media, but further investigation quickly revealed two possibilities. The night-watchman at the Red Lion in Cannon Row early on pointed out to a reporter for *The Star* an iron pillar next to the hoarding. A man could easily climb onto it and then over the hoarding – he had frequently seen men go onto the site at night (presumably to sleep); and he assumed that, once the killer was inside, it would have been a simple matter to unlock one of the doors. It was therefore possible for the murderer to have left his bundle near the gate, scaled the hoarding, then opened the gate from the inside and retrieved his parcel.[21] Inspector Marshall would, in due course, explain at the inquest that he had examined the hoarding in Cannon Row and agreed that a person could easily get over it there; however, in his opinion there was no indication that anybody had done so recently.[22]

It is anyway doubtful whether the murderer could have opened the gates, as it appears that they were securely locked. On the other hand, it transpired that the small gate in Cannon Row was not locked, but was fastened with a catch that was easily lifted by pulling a piece of string. It was the opinion of Inspector Marshall that the latch was not likely to have been noticed, except by someone acquainted with the building site. There were notices prohibiting strangers from entering, but no watchmen were on duty, even though tools had been stolen from time to time (which was why workmen hid their tools in the network of vaults).

The other theory was that the killer had brought the torso into the site on a cart along with building materials: it was realized that the road used by the carts was the nearest way to the recess where the body was found.[23]

All in all, the indications appeared to be that the torso had been dumped by someone who was intimately acquainted with the workings of the site, who knew how to get the torso onto the site, and who knew not only the intricacies of the labyrinthine passages, but even that they existed. Everything pointed to a current or former employee.

It was quickly determined that the body could only have been placed where it was found between Saturday night and Monday morning, because at about 3 p.m. on Friday, Charles Brown had been in the vault where the torso was found, along with several other men, including Mr George Erant, the clerk of the works, and a surveyor, Arthur Franklin, taking measurements. At 4.40 p.m. the following day, Ernest Hedge, left alone on the site to lock up, went into the vault to get a hammer in order to nail the door of a locker. He was certain that there had been nothing there then: 'I was in the very corner where the parcel was discovered.' He would later explain in some detail that the tools had actually been on the opposite side to where the torso lay. He had gone into the recess and struck a light to locate the tools. Then he saw them outside. He had taken a hammer and gone. (Later medical testimony would cast doubt on his story.)

The staining on the wall indicated that the bundle had been there for about three days, so the chances are that it was placed there on the Saturday night. It is not clear whether it would have been possible to lift the overhead planking and drop the torso into the interior; if it was, then no special knowledge of how to enter and exit the warren of corridors would have been necessary.

What particularly caught the public's imagination was the possibility that the murder had been committed by Jack the Ripper. The *Illustrated Police News* reported that – at least in the neighbourhood of Westminster – the discovery of the remains was 'the all-absorbing theme of conversation . . . and the horrors of the East End have lapsed as of minor importance'.[24] The *Daily Telegraph* also drew attention to the absence of the uterus, that particular organ also having been removed by the killer in the murders of Annie Chapman and Catherine Eddowes. Interestingly, in this case there was speculation that the murder had been committed by an illegal abortionist, who had got rid of the uterus to hide the evidence of an abortion that had gone wrong.[25]

As the days passed, people came forward to report missing relatives and friends. Every report was diligently investigated by the police under the direction of Chief Superintendent Dunlap and Chief Inspector Wren of 'A' Division, but they led nowhere.[26]

* * *

Various stories were also reported in the press. *The Star* stated that, at 5.20 p.m. on the Saturday, a respectably dressed man, aged about 35, was seen to climb over the hoarding from the site into Cannon Row and to walk quickly away. It said that the police had circulated a description of this man to all police stations.[27] The same newspaper also reported that a man named Edward Deuchar, a commercial traveller, had told police that, a little over three weeks earlier, he had boarded a tramcar from Vauxhall Station to London Bridge. One fellow passenger was a man carrying a parcel, from which there came a terrible smell. The parcel, which was done up in brown paper, seemed to be heavy and the man carried it under his arm with extreme care. This passenger, who was powerfully built, of rough appearance and rather shabbily dressed, was distinguished by a goatee beard. He looked ill at ease (hardly surprising: anyone carrying a stinking parcel, legitimate or otherwise, would probably look agitated!). Just after the tramcar passed the Obelisk in St George's Circus, the man jumped out. Mr Deuchar had also got off the tramcar and had found a policeman, to whom he pointed out the man.[28]

There were also moments of fresh horror. At about 8.30 a.m. on 6 October, the body of a woman was pulled from the Thames at Pimlico Pier. Examination showed that she had drowned and her death appeared to be suicide. She was identified as Elizabeth Jutsem, aged 52, of 21 Westmoreland Road, Pimlico.[29]

Rather more serious was a communication to Scotland Yard from Superintendent Berry of Guildford: on 24 August, the right foot and a portion of a woman's left leg had been discovered in a brown paper parcel on the railway line near Guildford railway station. The remnants appeared to have been either roasted or boiled. Detective Inspector Marshall went to Guildford and had the remains, which had been buried in the cemetery, disinterred and brought to London to be compared with the torso found at Whitehall. *The Star* would in due course publish a letter from someone calling him or herself 'Horresco Referens', claiming that a gentleman had returned from Russia with some bears' feet, considered there (and by the gentleman) to be a great delicacy. His friends, however, had not shared his tastes and he himself had tired of the diet, throwing away what remained in a railway tunnel. 'Suffer me to draw a veil over the rest of the tragedy, and to simply assure you that these facts are authentic', wrote the correspondent.[30]

* * *

On the afternoon of 8 October, Mr John Troutbeck, the deputy coroner for Westminster, opened the inquest in the Westminster Sessions House, Broad Sanctuary, took testimony from several persons, and then adjourned the inquiry for two weeks.

On 17 October 1888, the foundations of what would be New Scotland Yard yielded up the final remains – a left leg cut off above the knee, and an arm. With the permission of the police and Mr Grover (the building contractor), two journalists – Jasper Waring, the Tilbury representative of a London news agency, and a man named William Angle – had, together with Ernest Hedge and some others, taken a mixed-breed dog into the vaults. It at once appeared to have the scent of something underground at the opposite end of the vault to where the torso had been found. The earth was removed, and at a depth of less than six inches the dog seized what turned out to be a human foot. A little further away, buried about twelve inches deep, they found an arm. The discovery was reported to Inspector Wren, the acting superintendent of 'A' Division. That night the site was cleared of workmen, and policemen entered the vaults, which they illuminated with candles. As a thick fog descended (no doubt adding to the eeriness of the proceedings) a further search was made of the vaults, this time with a bloodhound which had earlier been demonstrated before Commissioner Sir Charles Warren in Hyde Park. The dog did not seem to be on best form and found nothing.[31]

Dr Bond was summoned by an Inspector Rose to the building site, where he saw the partly buried human leg. The soil 'gave unmistakable evidence of having covered the leg for several weeks ... Decomposition had taken place there, and it was not decomposed when placed there.' The leg was examined the following day, it being concluded that 'the leg had been divided at the knee joint by free incisions, and very cleverly disarticulated without injury to the cartilages'. Dr Bond and Dr Hebbert had 'no doubt that the leg belonged to the body and to the arm'.

Bond was now more convinced than ever that, despite the assertions of Ernest Hedge and others, the torso must have been where it was found for quite some time. 'I took the opportunity', he told the inquest, 'to examine the spot where the body was found, and I am quite sure that the last witness (Hedge) is wrong as to the body not having been there a few days before. The body must have lain there for weeks, and it had decomposed there.'

The reason, as Dr Bond explained in answer to a question from the coroner, was that 'The brickwork against which it had leant was deeply covered with the decomposed fluid of the human body turned black, and it could not have done that in a day or two. The stain is not superficial, but the brickwork is quite saturated. I should think it must have been there quite six weeks when found – from August.'[32] Also, the earth beneath it had sunk, indicating that the load of the torso had rested on it for a long time.

The inquest reopened on 22 October and more testimony was heard. Then the coroner summed up, concluding that there was no evidence as to the identity of the woman or the cause of death. It was to be supposed, he said, that the dissection indicated that the woman had been murdered, but it was for the jury to decide whether the verdict should be 'found dead' or 'wilful murder against some person unknown'.

The jury consulted briefly and returned a verdict of 'found dead'.

CHAPTER 8

'What a Cow!'

Annie Farmer (21 November 1888)

A T 12.30 P.M. ON 19 NOVEMBER 1888, THE BELL OF
St Leonard's, Shoreditch, tolled sombrely as a funeral cortège
left for St Patrick's Roman Catholic Cemetery in Leytonstone. The
coffin, lying on an open hearse, was decorated with two crowns and
a cross made of heartsease. Although the procession was followed by
few mourners, the public showed great interest. People had begun
to assemble an hour previously and now lined the funeral route:

> the people outside, who now numbered several thousands, mani-
> fested the utmost sympathy, the crowd, for an East-end one,
> being extremely orderly. Vehicles of various descriptions took
> oppositions outside the church railings, and traffic was completely
> blocked until the hearse moved off.[1]

This outpouring of public sympathy was remarkable, for it was the
funeral not of some well-loved dignitary or head of state, but of
Mary Jane Kelly, who had met her tragic death at the hands of the
Whitechapel murderer only ten days before. As the coffin was
placed on the hearse, women wept, crying out 'God forgive her',
while every man's head was bowed in respect. The emotion was
described as 'natural and unconstrained'.[2] The funeral itself was paid

for in full by Mr H. Wilton, sexton of St Leonard's, who let it be known that public donations were welcome and that, should there be a surplus, the money would go toward a tombstone. Mary Kelly was buried in an unmarked grave and no gravestone was forthcoming.[3]

The tremendous interest in Kelly's funeral was symptomatic of the great public concern within the East End, which by now had certainly seen its fair share of brutal murder. One can imagine how these horrible events were beginning to make their mark on the people of the area in more ways than just shock and fear. The emotions felt by the populace of Whitechapel and Spitalfields must have been raw, to say the least. But within forty-eight hours of Mary Kelly's body being consigned to the earth, the fear of Jack the Ripper was to rear its head again.

On 21 November, several evening newspapers published shocking news of yet another Whitechapel murder. The story had come from the Central News Agency[4] and appeared to be unequivocally reporting that the fiend of the East End had struck again:

> The Central News says the news that another terrible murder was committed in the East-end of London, last night, has caused another thrill of horror through London.
>
> The news flew like wildfire throughout the whole of East-end district, and in a short time hundreds of people were rushing in the direction of the scene, and the building is now surrounded by an excited throng.
>
> It was only when the room occupied by the poor woman was opened, shortly after nine this morning, that the terrible fact was discovered. The police were hastily summoned, and at once took possession of the building, making a thorough search in the house itself and in the surrounding district. No one is now allowed to enter or to leave the house. It is conjectured that the victim took her companion home with her last night, and that, as in the last

case, the crime was committed during the early hours of the morning.

The mutilations in this case were again of a most shocking character: but the full extent of these have not even yet transpired. Up to the moment of telegraphing there are not the slightest traces of the assassin, and it is doubtful whether even in this case the police will secure any tangible clue. The excitement is growing momentarily throughout the district.[5]

Word of mouth had seen to it that a major panic was in the offing, and the Central News had succeeded in confirming local fears. News spread fast, even reaching the American press before the day was out, with headlines such as 'Another Whitechapel Horror'[6] and ' "Jack the Ripper" – again'.[7] The Press Association said more about where the alleged incident had taken place:

> another murder of a woman was discovered about 10 o'clock, at 19, George-street – a street running from Flower and Dean-street to Thrawl-street. The woman's throat had been cut, and it is stated there were a number of stabs on the body. The police were at once informed, and took possession of the premises. The house is a small two-storied building fronting on to George-street, and the right opposite the Lolesworth Model Dwellings, and is within a few hundred yards of Miller-court, Dorset-street, where the last murder occurred. The houses in George-street are mostly let out as lodging-houses, some of them being used by the women of the streets.[8]

No. 19 George Street, the common lodging house where Martha Tabram had been staying at the time of her death, sat in the heart of the disreputable enclave of streets and courts to the east of Commercial Street; immediately next door was No. 18, where Emma Smith had been lodging around the time of the fatal attack on her near Osborn

Street in April. The premises themselves, registered to lodging-house keeper John Satchell,[9] were a three-storey affair, with two rooms on each floor and a communal kitchen on the ground floor. Legally it could house fifty-nine lodgers, but like most 'doss-houses' in this neighbourhood, the reality was somewhat different: apparently it held no fewer than thirty-two double beds, thirty beds for single men and sixteen more for single women.[10] And like many of the local houses, it would no doubt be used by prostitutes, who could take advantage of the discreetness offered by those beds hidden by partitions.

Regardless of the press agencies' assured claims that another Whitechapel atrocity had taken place, the newspapers were quick to get to the bottom of the real story.[11] Once the fog of rumour and sensation had dissipated, it transpired that no murder – by Jack the Ripper or anybody else – had occurred. Nonetheless, a rather note-worthy incident had taken place.

At about 8 a.m. on 21 November, the watchman at No. 19, a mulatto who went by the nickname 'Darkie', admitted a man and a woman. The man paid 8d for a partitioned double bed on the first floor. 'Darkie' thought no more of it, and the next hour or so passed quietly.

Around 9.30 a.m., Ellen Marks[12] was standing outside 18 George Street with Mary Callaghan, talking to Frank Ruffell, who was delivering coke to No. 17 next door. Marks was barefoot at the time, as she was having her boots rebuttoned. Presently, a man dashed out of No. 19 exclaiming 'What a cow!'[13] He appeared to be about 5ft 7in in height, with a fair moustache, and of very sallow complexion. There was the scar of an abscess on the left side of his neck. He wore a blue-black overcoat, speckled grey trousers and a hard black felt hat, and there was a white kerchief round his throat. There was blood on his mouth and a scratch, and his hands also had blood on them. The man appeared to be excited and, panting heavily, he ran towards Thrawl Street. As he approached the corner with Thrawl Street, a woman appeared at the door of 19 George

Street and exclaimed that the man had tried to cut her throat. From then on, things happened very quickly.

The commotion had come to the attention of several people in the lodging house. William Sullivan, a dock labourer who had returned home early after failing to find work, was standing near the front door when the woman appeared. Since he saw nobody else, it is assumed he had missed the man by moments. Philip Harris, a hawker, was sitting in the communal kitchen with eight or nine other men. On seeing the woman appear and hearing her shout, they all ran out into the street. Asking the coke-man Ruffell if he had seen anybody, their attention was caught by the fleeing man, who had just turned into Thrawl Street. They gave chase, with Ruffell joining them. Two of the men in the group – John Whitehead and a man who went by the name of 'Bones' – were known to John Bennett, a resident of 10 Flower and Dean Street, who at the time had been standing on the corner of George Street. He had seen the fleeing man, whom he described as 'short' and with a moustache, also noting that he had blood on his hand and a scratch on his face. Bennett saw the man run down Thrawl Street and disappear down a court,[14] but did not give chase himself; he later said that: 'If any alarm had been raised that the man was the East-end murderer I should have followed him.' It was also said that the man had passed two policemen who failed to respond.[15]

The pursuers continued down Thrawl Street, but almost immediately lost sight of the man. Frank Ruffell continued into Brick Lane, where he encountered a policeman at the corner with Heneage Street and informed him of what had happened.

But what really had happened, and who was the injured woman? Clues as to her identity were, in the first instance, fairly flimsy, with early reports calling her 'Tilly', 'Flossie',[16] 'Dark Sarah'[17] and 'Laughing Liz'. Not many of those involved recognized her, and it was believed that she had not been seen at that particular lodging house before; however Mary Callaghan seemed to know the woman as Annie Farmer, and in due course her true circumstances came to light.

Annie Farmer was about 40 years of age and was married to a respectable tradesman, although 'Farmer' was believed to be her maiden name.[18] They had long separated, owing to Annie's dissolute habits, and she was said to have been living at 1 Featherstone Street,[19] near City Road. Her estranged husband supported their three children, who were all in school (Annie herself was described as well educated),[20] and had originally allowed her ten shillings a week, though he had stopped making payments after discovering his wife's immoral lifestyle;[21] like many others in her situation, Annie Farmer had resorted to prostitution to support herself.

At about 7 a.m. on 21 November, she found herself penniless and aimlessly roaming the streets of Spitalfields. On Commercial Street, she was approached by a man whom she had first met twelve months previously. He had asked her why she was up and about at such an early hour. They chatted briefly before going to a pub, where the man had treated Annie to enough drink to render her slightly intoxicated. After an hour, he suggested that they find a lodging house, choosing 19 George Street and paying 8d for a double bed. It was at 9.30 a.m. or thereabouts that Annie, perhaps half asleep from the drink, awoke to find a knife at her throat. A brief struggle ensued, whereupon the injury was inflicted. When Annie cried out, the man fled from the house into the street.

Annie, descending the stairs from her first-floor room, was partially clothed and bleeding profusely from the wound to her throat. As the various onlookers attempted to give chase to the man, the lodging house deputy proceeded to wrap the wound with a piece of rag. The police were called for and arrived soon after. Searching the property, they found no weapon. As the cut in her throat did not appear too serious, Annie was encouraged to dress herself, and before long Dr George Bagster Phillips and his assistant arrived. Dr Phillips stitched the wound and, noticing that a crowd was

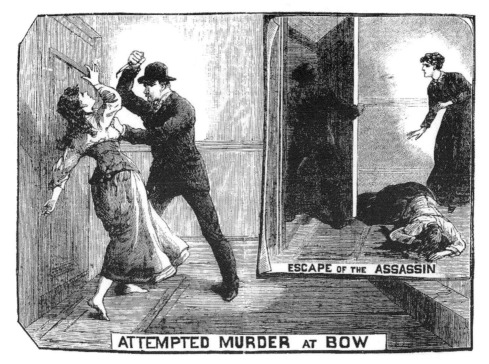

1. A dramatic contemporary interpretation of the attack on Ada Wilson at her home in Maidman Street, Mile End, in March 1888.

2. A press illustration from 1891 of 'Spitalfields Chambers', 8 White's Row, where Annie Millwood went after she was attacked with a knife in February 1888. Frances Coles, who also later became a victim, was resident there in 1891.

Text within the illustration:

THE FIRST OF THE SERIES OF WHITECHAPEL HORRORS.

I WAS FOLLOWED BY STRANGE MEN AND ASSAULTED AND MUTILATED

THE OSBORN ST MURDER

TAKING THE DYING DEPOSITIONS OF THE FIRST VICTIM OF THE WHITECHAPEL MONSTER

3. Emma Smith dies in the London Hospital after her savage assault in April 1888. This illustration appeared many months later when the 'Whitechapel murders' were well and truly underway, suggesting that the press were making a link with some of these earlier crimes.

4. Gunthorpe Street, formerly George Yard, as it is today. Martha Tabram was found dead in George Yard Buildings, which were located at the far end of the street.

5. A later depiction of John Reeves' discovery of Martha Tabram's body, from *Famous Crimes Past and Present* by Harold Furniss, 1903.

HORRIBLE DISCOVERY OF HUMAN REMAINS AT RAINHAM.

6. The *Illustrated Police News* thrived on salacious images such as this one, depicting the discovery of a woman's remains at Rainham in 1887.

7. The former headquarters of the Metropolitan Police at Scotland Yard, Whitehall. During its construction in 1888, the torso of a woman was found in the foundations in what has become known as the 'Whitehall Mystery'.

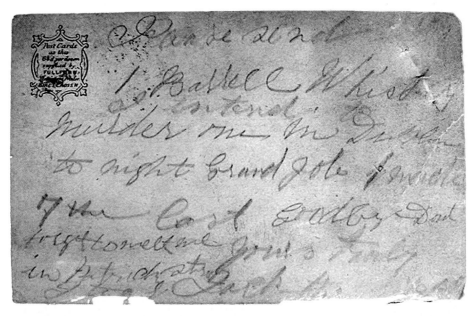

8. After the 'Dear Boss' letter – signed 'Jack the Ripper' – had been published, imitators were in abundance. Letters like this one, sent to the City of London Police and threatening to murder in Dublin, were not unusual. It was widely felt that the Ripper could strike anywhere.

9. More sensational imagery from the *Illustrated Police News* regarding the assault on Annie Farmer in the heart of the Spitalfields lodging house district. The illustration captures the immediate panic generated by the incident.

10. A contemporary (1888) sketch of the corner of George Street and Wentworth Street. George Street was at one time home to Emma Smith, Martha Tabram and Annie Farmer, as well as 'canonical' Ripper victim Mary Kelly.

11. High Street, Poplar. It was in a small yard off this busy thoroughfare that the dead body of Catherine 'Rose' Mylett was found on 20 December 1888. As always, thoughts turned to the Ripper, despite the lack of mutilation or evidence of strangulation.

12. A railway bridge near May Pen, west of Old Harbour, Jamaica – Estina Crawford's body was discovered on a railside road like this.

13. Joseph Davis, a gardener, finds part of Elizabeth Jackson in Battersea Park on 6 June 1889. Another sensational illustration from the *Illustrated Police News*.

14. PC Walter Andrews finds the body of Alice McKenzie in squalid, lonely Castle Alley on 17 July 1889. Alice McKenzie was considered a Ripper victim at the time by Dr Thomas Bond – an opinion not shared by Dr George Bagster Phillips, whose experience of the Whitechapel murders was considerable.

15. 'Clay Pipe' Alice McKenzie, as photographed in the Whitechapel Workhouse mortuary.

16. Spiritualist Robert Lees in later life. Lees' accounts of his visions and his attempts to get the London police to consider them have become a colourful part of Ripper lore.

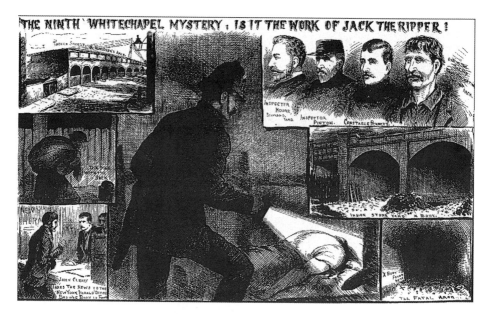

17. This *Illustrated Police News* illustration shows the discovery by PC William Pennett of the Pinchin Street Torso in September 1889. As was common, the main characters associated with the discovery are depicted, including Inspectors Pinhorn and Moore, as well as one of the men who had been sleeping rough nearby that night.

18. With each new murder, public excitement peaked. The death of Francis Coles in Swallow Gardens in February 1891 was no exception.

19. A contemporary press illustration of James Sadler and Frances Coles in their White's Row lodging house following their eventful trawl of the East End pubs.

20. The American Carrie Brown was also known as 'Shakespeare' owing to her apparent intelligence and culture. Her squalid death in a Lower East Side lodging house was the culmination of a life that had gone terribly wrong – a pattern shared by many of the victims of Jack the Ripper in London.

21. New York's Lower East Side, photographed here in the 1880s, was seen as the 'Whitechapel' of America's great city, reflecting similar issues of overcrowding, poverty and immigration.

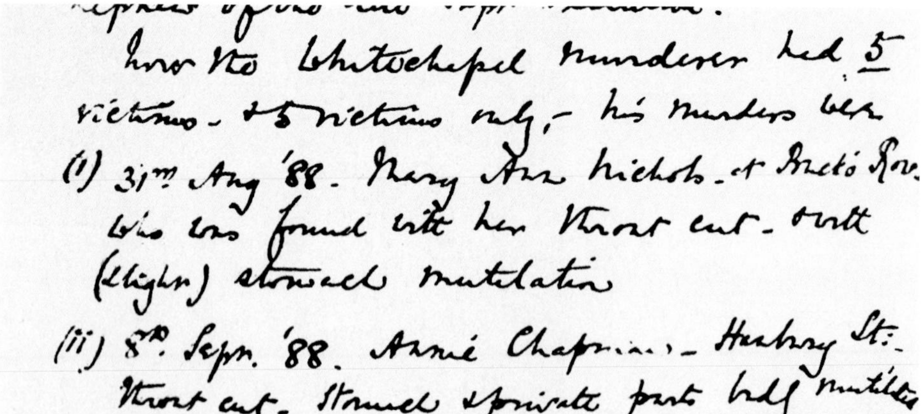

[handwritten memorandum]

how the Whitechapel murderer had 5 victims — & 5 victims only — his murders were
(i) 31ˢᵗ Aug '88. Mary Ann Nichols — at Bucks Row. who was found with her throat cut — & with (slight) stomach mutilation
(ii) 8ᵗʰ Sepr. '88. Annie Chapman — Hanbury St: throat cut — Stomach & private parts badly mutilated & some of the entrails placed round the neck.
(iii) 30ᵗʰ Sepr '88. Elizabeth Stride — Berner's Street.

22. Sir Melville Macnaghten's 1894 memorandum not only mentioned the names of three contemporary police suspects, but also made the assertion that Jack the Ripper only had five 'official' victims. The discovery of this significant document in 1959 changed how these murders were perceived for many years, and it still has a great influence today.

beginning to form, suggested that Annie be taken to Commercial Street police station.[22]

Although she appeared fit enough to walk to the station, despite still being under the influence of alcohol, it was suggested that Annie should be taken there on a stretcher – perhaps an unwise decision, given the growing excitement of the assembled crowds. As the stretcher made its way to Commercial Street, the spectacle encouraged word to circulate that there had been another murder.[23] In a very short time, the neighbourhood around George Street was thronged with people, anxious that Jack the Ripper might have struck again in their very midst. The same excitement could be found outside Commercial Street police station, but once Annie was inside, the doors were resolutely shut.

The lodging house where the incident took place was already being examined by the police, as was the surrounding neighbourhood, and by mid-morning descriptions of the assailant had been circulated to all police stations in the Metropolitan Police district. Detectives Thick, Dew, MacGuire and others were instructed by Superintendent Arnold to endeavour to trace the wanted man. His description, based on the generally consistent accounts of those who saw him, read thus: 'Wanted, for attempted murder, on the 21st inst., a man, aged 36 years; height, 5ft. 6in.; complexion dark, no whiskers, dark moustache; dress, black jacket, vest, and trousers, round black felt hat. Respectable appearance. Can be identified.'[24]

The reluctance of the police to give any information regarding the incident did not go unnoticed by elements of the press, which found the authorities' tight-lipped demeanour frustrating and even irresponsible in light of the panic that was now developing. A sergeant posted at the door of the station denied journalists entry, and even refused to comment on whether the woman was alive or dead. The refusal of the police to clarify the situation only inflamed the growing unrest. As one reporter commented, 'at present they look at you, smile, and assume an important demeanour. One might as well try to obtain information from a sphinx.'[25]

As the days passed, all attempts to trace the mystery attacker failed. More information regarding the attack itself was forthcoming, however. The throat wound itself was deemed not to have been made with a sharp instrument. More significantly, it transpired that while she was in the police station, Annie Farmer was found to have some coins concealed in her mouth. This led to the suggestion that the whole incident had been triggered by an attempt to trick the man out of money.[26] Although Annie claimed to have known the man and said that he had 'ill-used' her before,[27] she never gave any clue as to his identity.[28] For days afterwards, the streets were still being pounded by amateur detectives in their quest to capture the attacker, but with no result. Some took their investigations a little too far: one would-be sleuth had armed himself with a revolver and, when he unwisely decided to show the gun to a police officer, had been arrested for unlawfully possessing a firearm.[29]

Annie Farmer, having unwittingly found herself, albeit briefly, at the centre of the Whitechapel horrors, quickly faded into obscurity, as did the man who put her there; the hope that he might give himself up once it was announced that the police did not believe him to be Jack the Ripper proved a vain one.

This case, if anything, demonstrates the volatile state of the East End in 1888. It shows how a moderately sensational incident could be blown out of all proportion by the general fear of an unknown killer and emphasizes the knee-jerk response of a wide spectrum of the public that harboured that fear. But strangely, the story of Annie Farmer's assault in George Street did have a certain staying power and was still in the memory of some the following year, after the murder of Alice McKenzie in July 1889 (covered in Chapter 12). Frank Ruffell, the coke delivery man who had been part of the group that had pursued the mystery assailant, was interviewed by the American press. In a syndicated story that ran across three separate newspapers,[30] Ruffell, along with Annie Farmer – referred to as 'Dark Sarah' – were deemed to have seen Jack the Ripper. This implied that the knife attack in the George Street lodging house had indeed been the work of the Whitechapel murderer, and that it was his 'first botched job'. Even eight months later, Ruffell, who was by then working as the driver of a greengrocer's wagon,[31] claimed that he would recognize the man again.

It is very unlikely that Annie Farmer's assailant was the Ripper; the newspapers of the time were full of stories from around the country of knife attacks on women which immediately sparked comparisons with the fiend of Whitechapel. But the rounded description of her attacker did, according to one newspaper at least,[32] resemble that of a man who had accompanied Mary Kelly to her room on the morning of her murder.[33]

Unfortunately, all we have to go on today are the press reports, as no official Metropolitan Police documents relating to this case have been located. It is obvious that statements and reports would have been taken and filed; but the fact that such papers do not appear in those files perhaps shows that the police did not consider the Annie Farmer case to be related to the Whitechapel murders. Of course, there is always the possibility that the statements may exist some-where else, or may perhaps have been destroyed.

CHAPTER 9

Murder by Natural Causes

Catherine 'Rose' Mylett (20 December 1888)

SATURDAY, 7 SEPTEMBER 1940 WOULD CHANGE THE EAST END of London for ever. At 4.43 p.m., just as people were getting tea ready on that unseasonably hot day, the Blitz began. Some 364 bombers and 500 escort fighters darkened the bright sky – enemy planes as far as the eye could see. The death and destruction wrought that day, in two separate waves of bombing, marked the start of the transformation of the East End. It was not just the landscape that was changed, though; so was the public perception of the inhabitants – from poor, destitute and criminal people into plucky cockneys waving a fist at the sky and daring Hitler to do his worst.

Among the many buildings that were hit by incendiary bombs on that first day of the Blitz was the former Poplar Town Hall. Though essentially a functional building and architecturally undistinguished, it had served the community well over the years. It was also where the inquest into the death of one Rose Mylett had been conducted.

* * *

On Friday, 21 December 1888, the coroner, Wynne E. Baxter, entered the building, passed through the octagonal central hall and climbed the staircase to the public hall on the first floor. The inquest was due to begin at 11 a.m. Inspector Parlett of 'K' Division was there to watch the proceedings on behalf of the Metropolitan Police. He was probably anticipating a quiet hour or so, with a few witnesses explaining what they had seen or heard and recounting the discovery of the body, and with the doctor wrapping things up by describing how Rose Mylett had died of natural causes.

And indeed that is how the inquest proceeded – initially. But then it was the turn of the veteran divisional surgeon, Dr Matthew Brownfield, to speak. And Brownfield stated that Mylett had been murdered.

* * *

Rose Mylett's real name was Catherine and sheß was 29 years old, 5ft 2in tall, had light frizzy hair cut short, and hazel eyes. She was born in Mile End on 8 December 1859, the third child of Henry Mylett and his wife Margaret (née Haley). Henry, who hailed from Lough Lynn in Roscommon, Ireland, had worked as a labourer in a starch factory. By 1880, Catherine seems to have been living with a man named Thomas Davis, a commercial traveller. She claimed they were married, but no trace of a wedding record has been found. On 12 September 1880 she gave birth at 6 Maidman Street[1] to Florence Beatrice, whom she called Florrie or Flossie. According to Catherine's mother, the couple argued a lot and eventually separated.[2] Florence was sent away to school. She may possibly be glimpsed in the 1891 Census records among the children at the Kensington and Chelsea District School. Or she might have been at the so-called 'cottage homes' in Banstead, Surrey. By the second half of the nineteenth century it was recognized that the workhouse was not the place for destitute and pauper children, and instead they were cared for in a 'cottage home' (a large house catering for as many as thirty children), several of which would be grouped together. The cottage homes near Banstead were comparatively new, having been opened in 1880.

Catherine's movements over the next few years are unknown, but she clearly became increasingly dependent on alcohol, as her nickname of 'Drunken Lizzie Davis' indicates. Prostitution appears to have become her main source of income. She may also have had health problems: Elizabeth Usher, the head nurse at the Stepney Sick Asylum, would later check the infirmary records and find that over the previous few years Catherine had been admitted four times, each time as Rose Mylett or Rose Davis and each time for the same, unspecified condition. She was last admitted to the hospital on 20 January 1888 and stayed there for two months, discharging herself on 14 March 1888.[3] Catherine regularly took herself to Poplar, where she was known as a prostitute.

Poplar was a once prosperous place just a few miles from Whitechapel. By tradition, it had derived its name from a wood of poplar trees, or possibly from one tree growing on rising ground and visible from a distance. Over the years, the neighbourhood had developed into a quiet hamlet, with a single main street (unimaginatively called High Street). It had been described as 'a quaint straggling length of gabled houses, many built of wood, little gardens and trees in front of many of them'. This image of quaint rural tranquillity was spoiled somewhat by the further description that 'almost every second house' was 'an inn, beer house or place of refreshment'.

It was in the sixteenth century that Poplar had boomed, at least after a fashion: in 1597 Lord Wentworth granted the East India Company a 500-year lease on a parcel of land at Blackwall, where the company established a shipyard. The High Street provided an indirect route to the shipyard, and while the population of Poplar remained relatively small (about 2,500 in 1665, when the Great Plague struck), its businesses prospered. By the start of the nineteenth century, however, it had become evident that a more direct route to the docks was needed and East India Dock Road was laid out and built. This sounded the death knell for Poplar. High Street declined rapidly, and by the 1880s William Booth's survey recorded that 'Many shops have been empty for years.'

The High Street was nearly two-thirds of a mile long, averaged 30 feet in width, and was lined on either side with just over 300 narrow houses. Most had a shop in the front downstairs room, while the back parlour was used as the living room; there were two bedrooms upstairs. Though business was generally hard, the street's seventeen public houses seem to have done a flourishing trade, and most were well maintained, one even becoming a major music hall. The north side of the street was regarded as the better side and commanded higher rents, though by the 1880s both sides were poor (albeit with a semblance of respectability). Typically, the small courts that ran off it were lined by very poorly constructed housing that was deemed unfit for human habitation, but which nevertheless was overcrowded with people who could afford no better. By 1888, the High Street was described in one newspaper as 'a dirty, narrow thoroughfare'.[4]

Poplar generally appears to have been poorly lit, and a juror at the inquest into Mylett's death expressed the opinion that it was quite a dangerous place and poorly policed. He said he had seen 'a fight lasting over an hour take place in High Street, and people screaming, without ever a constable appearing on the spot'. Indeed, he thought the inhabitants were 'far more unprotected than the people of Whitechapel'.[5]

Between 184 and 186 High Street was a long, narrow passage that widened into a large yard called Clarke's Yard (because a builder named George Clarke stored old materials there). The yard contained a few small workshops and stables and was surprisingly busy – most evenings it was in use by at least one or two tenants until midnight. The yard (which no longer exists) was completely unlit, and even at the High Street entrance the only light was the meagre illumination provided by some nearby houses.

Until recently there had been gates at the entrance to Clarke's Yard, but they had mysteriously gone missing and the yard was known as the haunt of prostitutes, the darkness providing good cover for their activities. It was here, a short way up the passage leading into the yard, that Catherine Mylett's body was found on 20 December 1888.

Nothing much is known of Mylett's movements in the days leading up to her death. In or around October of that year, Catherine had moved into a common lodging house at 18 George Street, Spitalfields,[6] with a man named Ben Goodson. According to Mrs Mary Smith, the deputy keeper at the lodging house, Mylett and Goodson had separated about two weeks before her death.[7] Smith also said that Mylett, who was drunk more often than sober, had recently been imprisoned for five days.[8] Other women living at the house would confirm these details: Alice Graves, who was to feature more prominently in the story, said Mylett was known as 'Drunken Lizzie';[9] Lizzie Hanlon confirmed that Mylett had been living at the lodging house for about three months;[10] and Elizabeth Griffen referred to the man named Goodson.[11] Over in Poplar, Jane Hill, who kept a boarding house at 152 High Street,[12] said she had known Mylett for five years as Alice Downey, alias 'Fair Alice' and 'Drunken Liz'.

On Monday or Tuesday, 10 or 11 December, Catherine had visited her mother at her home in Pelham Street, off Brick Lane. They arranged to meet at the top of Brushfield Street, near Christchurch, Spitalfields, at 4 p.m. on 13 December, but Margaret Mylett was late and her daughter had gone by the time she got there. Mrs Mylett would never see her daughter alive again.

On Wednesday, 19 December 1888, between 6 and 7 p.m., Mary Smith saw Mylett in the lodging house and generously gave her 2d to pay her tram fare to Poplar. Catherine was sober at that time and was dressed in a double-breasted tweed jacket, black alpaca dress, brown stuff skirt, and a lilac print apron; she wore a red flannel petticoat and blue and red striped stockings, and side-spring boots. A blue-spotted kerchief was loosely knotted around her neck. When she did not come back to the lodging house the following day, Mrs Smith assumed she had been arrested.[13]

At 7.55 p.m., Charles Ptolomey, a night attendant at the Poplar Union Infirmary, was on his way to work. Passing up England Row, nearly opposite Clarke's Yard, he saw two sailors with a woman whom he later identified as Mylett. She was sober and the shorter of the two sailors was talking to her, while the other was pacing up and down. Ptolomey heard Mylett say 'No! no! no!' several times. He felt he would be able to identify the men again.[14]

Thomas Dean, who worked for a blind-maker at 159 High Street, Poplar, and who slept in the shop, left his workshop in Clarke's Yard about 10 p.m. He saw no one in the yard and heard no noise during the night.[15]

It was between 1.45 and 2.30 a.m.[16] on 20 December that Alice Graves claimed to have seen Mylett walking past the George pub in Commercial Road and heading towards the City with two men, one on either side of her. She was drunk and staggering, but Graves was not sure if the men were intoxicated and she paid them scant attention. Graves said that Mylett was wearing a hat (she was not when the body was found, and nor was a hat found in Clarke's Yard). As Alice Graves passed the George, she glanced at a clock illuminated by the gas light in the window before making her way home.[17]

The dog belonging to Mrs Thompson, the landlady of the East India Arms in High Street, began barking about 3 a.m. Mrs Thompson looked out of her window, but could see nothing.[18] A little while later, probably about 3.45 a.m., Benjamin Payne, who managed the William Brothers' grocery shop at 184 High Street, just by Clarke's Yard, finished a long night of paperwork. The ventilator in the shop had been open all night, but he had heard little apart from ordinary street rows – certainly nothing to excite alarm. Richard John Ashby, a letter-carrier (postman) living at 186 High Street, whose bedroom looked onto Clarke's Yard, had gone to bed at 11.30 p.m. and had woken at 3 a.m., but had heard no noise or shouts to alarm him.[19] Curiously, despite these reports that neither man had heard anything, in its story *The Times* recounted that both men had heard voices coming from the yard.[20]

It was at roughly 4.15 a.m., as Sergeant Robert Golding and PC Barrett were passing Clarke's Yard, that something lying by the wall in the yard caught Golding's eye. He took a closer look and discovered that it was the body of a woman, whom he recognized as one of the local prostitutes. She was lying parallel to the wall, her head about a foot from it and pointing away from the street. She was on her left side, with her left cheek on the ground and her left arm underneath her; her left leg, on which there were marks of mud, was slightly drawn up. The right arm and leg were stretched out. A little bloodstained mucus was issuing from the nostrils. Sergeant Golding's initial impression was that the woman had been leaning against some posts near the wall and had fallen down. There were no signs of mutilation or of any other injury, as far as Golding was aware; the woman's clothes were not disarranged and the presence of money (over a shilling) in her dress pocket suggested that robbery had not played a part in her death. Along with the money, Golding found in her pocket an empty phial or small bottle.

Leaving PC Barrett to look after the body, Sergeant Golding went to 170 East India Dock Road for Matthew Brownfield, the divisional surgeon. Since he was not immediately available, the policeman returned to Clarke's Yard with Brownfield's assistant, Dr George James Harris, who made a brief examination and declared that the woman was dead. Golding then sent for an ambulance and the body was removed to the mortuary.[21] Sergeant Golding conducted an examination of the yard, which was not paved but was composed of soil, and found nothing relevant. There was no evidence of any struggle having taken place.[22]

At 9.30 a.m. Curtain T. Chivers, the coroner's officer and mortuary keeper, saw the body and noticed a mark around the neck and some scratches. The mark was about an eighth of an inch deep, and the scratches were above it. He mentioned the fact to Dr Harris, who said that he had not noticed it in Clarke's Yard, but promised to look carefully for it when he conducted the post-mortem examination.[23]

Dr Brownfield and Dr Harris undertook the post-mortem at 9 a.m. the following day, 21 December. It was during this examination that Brownfield came to suspect murder. The two men found that the body was that of a well-nourished woman, who they estimated was aged about 30. There was a slight abrasion on the right side of the nose that might have been caused by any slight violence, and there was an old scar on the left cheek. On the neck was a mark that had apparently been made by a cord. It extended from the right side of the spine, round the throat to the lobe of the left ear; there were two or three inches at the back of the neck that had not been marked. Dr Brownfield established to his satisfaction that this sort of mark could be made by a piece of four-fold cord, described in a report by Commissioner James Monro as 'equal to packing-string of very moderate thickness'.[24] On the neck Brownfield also found abrasions of the sort that would be made by thumbs and middle and index fingers. They ran perpendicularly to the rope mark, and Brownfield thought these had been made by Mylett in her efforts to pull off the cord. There were no injuries suggestive of a violent struggle. Dr Brownfield thought someone had wrapped the cord around his hands and, standing behind and slightly to the left of Mylett, had pulled the cord over her head and drawn it tight, crossing his fists; where the hands crossed was where the marks of the cord were absent.

An internal examination showed the brain engorged with blood of a very dark colour. In an interview with *The Star*, Dr Brownfield said:

The left side of the heart was full of fluid black blood – particularly fluid and particularly black – and the lungs were gorged with the same fluid black blood, meaning that for the space of several respirations she had not breathed before the heart ceased to pulsate. Looking at the condition of all the organs in conjunction with the mark round the throat, my opinion is that death was caused by strangulation by means of a cord being pulled tightly round the neck.[25]

He went on to conclude that Mylett had been murdered no more than three-quarters of an hour before she was found – that is, at about 3.30 a.m., nearly two hours after the last reported sighting of her alive.

The stomach contained some food that had only very recently been eaten, but there was no sign of any poison or alcohol. According to Dr Brownfield: 'I smelt the stomach, and was unable to find any trace of alcohol at all. Neither should I say from the condition of the organs that she was a woman who was much given to drink.'[26] This is very curious, because Mylett was said to be a heavy drinker ('Drunken Lizzie') and Alice Graves testified that at 1.45 a.m. Mylett had been drunk and staggering.

One can only assume that her intemperance had not ravaged her body. But, assuming that it was indeed Mylett that Graves had seen, it is difficult to account for the absence of alcohol in the stomach – unless smelling the stomach contents was not a reliable way of detecting the presence of alcohol.[27]

Crucially, Dr Brownfield failed to communicate his conclusions to the police.

At 11 a.m. that same morning, Wynne E. Baxter opened the inquest into the death of the yet-to-be-identified woman. After hearing Dr Brownfield's startling conclusion, he adjourned the inquest, as 'it seemed very much as if a murder had been committed and that it would be better to adjourn to give his officer and the police time to make inquiries'.[28] *The Times* commented that 'The mystery surrounding the murder can only be compared to that which attended the recent series of crimes in the same district [i.e. the East End].'[29]

This all came as a shock to the police and caused a minor furore at Scotland Yard, because the police thought that Mylett had died from natural causes, nobody having intimated anything different. As James Monro expressed it in a report to the Home Office, the idea that Mylett had been murdered 'was certainly a matter of surprise to the police'.[30] Neither the policemen who discovered the body nor Dr Harris, who made the initial examination, thought there had been foul play; the body exhibited no obvious signs of strangulation (such as a protruding tongue or bulging eyes) and the evidence at the scene – or rather, the lack of it – did not suggest that a struggle had taken place.

The crucial question was whether or not Mylett had been murdered by Jack the Ripper. A journalist for *The Star* put the question to Dr Brownfield, who by way of reply posed a question of his own: had Jack the Ripper strangled or partially strangled his victims before cutting their throats? Complete or partial strangulation, he said, would have had the advantage of rendering the victim insensible. That would have made it easier and cleaner to cut the throat, and could explain why several of the victims appeared to have been laid on the ground before the throat was cut. The newspaper went on to add its own observation that, according to Dr George Bagster Phillips, Annie Chapman had been strangled. A journalist went to interview Dr Phillips, who declined to comment. However, the indefatigable newspaper reported that, via another, unnamed source, it had learned that privately Dr Phillips thought Mylett had probably been killed by the same man as Chapman.

This opinion was based not on anything substantial, however, but on Dr Phillips' conviction that Annie Chapman had been murdered by someone with anatomical knowledge and that Mylett had evidently been murdered by someone who had studied the theory of strangulation and knew where to place the cord so as to throttle her quickly and with the absolute minimum of struggle. The murder recalled the activities of the Indian religious murderers, the Thugee, and the newspaper commented rather melodramatically: 'The swift and silent method of the Thug is a new and terrifying feature in London crime.'[31] It was an unintentionally prescient comment, because Wynne Baxter would allude to the Thugs in his concluding remarks at the inquest.

It was rather embarrassing for Scotland Yard to find that Mylett was now being touted not just as a murder victim, but as a victim of Jack the Ripper. After all, it had previously been thought that she had died of natural causes. As Commissioner James Monro would eventually report:

> The absence of all signs of violence when the body was discovered & examined by the police and the assistant to the Divisional Surgeon – the fact that there were absolutely no signs of any struggle – The perfectly placid state of the features – The circumstance of a handkerchief having been found loosely folded round the neck of the corpse – all these circumstances, I am bound to say, made me rather hesitate to accept, without further confirmation the statement of the Divisional Surgeon as conclusive with reference to the cause of death. My experience in cases of strangulation led me to believe that the features of a woman so murdered would be swollen, livid, & discoloured, probably protruding – That the eyes would be staring – and that there would have been the livid *marks of the cord on the neck, accompanied probably with abrasion of the skin.*[32]

The problem, it seems, was a straightforward breakdown in communication: the police found no sign of violence on Mylett's body and no sign of a struggle in Clarke's Yard, and nor had Dr Harris when he briefly examined the body and pronounced Mylett dead. The police had accordingly released the body to the coroner in the expectation that the verdict of the inquest would be natural causes or suicide. The police inspector had seen Dr Brownfield, but (according to the inspector at least) the doctor had not intimated to him his opinion that Mylett had been strangled. And so the first the police heard of it was when Brownfield gave his evidence at the inquest. That Dr Brownfield was reported as attributing the murder to Jack the Ripper added insult to injury.

The police were clearly dissatisfied with Dr Brownfield's conclusion and Commissioner Monro asked Assistant Commissioner Robert Anderson to make further inquiries, directing Dr Bond, 'A' Division's surgeon, to conduct another examination of the body. Dr Bond was not available, so Monro asked the chief surgeon, Alexander MacKellar, to examine the body instead. We do not know in any detail what MacKellar thought, but in a report to the Home Office, Commissioner Monro said: 'I saw Mr. MacKellar on his return, and that gentleman fully supports the Divisional Surgeon in his opinion that death was produced by strangulation.'[33] It also so happened that Monro's letter to Dr Bond had been opened by Dr Charles Hebbert, demonstrator of anatomy at Westminster Hospital and assistant divisional surgeon to Dr Bond, who also went to the mortuary to inspect the body.

Dr Bond eventually examined Mylett's corpse on Monday, 24 December, comparing his observation with notes supplied by Dr Hebbert from his own examination conducted on the previous Saturday, when he was accompanied by Brownfield and Harris. They appear to have agreed about everything except the mark on the throat, which was not present when Bond examined the body; nor were there any injuries to the skin where the mark had been. The other marks, described as fingermarks, were present. While Dr Bond agreed with the deductions of Dr Brownfield, Dr Hebbert and Dr Harris that the deceased had died from strangulation, in his opinion it was not murder: rather the woman had fallen down while drunk and had compressed her larynx against the neck of her jacket;

the mark described as that of a cord must have been produced by the edge of her jacket's collar. He did *not* think Mylett had been strangled by the collar, which was not stiff enough; only that it was responsible for the mark. Dr Bond's conclusion was based primarily on the absence of any facial contortions or other signs that would have accompanied violent or quick strangulation.[34]

Although Dr Bond said that he had taken the contents of the stomach and had sent what remained to be analysed, either the results of the analysis were not available when the inquest reopened on 2 January 1889 and Dr Bond gave his testimony, or they were not reported in the press. Thus the crucial support for his hypothesis – that Mylett was drunk – is still unknown. Dr Brownfield said that he had detected no alcohol in Mylett's stomach. If true, this makes Bond's theory that Mylett fell down when drunk look unlikely; but Brownfield merely smelt the contents and failed to detect alcohol. An analysis of the stomach contents, as requested by Bond, might well have determined the presence or absence of alcohol once and for all.

On the last day of the inquest, 9 January 1889, Wynne Baxter summed up:

After Dr. Bromfield [*sic*] and his assistant, duly qualified men, came to the conclusion that this was a case of homicidal strangulation, someone had a suspicion that the evidence was not satisfactory. At all events, you've heard that doctor after doctor went down to view the body without my knowledge or sanction as coroner. I did not wish to make that a personal matter, but I had never received such treatment before. Of the five doctors who saw the body, Dr. Bond was the only one who considered the case was not one of murder. Dr. Bond did not see the body until five days after her death and he was, therefore, at a disadvantage. Dr. Bond stated that if this was a case of strangulation he should have expected to find the skin broken, but it was clearly shown, on reference being made to the records of the Indian doctors in the cases of Thug murders, that there were no marks whatever left. Other eminent authorities agreed with that view.[35]

The situation was obviously complicated and potentially confusing for the coroner's jury. Nonetheless a verdict of 'murder by person or persons unknown' was duly given and cause of death was described on the death certificate as 'Violent suffocation by strangulation by a cord which has not yet been found.'

The matter was far from over, however. Superintendent Steed, who had attended the inquest on behalf of the police, returned with the verdict to Robert Anderson, requesting further instructions. Anderson later sent a report to Monro, which included the following lines:

I have thought it only fair to him and his officers to tell him plainly that neither the evidence given at the inquest, nor the verdict arrived at, affects the judgment I formed when I personally investigated the case on the 22nd ult., and that I did not intend to take any further action in the matter.[36]

It appears that Anderson was content that the death of Catherine Mylett was not murder. It has since been suggested that he wilfully pushed for a non-homicide verdict – hence the involvement of numerous doctors, at the behest of the police, without notification being given to the coroner, Wynne Baxter.[37] It is possible that the above statement suggests that the police, despite the murder verdict, intended effectively to wash their hands of the case.

We do not know what (if any) explanation Dr Brownfield gave for not informing the inspector that he thought Mylett had been murdered. In a letter of 30 January 1889 to Dr MacKellar, he indignantly commented that he had received the coroner's order during the night, had conducted a post-mortem examination at 9 a.m. the following morning and was told that the inquest would open at 11 a.m.

He wrote that he was told a police inspector would be present, but he makes no mention in the letter of meeting or talking to him. It may be that the doctor was pressed for time, or saw the inspector only shortly before the inquest began – or simply assumed that a death from strangulation would have been treated as murder and routinely investigated. Regarding the reports in *The Star*, he wrote 'I hope you do not think me responsible for their reporter's articles',[38] but he continued to be pressed on the point. On 7 February 1889, he wrote: 'In answer to yours of the 6th inst. I deny that portion marked with blue lines & shown to me in your "Star" and further was most careful not to state to anyone more than what I had said at the inquest.'[39] Despite this denial, the matter rumbled on, the police seemingly eager to lay the blame at Dr Brownfield's door. The following week, even the chief surgeon sounded a little testy when he wrote to James Monro:

> Sir,
>
> In reply to your letter 98.122/3 I have the honour to inform you that in my opinion Divisional Surgeons should not give information referring to any police question to members of the Press except with the knowledge and approval of the Police. The same rule should also be applied to private individuals. I further consider that Divisional Surgeons are bound to give Police the earliest possible information of cases of death to which suspicion of foul play attaches. I have every reason to believe that this is the opinion that obtains generally amongst the Divisional Surgeons.[40]

The death of Catherine Mylett presents a small mystery of its own. It is unlikely that she was a victim of Jack the Ripper. However, as the assault on Annie Farmer in November shows, after the death of Mary Kelly there was a great temptation – almost a knee-jerk reaction – to ascribe any death or attack to the Whitechapel fiend. In the words of Robert Anderson in his 1910 memoirs, indignant to the last, 'the Poplar case of December, 1888, was death from natural causes, and but for the "Jack the Ripper" scare, no one would have thought of suggesting that it was a homicide'.[41]

CHAPTER 10

The Ripper That Never Was

Estina Crawford (28 December 1888)

THE CARIBBEAN ISLAND OF JAMAICA, 4,568 MILES FROM Britain and with a continuously tropical climate, could hardly have been more different from the grey slums of Whitechapel. And yet in 1888–89 it, too, was touched by Ripper hysteria.

Ten miles west of the old capital of Spanish Town is Old Harbour, a ship-building town originally known as Puerto de Esquivella. In 1888 it was linked to the former capital by Old Harbour Road. This ambling road, which ran parallel to a railway line, went through fields for much of its length, and passed small, somewhat isolated communities known as 'Pens'. These had been livestock farms in the 1700s, before they were divided up and sold off as residential lots. The communities that developed came to be known by the name of the Pen on which they were built: along Old Harbour Road lay Bridge Pen, Church Pen and McCook's Pen.

It was on Old Harbour Road, near Bridge Pen, that the body of a 'respectably clad'[1] black woman was discovered on the morning of Friday, 28 December 1888. Joseph Easy, a planter who lived at Hartlands, near Spanish Town, found it at about 7 a.m.[2] He could see that the face was covered and that there were traces of blood on the neck. Noticing three men approaching, he told them of the discovery, but he had to go to a funeral and left the scene. One of the men must have notified the police at Old Harbour, for Sergeant Major DaCosta, accompanied by a constable, went to see the body and noted that the throat had been cut from ear to ear. The mouth was sliced along the length of the jaw and the legs were tied at the knees with a handkerchief.[3] Leaving the constable to guard the body, DaCosta returned to Old Harbour and telegraphed Inspector Ponsonby. DaCosta then made a further examination of the spot and found some stones spotted with blood, some coral beads and a tooth. By the head of the dead woman was a piece of board with some blood on it. Lying a foot or two away from the body was part of a string of beads that resembled the loose ones already found. DaCosta thought there must have been a struggle, as the string of beads was broken.[4]

Joseph Easy returned to the scene after the funeral, but he did not linger, as a small crowd had gathered round the body. He did, however, find an earring a short distance away and he gave it to a policeman. Another discovery was made about three-quarters of a mile along the road by 12-year-old Rosannah Chambers, who, while fetching water from the river at the water bridge near her home at McCook's Pen, found a hat on the bank. It was a white straw hat with a black ribbon, and there was blood on it, which caused Chambers to wash it in the river before handing it over to Detective J. G. Hewett. Another resident of McCook's Pen, Thomas Cadbury, found a tooth, which he passed on to Sergeant Major DaCosta.[5]

William Dailey Neish, the district medical officer for Old Harbour, was called, and after he carried out a quick examination at the scene, the body was taken away. He conducted a post-mortem at 2 p.m. According to Neish, the victim was a black woman aged about 25. She had suffered a tremendous blow to the face, powerful enough to have been potentially fatal; however, the actual cause of death was haemorrhage and shock from the division of the left carotid artery. The injury to the face had been caused by a blunt instrument, and one heavy blow would have caused the injuries to the head. The upper and lower jaw, the nasal bones, the left orbit and the forehead bones were fractured. Two teeth were found lying loose in the mouth. The feet were soft and Neish thought the woman had been accustomed to wearing boots. He believed she had been dead for some fourteen to sixteen hours when he examined her, which would put the time of death somewhere between 10 p.m. and midnight on 27 December.[6] DaCosta had also cut some pieces of clothing from the body with the intention of using them in any potential identification.

The body, with its face covered, was guarded by Eliza Reid and Constable Samuel Thomas. They were present to allow potential witnesses to view the woman, in the hope that some identification could be made. At about 10 a.m. on 29 December, there was a curious incident, when a man arrived with a mule and cart to view the body. Reid took the man over but, as she raised the cloth from the face, the man seemed shaken and stepped back as though frightened. He was asked why he seemed to be trembling, but he made no reply, got in his cart and drove away. That afternoon the body, still unidentified, was buried in the Strangers Ground at the parish church of Old Harbour.[7]

On the evening of 29 December, Sergeant Major DaCosta received information from a woman named Mary Ann Richards, who claimed that she had seen the woman in a cart with a man the night before the body was found. Richards had been in Free Town at a dance and had left at 11 p.m. with her friend Louisa Armstrong and a man named Bonner. As they were walking along, a cart caught them up. The driver was a man, and he was accompanied by a woman. Bonner asked the man for a light, but he refused. Then Richards asked for a lift. The driver asked his female companion a question in Spanish, to which she replied 'yes' and a lift was offered. However, the driver would only take the women, as he felt that Bonner was more than up to the task of going home on foot. The two friends got into the cart and sat on a board that was lying in it. The woman sat with them and laid her head on Richards' lap, before asking the man for a match to light her cigar. She introduced herself as Estina Crawford[8] and said that she had come from Costa Rica, but had left her belongings in the Jamaican capital of Kingston. A little while into the journey, she removed a hat, which was in danger of being squashed, from a bundle of clean clothing. The hat was white with a black ribbon. As the women looked at it, the man, who was apparently called 'Benjy', spoke for the only time on the journey. Mary Ann Richards and Louisa Armstrong finally alighted at Richards' front gate, just a quarter of a mile from Old Harbour, while 'Benjy' and Estina drove on.[9]

It was this information that put Sergeant Major DaCosta on the scent of the man, who obviously was now wanted for questioning. On the afternoon of 30 December, DaCosta arrested Benjamin Ranger at his home at the Vere Race Course on suspicion of the murder of the woman on Old Harbour Road. Ranger's initial reaction was to say 'No, it's not me' in both English and Spanish. He tried to escape, but was apprehended and handcuffed by DaCosta with the assistance of Constable Solon, before being put on a bus. Ranger had heard of the murder, but did not mention the name of the dead woman; however, as the bus travelled to the police station, he began to talk freely, without being questioned, after he was shown pieces of the woman's clothing and the coral necklace. He appeared to have been drinking, but was not actually drunk. Ranger said that the woman was Estina Crawford of St David's, and that she had been living in Port Limon (Costa Rica) and Colon (Panama) for around thirteen years. Ranger had been living with her for about six months. He then made a number of comments to those assembled in the bus: 'I don't know why I did it, better for me to have stopped at sea', he said to one passenger; 'Why should I tell a lie, the things shown me belonged to the woman', he admitted to Constable Solon.[10] It was, to all intents and purposes, a confession.

In order to confirm the identification, Estina Crawford's body was exhumed on 2 January 1889. Constable Elias Duncan had originally seen the body where it was found, but at the time had no idea who she was. However, after the exhumation, he was told about Crawford by Benjamin Ranger and came to the rather bizarre realization that he knew exactly who she was – he and the woman had been school friends in St Thomas-ye-East, Costa Rica, around 1867. He had last seen her alive in Costa Rica in 1880.[11]

The magisterial investigation commenced on Thursday, 10 January 1889, before Mr H. J. Bicknell, at the magistrate's room in Spanish Town. Benjamin Ranger was charged with the murder of Estina Crawford and a succession of witnesses gave evidence. Henry Nathan Hibbert, a shopkeeper of 138 Barry Street, Kingston, had rented a room to Ranger and Crawford on or about 7 December. They had left around 18 December to go into the country 'to introduce her to his mother and family, to be married'. When they left, they had locked the door and left some things in the room. Hibbert never saw Crawford again.

Robert Barclay, a coppersmith and plumber, was Ranger's uncle in Cocoafalls. He had rented a cart and a mule to him on 27 December to fetch some things from Old Harbour. Ranger, accompanied by Crawford, had departed in the cart in the afternoon. He returned later that evening alone, saying that he had left Crawford at home in Kingston as she was sick.

At 5 a.m. on the morning of 28 December, Ranger was seen on Oxford Road, some way out of Kingston, walking away from the railway station, by Charles Langley, a cook in Spanish Town. Ranger asked Langley for a light for his pipe and Langley duly provided one. Ranger then asked if there was anywhere he could leave a mule and cart while he was in Kingston, and Langley directed him to a Mrs Rosanna Bryan, where the matter was arranged.

A few hours later, at about 9 a.m., Nathan Hibbert saw Ranger at the Barry Street house. When asked where Crawford was, he merely said that she 'was sick'. Ranger took away a large trunk. Sometime between 11 a.m. and noon, Ernest Chambers bumped into him in Old Harbour, where they briefly talked about the latest murder before Ranger left to supposedly pick Crawford up from the station.[12]

Ranger returned, with mule and cart, to Mrs Bryan's later that day. After making some small arrangements, he set off into Kingston, returning later in the evening with a large trunk, a red blanket and a large basket. At this point there was still no sign of Estina Crawford.[13]

On the final day of the hearing, 15 January, Mr J. J. Bowery, the island's analytical chemist, was called to testify. On 2 January, he had received some items pertaining to the case, and these he produced at the trial proceedings: several pieces of wood or board, one of which was believed to be a piece of the cart that Benjamin Ranger had hired (which had earlier been located), and all of which had blood on them; a parcel of shavings which also had marks of blood on them; Estina Crawford's straw hat, which was not bloodstained; and a parcel containing a necklace of coral with the strings cut. There was blood both on the ribbon with which it was tied and on the beads themselves. In addition, Bowery produced a small packet containing a gold earring and a tooth, a coloured handkerchief containing stones, loose coral beads like those of the necklace, a number of dry leaves and a matchstick, all of which were stained with blood, including the handkerchief, and finally a bundle of torn female clothing, all more or less considerably stained with blood.[14]

Inspector Ponsonby reported the opening of the trunk in the presence of Ranger; inside were various statements of monies paid by Estina Crawford to one George Johnson, a lot of female clothing, spoons and other articles. Ranger stated that the clothing belonged to Crawford and that the accounts were washing accounts, which also belonged to her.[15]

It is clear that some form of rudimentary forensic investigation had taken place, as coral beads had been found in the back of the cart, along with traces of blood on the wheels. It was also reported that Ranger's trousers appeared to have some very small blood spots on them. All the evidence pointed to Benjamin Ranger having taken Estina Crawford out onto the Old Harbour Road, where he used the seating board from the cart to batter her head violently. After that, he must have cut her face across and slit her throat from ear to ear. Judging by the amount of blood found on the various artefacts from the case, it was a very messy affair. But was there a motive? It was hard to say. But Ranger had said that Crawford had about £38 with her, with which she intended to buy wedding things in Kingston, yet no money was found either on the deceased or on the prisoner.[16] It was never clear what had happened to the money; and as there appeared to be no rancour between Ranger and Crawford – after all, they seemed to be getting ready to marry – why events turned out as they did also remained a mystery.

The last day of the trial went on late into the evening. The defendant had no witnesses in his defence, and at the close of the day, the jury, after hearing the address of counsel and the judge's charge, returned a guilty verdict. Mr Bicknell thereupon delivered the usual address and pronounced the death sentence.[17]

As Benjamin Ranger spent his last week on earth in the Middlesex and Surrey county gaol, the press, ever quick to divine a link between any violent crime against women and the Whitechapel murders, reverted to type and published the most sensational claims:

JACK AT WORK AGAIN

The Terrible Whitechapel Fiend Transfers His Field of Operations to Jamaica

   Three Victims Added to His Awful List from the Low Women of the Island

Kingston Authorities as Helpless as Were Those of London –
Fourteen More to Die

The crews of the various steamers plying between this city
[London] and Kingston, Jamaica, are telling fearful stories of
crimes committed in Spanish Town, a village near Kingston. The
first of a series of diabolical and mysterious murders took place, so
the sailors say, Nov. 28 1888, in St. Catherine's parish, a few miles
distant from Spanish Town. The victim was a negress of the
lowest and most vicious class, whose name has never been discovered. She was found early in the morning, lying in a fence corner
by the roadside, her throat cut from ear to ear, her cheeks, nose
and forehead slashed in a manner that would indicate it to be the
work of a skillful butcher. Her clothing had, as in the cases of
nearly all the Whitechapel murders, been thrown over her head,
and the little crowd which had gathered there upon the discovery
of the body were horrified to see that it had been mutilated exactly
as had been done in the London cases.

If anything further had been needed to make the horror-
stricken crowd attribute the crime to the Whitechapel fiend it was
found on a card pinned to the unfortunate woman's body by the
blade of a small penknife. The card bore the inscription: 'Jack the
Ripper. Fourteen more then I quit.'

Of course a diligent search was made for the murderer but he
was not found.

On the morning of Dec. 13, in a field, lying by and partially
concealed under an old shed, was found a second body. In this
case the woman was a notorious creature of the lowest class, a
negress called 'Mag.' Her wounds were of the same nature as
those inflicted upon the other. The authorities made a hurried
investigation and burried [sic] the body as speedily as possible,
giving no one an opportunity to examine it. No mention of the
crime was made in the newspapers at the time, the officials
endeavoring by every means in their power to hush the matter up

and have it talked about as little as possible. No trace was ever found of the murderer, and it was forgotten save by the wretched women who belong to that class among which the unfortunates moved.

The third body was found on the Friday before New Year's day. This time the newspapers were compelled to notice the discovery. The scene of this third murder was about midway between the places where the former discoveries had been made, and the sailors insist that the crime was in every way an alogus [sic] to the others.[18]

The first murder mentioned obviously had noticeable parallels with the Ranger case, but where the stories regarding the other two murders came from is baffling. Apart from this report, there was no coverage of any more murders in Jamaica. Whether this was merely Chinese whispers or the overblown stories of excitable mariners making their way to the eager press is not certain. But suddenly the spectre of gloomy Whitechapel had crossed the Atlantic and was beginning to infiltrate the sun-drenched tropics of the Caribbean.

Benjamin Ranger was hanged within the precincts of the Middlesex and Surrey county gaol on the morning of 5 February 1889.[19]

The Nicaragua Ripper (January 1889)

With uncanny timing, the news suddenly spread the following day that Jack the Ripper had struck again – in Managua, Nicaragua.

The *Brooklyn Daily Eagle* carried a single sentence that was ominous in its simplicity:

The murder and mutilation of women has broken out in Managua, Nicaragua.[20]

The report itself was heavily syndicated, appearing in the USA on 6 February:

> Managua, Jan. 24.
>
> Either Jack the Ripper of Whitechapel has emigrated from the scene of his ghastly murders, or he has found one or more imitators in this part of Central America. The people have been greatly aroused by six of the most atrocious murders ever committed within the limits of this city. The murderer or murderers have vanished as quickly as Jack the Ripper, and have left no base for identification. The victims are all of the same class as those in London.

A little more light was soon shed on the events unfolding in Central America, showing that definite comparisons were being made. However, the reports said very little: the names of the victims were never disclosed and no reference to witnesses or to those who were supposed to have discovered the bodies was made:

> Two were found butchered out of all recognition, even their faces being horribly slashed, and in the cases of all the others their persons were frightfully disfigured. Like Jack the Ripper's victims, they have been found in out of the way places. Two of the victims were possessed of gaudy jewelry, and from that it is urged that the mysterious murderer has not committed the crimes for robbery. In fact, in almost every detail the crimes and characteristics are identical with the Whitechapel horrors.[21]

The reports found their way into the British press,[22] and the *Penny Illustrated Paper* had even got wind of the murder of Estina Crawford to bolster the story. This gave its journalists the opportunity to suggest the next move for Scotland Yard:

We now learn that at the beginning of January similar atrocities were taking place in Nicaragua, and that about the end of December equally barbarous mutilations are reported from Jamaica. It would be interesting to know whether any steamer left the Thames after Nov. 9, and after calling at Jamaica in December proceeded to Central America. If such a steamer exists there seems a strong possibility that the murderer will be found among her crew – at any rate, the clue is one which might well be followed up by our detectives.[23]

Here the British press was lagging behind somewhat, for the answer to the mystery of whether these crimes demonstrated that Jack the Ripper was loose in Central America had already been answered. Ironically, it was the *Mitchell Daily Republican*, the American paper that was one of the first to suggest that the Ripper had crossed the Atlantic, which deflated the story by announcing that the reports of the murders were all hoaxes. What is more, it even went so far as to say that these bogus cases were generated by the British police:

There is reason to believe that the intermittent stories of real or attempted outrages of a similar character in various parts of the world since the latest East London horror were really put in circulation by Scotland Yard detectives, presumably with the strategical idea, which cannot fail to awaken admiration for its brilliancy, of lulling to sleep the vigilance of the real monster and tempting him to add another to his list of victims. The reported outrages in Central America really appear to have been of this kind, and if their promulgation was truly due to the ingenuity of the inspectors here it reflects some credit on their powers of invention.[24]

Ingenious it may have been; however, there is no suggestion in the extant Whitechapel murders files that the idea of decoying the

Ripper into further outrages was ever considered by Scotland Yard. It appears that one, admittedly brutal, murder near Spanish Town, Jamaica, was the catalyst for sensational and misleading reporting. But in the end, it was the only one that was actually committed.

It is obvious that the profile of Jack the Ripper as a killer to be feared was too good to resist. It goes to show one thing, though: not only could attacks and murders that were undoubtedly not committed by him be attributed to him; he could also be held responsible for crimes that never happened at all.

CHAPTER 11

A Gruesome Jigsaw

Elizabeth Jackson (4–12 June 1889)

O N THE MORNING OF 4 JUNE 1889, JOHN REGAN, A WATERSIDE labourer living at Napoleon Street, Bermondsey, was, like many of his trade, hanging around George's Stairs, Horsleydown, in the hope of getting a day's work on the river. The neighbourhood of Horsleydown, situated on the south bank of the Thames, opposite Wapping and close to St Saviour's Dock, contained London's largest warehouse complex, which centred on a narrow and unusually named street, Shad Thames.[1] This commercial area had been completed in 1873, and its warehouses held huge consignments of tea, coffee, spices and other commodities that had been unloaded from ships and stored, ready for distribution across Britain.

At about 10 a.m.[2] something caught Regan's eye. Near the bottom of George's Stairs he saw a small group of boys playing on the shingle of the river shoreline. Such sights were not unusual when the tide was out, especially on fine days, and June's weather was already turning out to be a vast improvement on May's, suggesting that summer was well on its way. From now on, the Thames foreshore, easily accessible via the numerous stairs on both banks, would begin to lure the more curious children of London into small adventures.

Regan could see that the boys were throwing stones at an object that had been washed ashore. His curiosity piqued, he went down to

see what it was. To his astonishment, he found it was a parcel tied
with a stout cord and containing human remains. Presently, a
Thames Police boat passed nearby and Regan flagged it down. PC
Alfred Freshwater, one of the three officers on board, conveyed the
grisly discovery to the police station at Wapping, on the opposite
side of the river, where the remains were examined by Dr Michael
McCoy. He was of the opinion that they were the remains of a
woman who had been eight months pregnant at the time of death.[3]

Several experienced Scotland Yard detectives proceeded to
Wapping to commence investigations. Among the first on the scene
was Melville Macnaghten, who was only three days into his new
appointment as the assistant chief constable (CID). Dr Thomas
Bond was also summoned to examine the remains, which were
described as consisting of the lower part of a female body. Death was
deemed to have occurred recently, as Dr Bond noticed a slight trace
of blood seeping from the edges of the cut parts of flesh. Dr Bond
and Dr McCoy were both of the opinion that the body part was that
of a young woman 'very recently delivered [of child], but after death'
and that the child had been the deceased's first.[4] None of the press
reports described exactly what was found within the parcel to draw
such conclusions; however, what it actually included were flaps of
abdominal skin and the uterus of the victim, complete with umbilical
cord and placenta:

> The flaps of skin and subcutaneous tissue consisted of two long,
> irregular slips taken from the abdominal walls. The left piece
> included the umbilicus, the greater part of the mons veneris, the
> left labium majus and labium minus. The right piece included the
> rest of the mons veneris, the right labium majus and minus, and
> part of the skin of the right buttock. These flaps accurately fitted
> together in the mid-line, and laterally corresponded to the inci-
> sions in the lower pieces of the trunk. The skin was fair, and the
> mons veneris was covered with light sandy hair. The upper part of

the vagina was attached to the uterus; both ovaries and broad liga-
ments were present, and the posterior wall of the bladder. The
uterus had been opened on the left side by a vertical cut, six inches
long, through the left wall. The organ was much dilated the
vessels on the inner surface large and open and the mucus
membrane swollen and softened. The uterus measured 10in. long
by 7.5in. wide. The circumference of the os externum was 4in. . . . .

The cord measured 8in. and the distal ends showed a clean cut.
The vessels contained fluid blood.[5]

But this was not the only discovery of body parts in the Thames that
day. Earlier, three boys had been taking advantage of the good
weather to bathe in the river near the Battersea Park side of Albert
Bridge when they noticed a strange object washed up on the foreshore. On investigation they found it to be a human limb, wrapped
in white cloth. Hurriedly dressing, the boys took their find straight
to the police, who immediately notified Scotland Yard and sent for
the assistant divisional surgeon for Battersea, Dr Felix Kempster,
who identified it as a portion of a human thigh, from hip to knee,
approximately sixteen inches in length. His opinion was that the
limb had been 'roughly and unskilfully severed from the trunk' and
had been in the water 'not more than a day'.[6] The white cloth that
the limb was wrapped in was found to be a portion of an item of
ladies' underclothing, the waistband of which had the name 'L. E.
Fisher' written along it. Fastened to another bit of the material was
a piece of tweed, seemingly torn from the right breast area of a lady's
long Ulster coat. It appeared that the limb had been severed when
the clothing was still present.

Dr Bond examined the abdominal portion found at Horsleydown
and the thigh retrieved at Battersea, and concluded that the two parts
undoubtedly came from the same body: traces of sandy-coloured
pubic hair were evident on both, and the portions of clothing in
which they were wrapped corresponded. Further examinations of the

thigh, by Dr Felix Kempster in the presence of coroner Athelstan Braxton Hicks, found it to be the left one, and more than likely from a woman aged between 20 and 30.[7] Fingermark bruises were also found, and it was concluded that these had been made before death. It was thought that the two parcels had been thrown into the water from the Surrey side of the Albert Bridge on the morning of 4 June at high tide. The bundle containing the portion of leg had sunk, and was discovered on the Battersea foreshore only when the tide had receded. The contents of the other package, however, were more buoyant: they were found floating at Horsleydown, evidently having been brought down with the tide.[8]

Several inquiries were made at Battersea police station regarding missing persons, but without result. The police attached great importance to the name 'L. E. Fisher' and invited any assistance that could identify either the clothing or the remains. In the meantime, it was not long before tentative comparisons were being made with the events of 1888, the body parts being described as 'mutilated horribly, like the victims of the Whitechapel fiend'. It was also reported that the discoveries had 'created wild excitement'.[9]

On Wednesday, 5 June, Wynne Baxter opened an inquest at the Vestry Hall, Wapping, into the remains found at Horsleydown. It was an unusual case, and Baxter initially expressed doubt as to whether an inquest was appropriate in this instance.[10] Nonetheless, a jury was summoned and an inquest convened. John Regan and PC Alfred Freshwater of the Thames Police gave their testimonies, and with that the inquest was adjourned until 3 July, while the remains were sent over to Battersea, where it was expected that a reconvened inquest would be held.[11]

The following day, however, the situation took a dramatic turn. At about 1.40 p.m. on 6 June, Joseph Davis, a gardener employed at Battersea Park, was working near a shrubbery on a piece of ground that was closed to the public and that was a mere 200 yards from the shore of the Thames.[12] There he found a parcel on the ground that was giving off an offensive odour. A quick glance at its contents sent him in search of a police officer: Davis had found another batch of human remains. The scene was attended by PC Walter Augier, who took the parcel to Battersea police station in a garden basket, accompanied by Davis. Dr Kempster's surgery was only a few yards from the police station, and he was quickly alerted to the find by Sergeant Viney, who was in charge of local inquiries into the case, and Sergeant Briggs. Scotland Yard was immediately informed by telegram.

The remains consisted of the upper trunk of a woman, minus the portions already found at Horsleydown. The chest cavity was empty, but the spleen, both kidneys, a portion of the intestines and a portion of the stomach were still extant. There was also a portion of midriff and both breasts. The chest-bone had been cut 'right down the centre, as if by a saw'.[13] Decomposition was well advanced, but Kempster was of the opinion that they were probably looking at 'the upper portion of a woman's body, undoubtedly forming part of the body of which portions were found in the Thames on Wednesday'.[14] The parcel itself consisted of a piece of dark plum-coloured skirt with two flounces and with red and white selvage. The skirt pocket contained a small black vulcanite button, and a large brass blanket pin was found pinned in the waistband, which was made from a fabric with a blue and white check upon it, resembling an ordinary household duster.[15] All this was contained within a square piece of brown paper; some white blind cord and ordinary string had been used to secure the parcel.

Later that day, around 4 p.m., Charles Marlow, a bargee at Covington's Wharf, close to the London, Brighton and South Coast railway at Battersea, noticed a parcel floating up the river (coincidentally, almost immediately opposite the spot where an arm belonging to the 'Whitehall torso' had been found the previous year). It was in 10–12 feet of water but floating on the surface, so Marlow fished it out with a broom. This bundle was wrapped in a piece of what looked like a woman's dark skirt and was tied up with ordinary string. Unwrapping the bundle, Marlow realized that the contents were human remains; a few leeches were feeding on the fresh blood that was probably still inside the pieces of flesh. At that moment, a police boat, towed by a steam-tug, passed by and Marlow attracted the attention of the officers, who took possession of the remains and conveyed them swiftly to Battersea mortuary.[16]

With what appeared to be increasing regularity, Dr Kempster was summoned. His examination revealed that the bundle contained the missing half, or upper portion, of the trunk that had been found earlier that day in Battersea Park. The arms had been cleanly cut off at the shoulder joint and the head had been separated from the body close to the shoulders. The chest-bone had been split in a way that matched the other portion, and two upper ribs that were absent from the other part of the trunk were in the bundle, together with the collar-bone, two shoulder blades, and all the skin of the back. A portion of the windpipe remained, but the lungs were missing. The hair on the body corresponded to that on the pieces of the body previously discovered.

The police had been building up a description of the deceased woman, based on the parts found and measurements taken from them. This description was now circulated. The woman was apparently about 25 years of age, 5ft 6in in height, and with bright auburn hair. It went on: '. . . judging by appearances, the police are inclined to believe that the woman met her death by foul means'.[17]

This description led to several reports by members of the public of missing female relatives. The Metropolitan Police received a letter from Oxford suggesting that the murdered woman had been a resident of the city named L. E. Fisher: the published description of the remains matched almost exactly the appearance of a red-haired young woman who had gone to London to enter service in a good family. So important was this information considered to be by Commissioner Monro that the Oxford police were instructed to make inquiries, assisted by Detective Inspector Turrell.[18] Another notion was that the dead woman may have been Laura E. Fisher, a barmaid at the Old Cock Tavern in Highbury, North London, who had stopped working there eighteen months previously. The landlord seemed to recall that she had had auburn hair, but her present whereabouts were not known.[19] However, both women were later found safe and well.

On Friday, 7 June, Battersea police station was inundated with telegrams, as several other missing portions of the body were discovered throughout the day. A gypsy named Solomon Hearne, who lived on a dust-heap in the area known as Lammas Land,[20] found a section of the lower right leg and foot on the Thames foreshore near Wandsworth Bridge at Fulham, wrapped in fragments of the same Ulster coat as the previous finds. The left leg and foot, wrapped in the sleeve of the coat, were found by lighterman Edward Stanton floating in the river near Limehouse.[21] Again, the remains were taken to Battersea, where Dr Kempster, clearly being kept busy by the developing case, confirmed that the legs belonged to the dead woman, whose body was now slowly coming together piece by piece.

The police and large numbers of volunteers, including from the Royal Humane Society,[22] conducted organized searches along the river in the Battersea area. As a result, a portion of lung was discovered at Palace Wharf, Vauxhall, and again brought to Dr Kempster at Battersea. All the pieces found were preserved in spirits. Portions of the clothing that contained the various recovered remains were taken along to Bridge Road police station at Battersea and made available for inspection by anyone who may have a missing female friend or relative who fitted the circulated description.

That evening, 7 June, an inquest was held at Pimlico that focused on the body of a newborn female child found bundled in ragged, filthy clothing near Ebury Bridge. There was some initial suspicion that this may have been connected with the case of the unidentified woman, due to several assertions that the woman had given birth prior to her death and dismemberment. The cause of death of the mystery child could not be ascertained. But just before 8 a.m. the following day, a wharf labourer by the name of William Chidley found a left arm and hand floating in a brown paper parcel in the Thames off Bankside. Again, Dr Kempster received the remains via the Thames Police and again declared that they were part of the steadily growing collection of remains from the same woman. The limb had apparently been removed with a clean cut, and there appeared to be four vaccination scars on the upper arm.[23] There was apparently no mark of any ring on the fingers (though later medical evidence suggested otherwise), leading to the conclusion that the woman was unmarried.[24] The skin was described as fair.[25] In fact, one report went so far as to claim that the hand was 'well-shaped and evidently that of a person in a superior position of life, as the nails appear to have been well cared for and the whole limb is very clean'.[26]

On the afternoon of Saturday, 8 June, the buttocks and pelvic area, minus any internal organs, were found in the mud between Albert Bridge and Battersea Bridge by Sub-Inspector Joseph Churcher of the Thames Police. A peculiar observation was made on closer examination of the buttocks: a piece of fine linen, about nine inches by eight inches, probably a handkerchief, was found 'rolled and pushed into the body'.[27] This suggested that the cloth had been inserted into the rectum or what remained of the lower portion of the vagina. No reason for this peculiarity was ever ventured.

The right thigh, much decomposed and again wrapped in a piece of the familiar Ulster coat, was found the same day under some bushes in the garden of Sir Percy Shelley's house on Chelsea Embankment by a reporter from *The Star*, Claude Mellor.[28] On the afternoon of Monday, 10 June, the right arm and hand were found by lighterman Joseph Squire floating in the Thames off Newton's Wharf at Bankside, close to Blackfriars Bridge. By now, the only portions of the body unaccounted for were the heart, lungs, head and neck, the intestines and the missing foetus. The *Portsmouth Evening News* gave a summary of what was known of the woman from her remains, although some comments appeared to contradict earlier evidence:

> She was a woman not more than 25 years of age, her height being from 5ft. 4in. to 5ft. 6in. She had bright auburn hair, and well-shaped hands and feet; but the nails of both hands were cut or bitten close to the quick. On the ring finger of the left hand there was a mark apparently showing that a ring had been forcibly removed. There were no marks indicating that she had been engaged in any work. There is no doubt whatever that the deceased woman was undelivered at the time of her death. She had been from seven to eight months pregnant. The body was cut up in a similar manner to the Rainham and Embankment cases. The police have been actively pursuing their inquiries, and from the results of these it is considered extremely improbable that the deceased's name is L. E. Fisher.[29]

One final development came in the form of a shocking discovery by the Thames Police. A jar, thought to be like those used for pickles, was found floating in the river at Whitehall. It contained a male foetus, believed to be of 5–6 months' gestation.[30] However, just as in the case of the abandoned newborn at Pimlico a few days before, it was impossible to connect this incident with the events of the previous eight days.

Several newspapers, particularly overseas, had linked this 'Thames Mystery' with the Whitechapel murders right from the first discovery of pieces of body; Washington's *Evening Star* stated that 'it is generally believed that "Jack the Ripper" has resumed his bloody work',[31] and similarly the *Newark Daily Advocate* put out the headline 'Jack the Ripper again spreads terror through Whitechapel'.[32]

Reports that two letters, supposedly from Jack the Ripper, had been sent to Leman Street police station made an early appearance in the press. The first letter – which arrived three days before the first set of remains was discovered – was headed, 'He is not dead, but liveth.' It was signed 'Jack the Ripper' and suggested that the writer was about to 'recommence operations' in the East End. No particular attention was paid to this letter at the time, until the discovery of the remains at Horsleydown and Battersea. On 6 June, another letter was received, making specific reference to unfolding events: 'I see you have been finding the pieces. How is it you have not caught me yet? Look out for more pieces.'[33] Still, the letters were given little consideration by the police, used as they were to such missives.

The domestic press, however, was circumspect about jumping to conclusions. Still, once the finding of human remains in the Thames had all but ceased, one paper was moved to comment: 'This would point not to isolated and intelligible murder, but to one more crime in an unexplained series – possibly, but not certainly, the same series as that which is associated with the Whitechapel mysteries.'[34]

With the mighty river refusing to offer up any new remains, the inquest into the death of this woman whose dismembered body had been strewn about the Thames foreshore began on Saturday, 15 June, at the Star and Garter pub in Battersea. It was presided over by Athelstan Braxton Hicks, coroner for mid-Surrey. The inquest created a great deal of excitement and attracted many people who lingered outside the court. Pointing out that no fewer than twenty-three witnesses would be appearing to give testimony, Mr Braxton Hicks decided that medical evidence should be given first. Dr Thomas Bond was called. He handed over the medical report, which was read out:

> . . . the remains were those of the same woman, and that the deceased was about 20 or 30 years of age, fair and plump, with bright, sandy hair. From the length of the thighbone the witness

was of opinion that the deceased was about five feet four inches or five feet six inches in height. The head had been separated from the neck at the sixth cervical vertebra, the tissues having been divided by a series of sweeping cuts. The legs and arms had been very neatly disarticulated. As a result of his examination of the abdomen, witness was of opinion that the woman was about eight months advanced in pregnancy, and that she was undelivered at the time of her death, which probably took place within 24 hours of the first portion of the body being discovered. The condition of the ring finger showed that a ring had been forcibly removed, either just before or after death. The palms of the hands denoted that the deceased was not used to manual labour. The system of mutilation showed skill and design, not the anatomical skill of a surgeon, but the technical skill of a butcher or horse knacker, or any other person accustomed to deal with dead animals. There was a great similarity of design in the cutting up in this case with that of the Rainham mystery and the more recent case in Whitehall.[35]

Dr Bond went on to say that, as the neck and the stomach were missing, it was impossible to say whether the throat of the woman had been cut or whether she had had drugs administered to her; the cause of death could not be determined, as the head, throat, lungs and heart had never been recovered. (Fruitless attempts had been made to find the head, using a dog named Smoker, which had previously been successful in discovering missing parts in the 'Whitehall Mystery'.[36])

The numerous witnesses ranged from the unwitting discoverers of the various body parts[37] to the police officers who conveyed them to the various police stations and mortuaries. One witness was Sub-Inspector Joseph Churcher, who had found the buttocks and pelvis and who again mentioned the piece of fine linen that had been found 'inside' the remains – something that previously only the

Lloyd's Weekly Newspaper had reported. After a long day, the inquest was adjourned for two weeks.

A syndicated news report circulated after the first day of the inquest suggested that an 'illegal operation' (abortion) had been performed on the woman and that members of the woman's family may have been complicit in the deed by arranging the operation. It was likewise suggested that 'if, as is now believed probable, the woman found mutilated at Rainham and on the Embankment met their deaths in the same way as this latest victim, it is evident that there exists in London an establishment where illegal operations upon women are regularly performed, and to the discovery of this the police are directing all their attention'.[38]

On 26 June, the news broke that the dismembered woman had been identified 'in the most positive manner' as an unfortunate named Elizabeth Jackson. The news brought with it the further belief, courtesy of the Central News Agency, that 'she was really a victim of the Whitechapel fiend, Jack the Ripper'.[39] Reference was made to the 'nameless indignity' that had been inflicted on the corpse – that is, the piece of linen that had been found inside the pelvic remains – though the exact nature of the discovery would never be specifically described in the press.

Elizabeth Jackson was born in 1865, the daughter of John Jackson, a stonemason, and his wife Catharine. She had gone into domestic service in the neighbourhood of Chelsea at the age of 16. By the late 1880s Elizabeth was well known to the police in the area. Apparently, she was last seen alive by her family on 31 May 1889. After that date there is no evidence of her having stayed in any of the various lodging houses or infirmaries in the London area. Her father had expressed concern in a letter to another of his daughters that the Thames victim may have been his missing daughter Elizabeth.

The police had been able to identify the clothing that was used to wrap many of the individual fragments of remains: they were traced to a Mrs Gerards,[40] 'a lady in a good position in society, who, upon her marriage some five or six years previously, gave it away with other cast-off underclothing and wearing apparel'.[41] By tracking the garments from owner to owner, the police eventually found someone who had given them to Elizabeth Jackson.

Elizabeth's sister Mary informed the police that Elizabeth had a small scar on one of her wrists, caused by a broken vase when she was about 12 years old.[42] This lead was duly followed up: although the remains of the arms in the mortuary had become quite decomposed, by lifting a portion of skin in the appropriate place, the scar tissue was revealed.[43] Mary, along with another sister Annie, confirmed that the last time they had seen Elizabeth, she had been 'in the family way'.[44]

The police traced Elizabeth's movements up until the time of her disappearance at the end of May. She had been a frequenter of common lodging houses in the Chelsea area and was last known to have lived at a house at 14 Turk's Row,[45] close to the Chelsea Barracks. Jenny Lee, who also lived at Turk's Row, said she had known Elizabeth for about two years and reported that she had been leading a 'loose life' for the previous seven months.[46] Elizabeth had gone to Ipswich with a man in January and had returned at the end of March; they had frequently quarrelled, and Elizabeth was once wounded with a knife.[47] From that time on, Jenny noticed Elizabeth going out with various men. The last time she had seen Elizabeth was outside the Royal Hospital Tavern on 3 June, when she had been with another woman (Elizabeth Pomeroy) and a man, described as wearing light moleskin trousers, a dark cloth coat and a rough cap, as worn by men who worked on the roads. Elizabeth had been wearing the same check Ulster coat that was to take on so much significance in the coming days.[48] It was clear that Elizabeth Jackson had been alive barely twenty-four hours before her first remains were discovered in the river.

'Ginger Nell', another of Elizabeth's friends, told how she had last seen Elizabeth on 2 June, when she had claimed to have nowhere go. She had been promenading near Battersea Bridge and the Albert Palace,[49] and sleeping on benches along the Chelsea Embankment. 'Ginger Nell' warned Elizabeth of the perils of the dangerous class of watermen who infested that locality. Elizabeth had also boasted that she had been in the habit of remaining in Battersea Park after the park gates were closed. This park was also known as one of the areas where the unfortunates 'promenaded'. The information gave rise in some newspapers to the idea that Elizabeth had been accosted, murdered and dismembered in the park itself. Reports suggested that there were two main theories being pursued: the first involved an 'illegal operation'; the second was that Elizabeth may have fallen victim to one of the rough watermen of the Thames and been murdered either outdoors, by the side of the river, or onboard a vessel there.[50]

A great deal of fresh information was provided by friends and family when the inquest resumed on 1 July. This confirmed beyond doubt that it was indeed the unfortunate Elizabeth Jackson whose body had been carved up and disposed of in such a brutal manner. It emerged that, up until late April, Elizabeth had been living and travelling with a millstone grinder named John (or Jack) Fairclough.[51] Witness Kate Paine of Millwall said she had let a room to Elizabeth and Fairclough on 18 April at four shillings a week. Elizabeth wore a ring, called Fairclough her husband and was five months pregnant at the time. But Fairclough was abusive to Elizabeth, knocking her about, and he eventually left her on 28 April. Elizabeth departed the following day, owing six shillings and taking the bed quilt with her. Mrs Paine remembered Fairclough (also known as Smith) well, and had described him to the police: age – about 37; height – 5ft 9in; complexion – fair, clean-shaven, slightly pitted with smallpox; and deaf. His nose was twisted as if it had been broken. He was broad-shouldered and had 'steelmarks' on the left hand. The last time she saw him, he was dressed in a light green and black striped jacket and light striped trousers with a piece of light check sewn into the waist.

He also had on a blue and white striped Oxford shirt, a white muffler, laced boots and a light grey or mouse-coloured felt hat. He was carrying a soft cap with a peak of the same material.[52]

The police were keen to interview Fairclough, whose photograph was in the process of being circulated around various parts of the country. The inquest was adjourned so that he could be located and brought in for questioning. At the end of the day, the coroner, Braxton Hicks, ordered that the remains be buried under the name of Elizabeth Jackson.

The inquiry resumed on 8 July, after John Fairclough had been located in Tipton St John, Devon, apparently wearing the same clothes as had been described by Mrs Paine.[53] He 'expressed himself perfectly willing to proceed to London and to give any information in his power'.[54] Though uneducated and apparently illiterate, he showed a marked intelligence, promptly answering all the questions that were put to him. He said that he was 36 years old, a native of March in Cambridgeshire and a millstone dresser by trade. He had first met Elizabeth Jackson towards the end of November 1888 at a public house on the corner of Turk's Row, Chelsea, where she told him that she had been living with a man named Charlie. He remembered that it was a Sunday night. The following day he had to go to Ipswich for a few months to work, and Elizabeth agreed to accompany him. He described her as a sober woman, and they only quarrelled now and then. On 30 March 1889, they left Ipswich and took the train to Colchester. From there they walked to London, where they stayed for five days at a Whitechapel lodging house, after which they lived at Mrs Paine's in Millwall.

Fairclough had wanted Elizabeth to go with him to Croydon, but she refused, preferring to stay with her mother in Chelsea until the baby was born (by now she was heavily pregnant with his child). He went to Croydon alone, having no money to give her, and got a few days' work at Waddon Flour Mills. From there he went to Wandsworth, then tramped huge distances to Isleworth, Uxbridge,

Ware, Bishop's Stortford, Saffron Walden, St Ives (Cambridgeshire), Huntingdon, St Neots, Biggleswade, Hitchin, Luton and St Albans, reaching Harpenden on 31 May. He also went to Watford, and on 3 June (the last day Elizabeth was seen alive) he was at High Wycombe and called at Great Marlow on his way to Reading. He subsequently Odiham (where he was bitten by a dog and had the wound treated by the parish doctor) and on Whit Sunday he was at Basingstoke. Then he continued travelling until he reached Tipton, near Ottery St Mary, where the police found him on Saturday, 6 July. From the time he and Elizabeth had parted at Millwall, he had neither seen nor heard anything of her and, unable to read the newspapers, had heard nothing of the 'Thames Mystery'.[55]

It was as thorough an account of his movements as could possibly be given and (if true) would undoubtedly exonerate him of any involvement in Elizabeth's death. With so much information requiring verification by the police, the inquest was again adjourned to allow Fairclough's statement to be thoroughly checked. His story proved to be entirely accurate, demonstrating that he had not been in or anywhere near London for at least ten days before and after Elizabeth's disappearance.

On the final day of the inquest at the Star and Garter, on 25 July, the coroner stated that all the evidence that could be heard had been considered and that 'there was no doubt that the woman must have died under circumstances which were exceptionally suspicious, for had she died in the ordinary way it would have been wholly unnecessary to have disposed of the body in this revolting manner'.[56] It was also announced that the clothing bearing the name 'L. E. Fisher' on the band had been bought at a lodging house in Ipswich; it had originally belonged to a domestic servant at Kirkley, near Lowestoft, and had been sold 'as rags' by her mother when she was staying near her daughter in November 1888. The woman was eventually traced to Byker, near Newcastle, and her father, who had marked the clothing and recognized his own handwriting, was traced to Bill Quay, on the Tyne.[57]

On the coroner's advice, the jury returned a verdict of 'murder by person or persons unknown'.

The claims by the press that the murder of Elizabeth Jackson could be linked to the Whitechapel murders soon fizzled out – particularly after the murder of Alice McKenzie in Whitechapel. She was killed on 17 July, while the inquest into the 'Thames Mystery' was still ongoing.

CHAPTER 12

Jack the Ripper or Not?

Alice McKenzie (17 July 1889)

CASTLE ALLEY IN WHITECHAPEL WAS RARELY OUT OF THE newspapers, mainly because of the outbreaks of disease, not to mention the crime and sheer human brutality that had existed there since the turn of the century.

In July 1823, an Irishman named Cornelius Cain had returned home to find that a six-week-old baby had apparently been abandoned by its parents and left in the care of his wife. The hungry child was crying loudly; Cain flew into a rage, grabbed it, took it outside and threw it onto a dunghill, where it was found by the parish watchman, who took Cain to the watch-house and the baby to the workhouse.[1]

During the cholera epidemic of 1849, there were several deaths in Castle Alley, one in particular that is worthy of special mention. Four-year-old William Elder lived with his parents in a room with walls that were black with dirt and mould. The room reeked almost unbearably. The landlord claimed (scarcely credibly) that he was forever cleaning and carrying out repairs, but the rooms were made dirty by the people who lived in them. In the cellar of the house was a cesspool and a privy, 'and the effluvium proceeding therefrom was indescribable'.[2]

Castle Alley was a hotbed of crime and had served criminals well since the 1700s: victims would be lured or forced into the narrow passage, and perpetrators would make their escape through it. In 1816, a gardener from Kent (appropriately named Timothy Root) was manhandled into Castle Alley by two women – Frances Sibley, aged 35, and Ann Tilling, aged 21 – and robbed of his purse containing £2 10s 6d. In those days, the cost of the purse was also considered, and that, together with a key it contained, were valued at an additional 1s 2d. Sibley and Tilling were found guilty and sentenced to death (though in both cases the sentence appears to have been commuted). Among the many who used Castle Alley as a means of escape was a man (never apprehended) who stole a watch from the splendidly named Ebenezer Ince of Merry and Son, a provisions merchant in Whitechapel Road. The man assaulted Mr Ince in the street outside the entrance to the alley, and then made good his escape up the alley itself while some confederates blocked the entrance to prevent pursuit.[3]

This unsanitary alley was frequently mentioned in newspaper reports of cholera or smallpox outbreaks; for instance, six deaths from smallpox were reported within a week in February 1863, four of them children living at 22 Castle Alley.[4] The death rate there was higher than in the area as a whole: fever, scarlet fever and febricula were very common, and scrofula and tubercular diseases were almost as frequent. One doctor claimed that he visited sick people in Castle Alley almost every day for fifteen years, and in 1875 the medical officer of health recommended that all the houses there be demolished:

As regards Castle Alley, I have on three separate occasions reported it to be unfit for habitation in consequence of the faulty construction of the houses, the want of ventilation and the impurity of its atmosphere. It contained in May last, on a house-to-house visitation by Mr Wrack, a population of 315 persons – viz. 208 adults and 107 children. There are 31 houses, in which there are 108 rooms. The entire area of the place is 1,496 square yards, which gives an average of about four square yards per person. Castle Alley is entered by a covered way several feet in length and only about 3ft in width, and owing to the filth which is daily deposited in its narrow passage it is always in an offensive condition. The backs of the houses in Whitechapel High Street completely prevent a free current of air from entering this densely crowded locality, so that the foul emanations which are given off by so many people congregated together in this narrow place, extending from the entrance in Whitechapel High Street to the new Board School, cannot escape, and hence the atmosphere is always close and fetid.[5]

Of course, nothing was done.

In order to enter Castle Alley from Whitechapel High Street one had to pass through a narrow covered passage only three feet wide, but several feet long. On one side of the alley itself was the high wall of a tea warehouse, which caused the thoroughfare to be in deep shadow even when the sun was shining. It was filthy: rubbish (of a kind unspecified by the newspapers) was dumped in the entrance and the smell was apparently indescribable. At night, local costermongers stored their barrows and other miscellaneous vehicles there, and up until about June 1889, two policemen had been watching the alley permanently, since it was thought to be a likely spot for a Ripper murder. The following month, that fear was realized.

November 1889 would witness an Indian Summer, but nobody could have imagined that earlier in the year. On the night of 16/17 July the sky was leaden, and occasional bursts of driving rain made it a less than ideal time to be pounding the beat around the East End. As PC Andrews plodded down Castle Alley from Wentworth Street, he came across a woman slumped on the pavement, apparently 'sleeping it off' in the comparative shelter of the alley. This was not uncommon. He turned on his lamp and tried to rouse her, but in the yellow light the woman's sightless eyes gazed back at him. There was a terrible gash in her throat.

Alice McKenzie is described as having been 5ft 4in tall, with a pale complexion and brown hair and eyes. The top of the thumb on her left hand was missing and she lacked a tooth in her upper jaw. She was dressed in a red bodice that was patched under the arms, a brown skirt, knitted brown petticoat, white chemise, one maroon and one black stocking, and button boots. She also wore an apron and paisley shawl. All her clothes were very old and there were no possessions on her body, although her old clay pipe was found beneath her.

Little is known about Alice McKenzie's background. She was believed to have been born in 1849 or thereabouts, and the man with whom she had lived for the last few years of her life, John McCormack, thought she came from Peterborough.[6] However, according to the Peterborough police, although six months before her death Alice had been arrested there on a charge of vagrancy, she was not a native of the city; they said she came from Scotland.[7] Elizabeth Ryder, the deputy of the lodging house where McKenzie frequently stayed, said she had often heard her mention that she had sons abroad, though the deputy did not know (or could not recall) where. McCormack was later quoted as saying that she had a son in America, that she was the last of her own family, and that her father had been a postman in Liverpool.[8]

Alice McKenzie had met John McCormack, a labourer who had been employed by Jewish tailors at Hanbury Street and elsewhere, in Bishopsgate around 1882. Since then they had lived in various common lodging houses in Whitechapel, eventually settling at 'Mr Tenpenny's'[9] at 52 Gun Street, Spitalfields, where, according to Elizabeth Ryder, they had lived on and off for about a year as man and wife.[10]

The last time McCormack had seen Alice was between 3 p.m. and 4 p.m. on 16 July, when he had returned to the lodging house after a morning's work. Apparently they had had an argument earlier in the day. When McCormack got back, and having just been paid, he gave Alice 1s 8d, making it clear that the eight pence was to pay for their bed, while the rest was for her to do with as she pleased.[11] And with that, no doubt weary, he went straight to bed. It would later transpire that Alice left the lodging house without paying the deputy, Elizabeth Ryder, the money owed.

The next 'sighting' of Alice McKenzie occurred at 7.10 p.m. and was unusual in that, according to a report made by Sergeant John McCarthy, it was made by George Dixon, a blind boy. He claimed that Alice had taken him to a pub near the Royal Cambridge Music Hall[12] on Commercial Street:

He heard Mrs. McKenzie ask someone if they would stand a drink and the reply was 'yes'. After remaining a few minutes Mrs. McKenzie led him back to 52 Gun St. & left him there. The boy Dixon says he would be able to recognise the voice of the person who spoke to Mrs. McKenzie in the public house.[13]

The location of the pub was not specified; however, inquiries were made at the public house next door to the music hall,[14] where the staff had no recollection of seeing Dixon and McKenzie.[15] Regardless of how many inquiries were made, Dixon's account could not be substantiated.

Back at Mr Tenpenny's, Elizabeth Ryder saw Alice a short time later, between 8 p.m. and 9 p.m., apparently the worse for drink. She appeared to be on her way out, and it was noted that she had some money in her hand. For a while it was assumed that she had gone out with a fellow lodger named Margaret 'Mog' Cheeks, a woman who had been separated from her husband Charles, a bricklayer, for three years.[16] At 3.30 a.m. the following morning, Mrs Ryder checked to see whether the two women had returned to the lodging house. They had not, and following the discovery of Alice's death, the welfare of Mrs Cheeks was a matter of grave concern. She eventually came forward to say that she had not gone out with Alice, but had spent the evening at her sister's.[17]

In the meantime, John McCormack had woken up between 10 p.m. and 11 p.m. to find no sign of Alice. Going downstairs, he met Elizabeth Ryder, who told him that Alice had not yet paid her the money for their bed.

A final, fleeting glimpse of Alice McKenzie occurred at 11.40 p.m. in Flower and Dean Street. A friend, Margaret Franklin, was sitting on the steps of a barber shop at the eastern end of the street, near Brick Lane, with Catherine Hughes and Sarah Mahoney, when Alice, seemingly in a hurry, had passed by, alone and heading in the direction of Whitechapel. Franklin shouted out, 'Hulloa, Alice!' to which Alice replied, 'I can't stop.' Nevertheless, she did pause briefly to exchange a few words before walking on.[18]

Around forty minutes later, at 12.20 a.m. on 17 July, PC Joseph Allen entered the gloomy archway on Whitechapel High Street which led into Castle Alley. Deciding the time was right for a quick bite to eat, he stood under a lamp and had a snack. It was all very quiet and Allen saw nobody else in the street and heard no noises from the backs of the houses opposite. After five minutes, he continued on his way toward Wentworth Street, noticing that on the corner with Newcastle Street the landlord of the Three Crowns pub was shutting up shop. About 100 yards down Wentworth Street, he passed PC Walter Andrews who was proceeding in the direction of Goulston Street.[19] After a brief chat, the two parted company, Allen continuing towards Commercial Street and Andrews making his way down Castle Alley, where he encountered nothing suspicious.

On the western side of Castle Alley stood the rear wall of Whitechapel Wash House. Built on neighbouring Goulston Street, it opened in 1847 and was London's first 'wash house'. In a neighbourhood such as Whitechapel, where hot water was frequently lacking in homes and lodging houses, such facilities were essential. Originally for men and boys only, Whitechapel Wash House was advertised the year it started operating as being open from 5 a.m. until 10 p.m., and costing 'first-class (two towels), cold bath 5d., warm bath 6d.; second-class (one towel), cold bath 1d., warm bath 2d. Every bath is in a private room.'[20] Sarah Smith, the wife of retired police officer Richard Smith (in July 1889, superintendent of the wash house), had her bedroom window at the back of the premises overlooking Castle Alley. At around 12.25 a.m. that morning, she was reading in bed. Had there been any disturbance, she would have been well placed to hear it; but the street outside was quiet.[21]

At 12.45 a.m. it again began to rain. Subsequent events happened quickly. PC Andrews set off from Wentworth Street in the direction of Castle Alley, bumping into Sergeant Edward Badham,[22] who was checking the constables' beats that night. After a brief exchange of pleasantries, Andrews continued on his way. As he approached the lamp where PC Allen had had his snack just twenty minutes earlier, he noticed somebody lying on the footpath between two costermonger wagons. Sergeant Badham had walked only a few hundred yards when he heard PC Andrews' two loud blasts on his whistle. Rushing to join Andrews in Castle Alley, his attention was drawn to a woman lying on her right side with her clothes pulled up, exposing her abdomen. He straightaway noticed a quantity of blood on the pavement under her head. PC Andrews commented on it being 'another murder', probably referring to the Whitechapel series, and as he leaned over to touch the body, he noticed that it was quite warm.[23]

Sergeant Badham, having instructed Andrews to stay with the body, went off to find reinforcements. In his absence, Andrews spotted Isaac Jacobs, a bootmaker who lived in nearby Newcastle

Street. He was on his way up Castle Alley to 'McCarthy's shop' in Dorset Street,[24] with the intention of finding some supper. Andrews made Jacobs wait with him. Presently, Badham returned with several officers, including PC Allen, who was sent to fetch Dr George Bagster Phillips. The doctor arrived shortly after Inspector Edmund Reid, at just after 1.10 a.m. On the instructions of Superintendent Thomas Arnold, several men were dispersed in different directions to make inquiries at various lodging houses and coffee houses to find out if anybody suspicious had recently come in. The body was taken by Sergeant Badham to the Whitechapel Workhouse mortuary in Old Montague Street, where it was examined by Inspector Reid. The bloodstains on the road were cleaned up and a thick layer of dust was thrown over any last traces, although splashes could still be seen under the street lamp.[25]

Almost immediately, the talk was of Jack the Ripper, as 'the murder threw Whitechapel into a condition of fearful excitement, and Castle alley was crowded all day. People from all quarters flocked to the scene and stories of the crime were on every tongue.'[26] Great crowds assembled at the mortuary where the body was being held, and inevitably newspapers began to draw the conclusion that the death of Alice McKenzie was the work of the Whitechapel monster. 'Jack the Ripper adds one more unfortunate to his bloody score', read one account, going on:

Jack the Ripper is back again. The horrible murder committed this morning enables him to cut another notch in the handle of his terrible knife. The details of this morning's crime leave no doubt that he is the murderer of Alice McKenzie.[27]

Another headline read: 'Jack the Ripper's Latest Murder Accepted as a Matter of Course'.[28]

The body was stripped by the mortuary attendants, who found a clay pipe, which had broken when the body was thrown to the ground. Following police inquiries around local lodging houses, the corpse was identified as Alice McKenzie, and John McCormack and Elizabeth Ryder confirmed her identity at about 2 p.m. on 17 July. Sarah Smith from the wash house also recognized Alice as somebody who occasionally frequented the baths, but she knew her as 'Kelly'.

Soon after, Dr Phillips conducted his post-mortem, by which time rigor mortis was well in evidence. As the ground beneath the body was dry, the time of death was put at around 12.45 a.m. The injuries were superficial compared with those inflicted on previous victims. The wound in the neck was four inches long, reaching from the back part of the muscles, which were almost entirely divided, to the fore part of the neck, reaching a point four inches below the chin. There was a second incision immediately below the first. The cause of death was syncope arising from loss of blood through the divided carotid vessels; death was probably immediate.[29] Dr Thomas Bond, who made a further examination of the body, accompanied by Dr Phillips, reported on the extent of the abdominal injuries:

On the right side of the abdomen extending from the chest to below the level of the umbilicus there was a jagged incision made up of several cuts which extended through the skin & subcutaneous fat & at the bottom of this cut there were 7 or 8 superficial scratches about 2 inches long parallel to each other in a longitudinal direction. There was also a small cut eighth of an inch deep, quarter inch long on the mons veneris. I think that in order to inflict the wound which I saw on the abdomen the murderer must have raised the clothes with his left hand & inflicted the injuries with his right.[30]

What is interesting about the McKenzie case is that the opinions of these two medical men – by now more than conversant with the

Ripper's handiwork – differed. Dr Phillips was firmly of the opinion that:

> after careful & long deliberation I cannot satisfy myself, on purely anatomical & professional grounds that the perpetrator of all the 'Wh Ch. murders' is our man. I am on the contrary impelled to a contrary conclusion in this noting the mode of procedure & the character of the mutilations & judging of motive in connection with the latter.[31]

Dr Bond, on the other hand, wrote:

> I see in this murder evidence of similar design to the former Whitechapel Murders viz: sudden onslaught on the prostrate woman, the throat skilfully & resolutely cut with subsequent mutilation, each mutilation indicating sexual thoughts & a desire to mutilate the abdomen & sexual organs. I am of opinion that the murder was performed by the same person who committed the former series of Whitechapel Murders.[32]

Chief Commissioner James Monro, who had visited Castle Alley at 3 a.m. on the day of the murder, appeared to agree with Bond, and in a letter to the home secretary declared: 'I am inclined to believe [the murderer] is identical with the notorious "Jack the Ripper" of last year.' He also observed that 'in spite of ample Police precautions and vigilance the assassin has again succeeded in committing a murder and getting off without leaving the slightest clue to his identity'.[33]

The conclusions of Bond and Monro were obviously not shared by the higher echelons of the CID. Although he had been on holiday at the time of the murder, Robert Anderson felt moved to mention the death of Alice McKenzie in his memoirs two decades later, suggesting also that Monro had at some point changed his mind:

I am here assuming that the murder of Alice M'Kenzie on the 17th of July 1889, was by another hand. I was absent from London when it occurred, but the Chief Commissioner investigated the case on the spot and decided it was an ordinary murder, and not the work of a sexual maniac.[34]

In fact, following the murder, Monro had seen to it that extra plain-clothes officers from other divisions were in place around Whitechapel for the next two months – three sergeants and thirty-nine constables.[35]

With the deceased successfully identified and a clear case of murder, an inquest was quickly convened at 5 p.m. the same day, presided over by the ubiquitous coroner Wynne Baxter at the Working Lads' Institute, Whitechapel Road. Aside from the police officers who had been on the scene immediately after the discovery of Alice McKenzie's body, several other witnesses were present, including McCormack and Ryder, who were able to furnish information on the character of the murdered woman and on the fateful events of that morning. The following day, more witnesses described Alice's movements on her last night and medical evidence was given. It was at this point that Margaret 'Mog' Cheeks made an appearance, safe and well, despite earlier fears that she had shared Alice's fate.

The funeral of Alice McKenzie, originally scheduled for 22 July 1889,[36] took place after a brief postponement on Wednesday, 24 July. The procession set off from a pub called the Tower at 19 Artillery Street at 1.30 p.m. The funeral expenses were paid by the proprietor of this pub, Alexander Solomon Parker, along with Thomas Tempany, owner of the lodging house in Gun Street that had been Alice's final home. The streets around Artillery Street were congested with 'rivers of heads and tides of human beings, there were walls of faces, both male and female, old and young'.[37] It was a handsome affair: with the hearse were two mourning carriages, each with a driver and attendant mute, and big black horses with glossy manes and black velvet cloths. Everything was decked out in solemn black. The mourners included nine women from the lodging house and three men, among them John McCormack.

The cortège wound its way through Whitechapel, passing many of the other murder sites en route to the cemetery at Plaistow: it drove along Commercial Street, past Dorset Street, then into Hanbury Street, passing by No. 29. Then, after proceeding down Old Montague Street (where earlier that day Alice's body had been laid out for people to pay their last respects), it turned into Baker's Row and the western end of Buck's Row. As the small procession turned into Whitechapel Road and then towards Commercial Road, the great crowds began to thin and the cortège trundled out of sight. As the coffin was lowered into its final resting place, women wept at the graveside.

The third and final day of the inquest was 14 August, when the all-too-familiar verdict of 'wilful murder against some person or persons unknown' was given. Coroner Baxter, in his summing up of the case, said that 'there is great similarity between this and the other class of cases which have happened in this neighbourhood, and if this crime has not been committed by the same person, it is clearly an imitation of the other cases. We have another similarity in the absence of motive.' He also took the opportunity to highlight the conditions in the neighbourhood of Castle Alley, which had gone unchecked for so long: 'Many of the houses in the neighbourhood are unfit for habitation. They want clearing away and fresh ones built. Those are physical alterations which, I maintain, require to be carried out there.'[38]

The jury concurred with Baxter's thoughts and requested him to forward a recommendation to the county council and the Whitechapel District Board of Works to remove the narrow passageway of Castle Alley and open it up to Whitechapel High Street as a proper street. Such alterations were eventually made, and the following year an article in the *Pall Mall Budget* noted that, though there had been little change to the district of Whitechapel as a whole in the aftermath of the murders, Castle Alley was finally undergoing the alterations it richly merited: 'There is some prospect at last of the vile hole known as Castle-alley, where the last murder occurred, being swept off the face of the earth, for the Whitechapel Board of Works have lately decided to convert it into a public thoroughfare.'[39]

* * *

In common with all the cases in the Whitechapel series, nobody was charged with the murder of Alice McKenzie. However, there is an interesting footnote to the case. A day or two after the crime, a man named William Wallace Brodie turned up at Leman Street police station to confess to the Ripper murders, and particularly to the most recent one. It was not the first time he had done something like this: the previous month, while on 'a spree' in Cape Town, South Africa, he had confessed to the murders. On that occasion, he appeared to be suffering from delirium and, when brought before the magistrate, was discharged and advised to give up drinking.[40] On 15 July 1889, he returned to England, working his passage as a fireman. A few days later he turned up at Leman Street, where he made his second confession.

Brodie was charged on his own admission of guilt, but the police quickly established that he had been in prison, convicted of larceny, from May 1877 until his release on 23 August 1888, having served eleven years of a fourteen-year sentence. He had gone to South Africa in early September, and his presence there for most of the period of the Whitechapel murders amply demonstrated that he was a time-waster. Moreover, according to a Mr Salvage of the Strand, Brodie was 'very drunk by 11 p.m. on the night McKenzie was murdered and had been put to bed at that time, not leaving until about 10.20 next morning'.[41] Brodie was examined by doctors and declared sane, but at the time of the confession was said to have been suffering from acute alcoholism that caused hallucinations. He was discharged, but immediately rearrested for defrauding a jeweller named Peter Rigley Pratt over a watch. At his trial, Brodie was often very aggressive and on a number of occasions had to be restrained by several warders.[42] He was found guilty and ordered to serve the remainder of his sentence for larceny, with an additional six months' hard labour for the fraud.

CHAPTER 13

The Body from Elsewhere

The Pinchin Street Torso (10 September 1889)

IN 1852, PARLIAMENT PASSED AN ACT ON THE CONSTRUCTION OF a railway line from Fenchurch Street station in the City of London to Southend-on-Sea in Essex, some forty miles to the east. The line was built by a company called Grissell and Peto, which was also responsible for a number of London's best-known buildings, among them the Lyceum, St James's Theatre, the Reform Club, the Oxford & Cambridge Club and, perhaps most notably, Nelson's Column. The railway line ran over a row of arches on the southern side of Pinchin Street, St George-in-the-East, between Back Church Lane and Christian Street. The arches sat opposite a row of run-down houses, and the whole neighbourhood was generally considered poor and miserable:

Like most parts of the district lying between Whitechapel and the notorious old Ratcliff Highway, Leman-street and neighbour-hood are densely crowded, a large proportion of the inhabitants being Germans, Poles, and Russians, who follow the pursuits of tailoring and bootmaking, polish walking sticks, hawk pictures, and engage in various callings of a similar kind requiring no great physical exertion. The whole district is squalid. No one would be a bit the worse if, by some other great public works, half of it were cleared altogether.[1]

By 1889, one of the arches was being used by the district Board of Works for storing stones. Access to it was generally blocked off by a hoarding, but this had been partly torn down and, like some of the other open arches along the street, had become quite easy to get into, providing an ideal shelter for the homeless and those in need of a place to spend the night. One such person was Michael Keating.

It was between 11 p.m. and midnight on Monday, 9 September 1889, when Keating, a shoeblack who usually stayed in a lodging house at 1 Osborn Street, Whitechapel, blearily wandered along the forbidding Pinchin Street. He was drunk and tired, but he had spent all the money he had for a bed on drink. He would later recall seeing people milling around in Pinchin Street,[2] but he did not notice anyone in particular, being more interested in the railway arches, which he thought looked like a quiet place for a sleep. He picked one out, went in, lay down and was soon dead to the world.

Unbeknownst to him, a few hours later he was joined in the next arch by two sailors. One of them, Richard Hawke, hailed from St Ives in Cornwall. On being paid off in London some seven or eight weeks earlier, he had gone into Greenwich Hospital, where he had stayed until he was discharged, penniless, that same Monday. He had walked from Greenwich to London and wandered the streets, but at some point he either made sufficient money to buy a few beers or had been fortunate enough to have been bought some. He had met up with another sailor in a pub near the Sailors' Home[3] and had drunk about three pints shortly before the pub closed. The two men then wandered the streets, arriving in Pinchin Street, where Hawke asked a policeman the time. It was 4.20 a.m. Feeling tired and seeing the arches, the two men went inside. They passed through the arch closest to Back Church Lane and from there entered the adjacent arch, settled down and soon fell asleep. According to Inspector Charles Pinhorn, the arches were well known as a place where vagrants slept and, although they were private property and technically the police had no right to enter them, they would turn people out of the arches almost nightly.[4] On this night, however, there was a new policeman on the beat.

PC William Pennett had gone on duty at 10 p.m. His beat took him through Pinchin Street every half hour, and he varied his route, sometimes entering Pinchin Street from Back Church Lane and sometimes from Christian Street. It was a short beat, dull and repetitive – the sort that numbed the brain. But as PC Pennett had never done it before, he was more conscious of his surroundings than he might otherwise have been.

At about 5 a.m., he woke up Jeremiah Hurley, a carman who worked for John Smithers in Well Street – policemen on some beats would often act as an alarm clock, the duty being known as 'knocking up'. Hurley had stopped PC Pennett the night before and had asked him to call at his home in Annibal [*sic*] Place all week at the same time. He then walked to Pinchin Street. There was a lamp about nine feet from the arch closest to Back Church Lane, and this cast enough light into the arch to make anything unusual visible to a patrolling policeman; but dawn was now breaking, and PC Pennett could see clearly inside the archway, where he spotted nothing of interest. He walked on along Back Church Lane and into Ellen Street, and from there to Christian Street. He saw nothing suspicious: nobody carrying a bundle and nobody pushing a handcart with a bundle on it. By 5.25 a.m., he was on his way down Christian Street and back into Pinchin Street. He crossed the road to where the railway arches were and glanced over at the arch where the hoarding had been torn down. Inside he saw what appeared to be a bundle. He went across to investigate and found that it was a human torso, minus head and legs. It lay on its stomach, about a foot from the right wall of the arch. The right arm was doubled under the abdomen and the left arm was lying under the left side. Over the surface of the neck and the right shoulder were the remnants of what had been a chemise. It had been torn down the front, and had been cut from the front of the armholes on either side. It was almost completely bloodstained.[5]

Policemen had been instructed that, in the event of any such discovery, they were to remain with the body and blow their whistle to summon assistance. An American newspaper, dripping with sarcasm, observed: 'The policeman blew his whistle as a signal for the murderer to get out of the way, and, after abundant time had elapsed for anyone to escape from the neighborhood, the police formed a cordon around the spot.'[6] In actual fact, PC Pennett realized that blowing his whistle would attract a crowd and, as there was no possibility that the victim was still alive and therefore no immediate urgency, he refrained from following instructions. Instead, noticing a man with a broom on his shoulder, he called him over and said, 'You might go and fetch my mate at the corner.' The man replied, 'What's on, governor?' and Pennett said, 'Tell him I have got a job on. Make haste.'[7]

The man went up Back Church Lane and soon two police officers appeared – an acting sergeant and a constable. The sergeant arrived first, and Pennett told him, 'You had better go and see the inspector, as there is a dead body here.'[8] The man set off for the police station while Pennett waited at the scene with the constable. Inspector Pinhorn duly arrived and at once gave directions for the arches to be searched.

Jeremiah Hurley, the man earlier woken by PC Pennett, came down Philip Street at about 5.35 a.m. On the corner with Pinchin Street, he saw a man who, he thought, was a tailor waiting to go to work. There was nobody else around at that point, but when he got to the railway arch he saw an inspector and an officer in plain clothes.[9] Pennett, meanwhile, had searched the arches as instructed and had found Richard Hawkes and his companion asleep in the last arch, and Michael Keating, the shoeblack, in the middle arch, lying asleep on some stones. Pennett woke them and they were taken to the police station.

From Leman Street police station an ominous two-word code was telegraphed to police stations throughout the district: 'Whitechapel Again!'[10] Within a short time Superintendent Thomas Arnold and Detective Inspector Edmund Reid of 'H' Division were on the spot and issuing instructions, and the Thames Police under Detective Inspector Regan embarked on a painstaking search of vessels in the river and the docks. Sergeants Moore, Francis, Howard, Davis and Scott at once got their various craft on the river and boarded all the vessels at the mouth of the Thames and in the docks. Attention was particularly focused on the cattle boats and ships from Spain and America. Among those vessels boarded in the London Docks were the *City of Cork*, the *Cadiz*, the *Malaga* and the *Galicia*, and the *Lydian Monarch* in the Millwall Docks. It took a considerable amount of time to search these vessels and the captains of the various vessels were able to give satisfactory accounts as to their crews' whereabouts.[11] Within half an hour of the gruesome discovery, Commissioner James Monro, Chief Constable Bolton Monsell and Chief Inspector Donald Swanson had arrived at Pinchin Street.

Shortly before 6 a.m., Dr Percy Clark, assistant to Divisional Surgeon George Bagster Phillips, arrived and examined the remains. After his initial examination, the body was placed on the ambulance and transported to the St George-in-the-East mortuary, a small brick hut in the grounds of Nicholas Hawksmoor's St George-in-the-East Church at the junction of Cable Street and Cannon Street Road. From the first examination and a fuller post-mortem later in the day, Dr Clark concluded that the torso was that of a woman who had stood about 5ft 3in, was stout, dark complexioned and aged between 30 and 40. On the abdomen was a wound 15 inches long. On the back were four bruises, all caused before death. One, about the size of a small coin (Dr Clark said it was the size of a sixpence) was over the spine, level with the lower part of the shoulder blade. An inch lower down was a larger bruise (about the size of a half crown) in the middle of the back; and there another on the top of

the hip bone that was about 2½ inches in diameter. The fourth
bruise, about 1½ inches in diameter, seemed to have been the result
of a fall or a kick. All of them appeared to be recent. On the right
arm were eight distinct bruises, and on the left arm seven; and on
the outer side of the left forearm, about 3 inches above the wrist, was
a cut about 2 inches in length, and half an inch lower down was
another cut, both made after death. The backs of both forearms and
the hands were badly bruised. The bruises on the right arm looked
as if they had been made by someone tightly grasping the arms. The
hands did not appear to be very work-hardened, and the hands and
nails were pallid. Rigor mortis was not present and decomposition
was just setting in.[12]

Dr Clark, Dr Hebbert, Dr Sargent and Dr Appleford would all
assist in the post-mortem, and Dr Phillips would examine the body
twice, on one occasion with Dr Frederick Gordon Brown. It was
reported that the severing of the head from the body had been 'skilfully done, without hacking, and the fact that a saw had been used
to sever the bones in a skilful manner, pointed to the possession of
a good knowledge of anatomy on the part the operator'.[13] Curiously,
an American newspaper, the *Trenton Times*, reported the following
titbit of fascinating information:

> A rumor is afloat, but cannot be traced to an authoritative source,
> that one of the doctors has pointed out that the surgical work of
> the fiend who committed the murder bears a remarkable resem-
> blance in certain features to peculiarities which have frequently
> been noted in the work of a well known London surgeon, a man of
> the highest standing in his profession, but exceedingly eccentric.[14]

So far as one can tell from the press reports, Dr Sargent was the only
doctor to have expressed the opinion that the dissection appeared
skilful. Indeed, Dr Phillips thought that the person responsible had
butchery skills, but no anatomical knowledge. The torso was 2ft 2in

long, 34 inches in circumference round the bust, and 31¾ inches in circumference below the breast. The length of hand was 6½ inches. The torso weighed roughly 67 lbs. In Dr Phillips' opinion, based on the absence of blood in the body and the pallor of the hands and nails, the woman had 'undoubtedly' died from loss of blood following her throat being cut and a main artery severed. He went on to say: 'I believe the mutilation to have been subsequent to death, that the mutilations were effected by someone accustomed to cut up animals or to see them cut up', but 'I have no reason for thinking that the person who cut up the body had any anatomical knowledge.'[15] The murderer had done his work with a strong knife, 8 inches or more in length. The condition of the liver suggested that the woman had been an alcoholic, and there were other indications that she neglected herself – the body appeared not to have been washed for some time. A curious feature of it was that marks on the waist showed that a cord had been tightly tied round it, but the doctors did not suggest a reason. The stomach contained 'a small quantity of fruit, like a plum'.[16]

Later in the day, the police issued a notice:

Found, at 5.40 this morning, the trunk of a woman under railway arches in Pinchin street, Whitechapel. Age about 40; height 5 feet 3 inches; hair, dark brown; no clothing, except chemise, which is much torn and bloodstained; both elbows discoloured as from habitually leaning on them. Post mortem marks apparently of a rope having been tied round the waist.[17]

It was suggested that the outrage was not the work of Jack the Ripper:

The most experienced of the detectives who have been engaged in connection with the Whitechapel murders do not believe that Jack the Ripper has anything do with the ghastly find. They are of opinion that the body has been a 'subject' in some dissecting-room, and that it was placed where it was discovered by some medical students who had obtained possession of it.[18]

Another possibility was that the woman had been murdered by the person or persons responsible for the dismemberment murders at Rainham and Whitehall (Chapter 7), and for the death of Elizabeth Jackson (Chapter 11): in each case the head had been severed and was missing.[19] The police and press also speculated that the woman may have died from an 'illegal operation' and the body dismembered to make it easier to dispose of.

It was quickly decided that no murder had taken place in the railway arch, but that the torso had been transported there and dumped not long before it was found. Given that the decaying torso smelt very bad, it had probably not been brought far (otherwise the person conveying it would have been noticed and very probably stopped). The police felt that the dismemberment had been carried out in the immediate vicinity of Pinchin Street, and accordingly began a house-to-house search of the surrounding roads. Everyone living in Pinchin Street itself was questioned, but nobody reported seeing anything unusual in the street; all the policemen on duty in the area were questioned and none had seen anyone carrying a bundle or pushing one on a handcart. During the afternoon, the police conducted a further examination of the surrounding arches, waste-ground and yards, but could discover no sign of the body having been dragged to the spot. During the search of the neigh-bouring streets, a piece of bloodstained cloth was found in nearby Hooper Street, but no connection with the Pinchin Street body could be established.[20]

Despite the authorities' assertion that Jack the Ripper was not responsible for the outrage, some elements of the press were initially happy to splash his name all over their headlines. On the day the news broke, one paper declared: 'Jack the Ripper at work again. The worst of the East End atrocities',[21] while another stated that he was 'again at his terrible work in London'.[22]

During the day of the discovery, crowds of people gathered at the entrance to Pinchin Street to gaze at the railway arch where the body had been found. By evening the site had been visited by thousands. Although the feeling in the area generally seems to have been one of great excitement, a Washington newspaper, the *Evening Star*, reported otherwise:

> The London newspapers picture Whitechapel in a state of panic-stricken excitement today. Whitechapel, however, is in a state of torpor. The people have become so accustomed to these tragedies that they cease to excite anything more than mild interest and a vague wonder in the minds of street-walkers as to which one will be taken next. When your correspondent visited Pinchin street under the railway arch at midnight tonight, a crowd had gathered about the police cordon, which for some inscrutable reason is drawn about the spot where the body was found. Numbers of women lay asleep on the sidewalk and others were talking and jesting with the policemen, but the great body of men, women and children only stared apathetically at the black hole where the bloody trunk was found, and perhaps found a species of gratification in conjuring up the probable details of the crime in their morbid imaginations.[23]

Large numbers of women applied to the constable in charge of the remains at the mortuary for permission to view them, but their requests were refused, as they could not possibly say to whom the torso belonged.[24] *The Times*, however, reported that the celebrated Stuart Cumberland had gained access to the mortuary and had viewed the remains, although the journalist did not know Cumberland's purpose.[25]

Stuart Cumberland – Mind-Reader

Stuart Cumberland was a fascinating character who enjoyed considerable fame in the 1880s and 1890s. He was rarely out of the press, and in 1888, the year of the Ripper murders, had written a widely serialized book entitled *A Thought-Reader's Thoughts*.[26] As well as being a writer and editor of the *Illustrated Mirror*, Cumberland (whose real name was Charles Garner) was perhaps the most celebrated mind-reader of his day (and possibly of any other day).

Cumberland never claimed to have supernatural or psychic abilities; he was instead a kind of human lie-detector. His great gift was an ability to skilfully detect the almost imperceptible muscle movements that betrayed somebody's thoughts. He was apparently so sensitive to these involuntary muscular variations that he could 'read the mind' of someone seated on the other side of a closed door and connected to Cumberland by a string passed through the keyhole. His 'mind-reading' feats astonished audiences around the world.

Some people believed that Cumberland actually had genuine telepathic gifts. His *Times* obituary acknowledged that 'Mr Cumberland was perhaps the most remarkable and gifted exponent of sign-reading or muscle-reading that we have had, and it seemed that in some cases he really possessed a certain power of thought-transference.'[27]

People did not really understand what Cumberland did, and news reports often described him as a clairvoyant. This was reflected in an interview he gave to the *Evening News* when Mary Kelly was murdered. Asked whether his powers could be used in the detection of crime, Cumberland explained that he was not supernaturally endowed and could do nothing unless confronted with a suspect – at which point he could probably determine whether he was guilty or not, and perhaps even elicit a confession: 'More I cannot do.' He was, though, 'pleased to help the police all I could if an opportunity offered. In fact, I am postponing my journey to Berlin for a week or so, on the chance of my services being of any use.'[28]

Cumberland's services do not appear to have been needed, but on 29 July 1889 he published an article in the *Illustrated Mirror*: 'My Vision of Jack the Ripper'. In it he described a dream in which he had seen the face of the murderer:

> The face was thinnish and oval in shape. The eyes were dark and prominent showing plenty of white. The brow was narrow, and the chin somewhat pointed. The complexion was sallow – somewhere between that of a Maltese and a Parsee. The nose was somewhat Semitic in shape, and formed a prominent feature of the face. The formation of the mouth I could not very well see, it was shaded by a black moustache. Beyond the hair on the upper lip the face was bare. It was not a particularly disagreeable face, but there was a wild intensity about the dark full eyes that fascinated me as I gazed into them. They were the eyes of a mesmerist![29]

Some newspapers claimed that Cumberland's dream was so vivid that he went to Scotland Yard and gave the authorities a minutely-detailed description. In the following issue of the *Illustrated Mirror* Cumberland described how, the day after he had had his dream, he was returning from a visit to his solicitor in a hansom cab when, in Regent Street, just above Piccadilly Circus, he passed another hansom, inside which he saw the man in his dream. He thought of turning and following the man, but considered it foolish in the circumstances to do so and continued on his journey – an act which, it would appear, he afterwards regretted.[30]

Up in Edinburgh, a Mr T. Ross Scott of 26 Queen's Crescent had been having a recurring dream since 4 July. In it a man stood in a small dispensary. Mr Scott had the impression that he was a ship's surgeon. Two weeks later he was still having the same dream when his attention was drawn to Stuart Cumberland's article. He recognized the man in his own dream as the one in Cumberland's vision.

A lady had likewise dreamt of the man and had later seen him sitting in a fashionable London church during evening service.[31]

In an article in the *Illustrated Mirror* of 27 August 1889, Stuart Cumberland prophesied that another Whitechapel murder would be committed within a fortnight. When the Pinchin Street Torso was discovered, many newspapers commented on the accuracy of Cumberland's prediction. It was against this background that Stuart Cumberland visited the mortuary and viewed the corpse. *The Times* may not have known Cumberland's purpose, but the *Birmingham Daily Post* claimed to: 'He is now attempting to solve the mystery of this crime.'[32] At the end of the month, several newspapers reported, slightly jocularly, that Stuart Cumberland and Dr Lyttleton Forbes Winslow[33] had announced that they intended to spend a few nights in the East End in pursuit of Jack the Ripper. 'It is to be hoped that they will not end up by capturing each other.'[34]

* * *

A week before the torso was discovered, a letter had been found at the rear of the London Hospital. In it the writer announced his intention of committing another murder. The letter had been handed to the police, but they received many such letters and so paid no heed to this one. On the night following the discovery of the torso, another letter was found in Whitechapel: 'I told you last week I would do another murder.'[35] The police endeavoured to compare the handwriting of the two missives, but nothing came of the curious incident.[36]

At 1.15 p.m. on Sunday, 8 September 1889 – two days before the gruesome discovery – a news vendor named John Arnold contacted the London office of the *New York Herald* to say that he had heard from an ex-police inspector he had met in Fleet Street that there had been a horrible murder in Back Church Lane and that it had been discovered by a policeman at 11.20 a.m. that day. Because he did not want his estranged wife to know his whereabouts, Arnold gave a false address (21 White Horse Yard, Drury Lane) and a false surname, 'Kemp'. Unfortunately this was noted down wrongly as 'Cleary'. Two reporters had driven rapidly to Back Church Lane and made a thorough search of the neighbourhood. They went down as far as the archway where the body was subsequently found, but all was quiet and there was no trace of any murder. They met two police officers, an inspector and a constable, and questioned them both about the story they had heard. The policemen had heard nothing, however.

From the moment the body was found in Pinchin Street two days later, however, the story took on greater significance and a hunt began for 'John Cleary', who, it was felt, must have had some inside knowledge of the deed.[37] At 21 White Horse Yard, the search hit an unexpected snag when it was found that nobody named Cleary lived there. In fact, none of the local residents had ever heard of a John Cleary – obviously the man had given a false address!

On learning that he was being sought, John Arnold came forward and identified himself to Sergeant Froest of the CID, eventually giving a statement. Arnold in fact lived at 2 Harvey's Buildings, Strand, and the man who told him of the murder in Back Church Lane was actually a soldier.[38] His original story was quite possibly sparked by a false report – it was suggested that it may have been based on the discovery of an unconscious woman in Whitechapel High Street at midnight on 7 September.[39] If that was indeed the case, here is a prime example of how even the most innocuous incident involving a woman in Whitechapel could trigger fears of another Whitechapel horror.

* * *

However, the case of the Pinchin Street Torso was anything but innocuous, and the police were faced with the mystery of who the victim was. Among local people at the time, it was suggested that the torso was that of a woman named Lydia Hart, who was well known as a 'dissipated creature' and had been missing for three or four days. Known as 'Lyddy', she rented a room in Ellen Street, a few blocks away from Pinchin Street, and this latest discovery set friends looking for her in infirmaries and hospitals. There was some genuine affection for 'Lyddy', it seems, as one friend told the press: 'Every now and then she goes on the drink and Lord knows what's become of the poor lamb.'[40] It appears that the missing woman was soon located (although in fact Lydia Hart was not her real name and she was not of the same 'character' as the previous Whitechapel victims). Her two sons found her at an infirmary, where she had been staying after going 'on a bit of a spree' and thinking it 'necessary to get medical treatment'.[41]

Coroner Wynne Baxter opened his inquiry into the death of the Pinchin Street victim at the Vestry Hall, Cable Street, on 11 September, with Detective Inspectors Reid and Moore watching the case on behalf of the CID. The jury went to the mortuary and viewed the body. After hearing evidence from PC Pennett and Inspector Pinhorn, Baxter adjourned the inquiry until 24 September because Dr Clark was engaged at the Old Bailey and Dr Phillips had not yet concluded his examination of the body. On that second day of the inquest, the time was spent more productively. Evidence was given by the two doctors, two of the men who had been sleeping rough in the arches and Jeremiah Hurley. In an incident not widely reported, it was suggested to Hurley that PC Pennett had been asked to wake him up at the time he did as a ruse to keep the officer away from his beat. Whether this was meant to imply that Hurley was complicit in the murder or disposal of the remains is unclear. However, he was quick to dispel the notion.[42]

Baxter, in summing up this uncharacteristically brief (for him) inquest,

> observed that they had not been able to produce any evidence as
> to the identity of the deceased, but the evidence of both medical

gentlemen engaged in the case clearly showed that the unfortunate woman had died a violent death. It was a matter of congrat-
ulation that the present case did not appear to have any connexion
with the previous murders that had taken place in the district, and
the body might have, for ought they knew to the contrary, been
brought from the West-end and deposited where it was found.[43]

The jury then returned a verdict of 'wilful murder against some
person or persons unknown'.

The identity of the victim was still playing on the minds of people
many weeks and months later. One claim that the remains had been
identified came from a rather unexpected source: a Mexican newspaper, *El Tiempo*, reported in late October that the parents of one
Emily Barker of Northampton had come forward to say they had no
doubt that the victim was their daughter. Apparently she had been
leading an 'unsettled life', and had recently been taken off the street,
half naked, by an Anglican priest. She had stayed with him for a
short while, and a few days after she left his house the torso was
found in Pinchin Street. The mother was quite confident that she
was correct, because she believed she had made the shirt that the
torso was wearing. It was also believed that she had recognized a
distinctive mark on one finger of the right hand. However, none of
these claims appear to have been confirmed by the press or the
police. Despite suggestions in the article that the Northampton
police had now joined the London force in the hunt for 'Jack el
Destripador',[44] nothing appears to have come of it. Indeed, it would
seem that Emily Barker had already been dismissed by the police as
a potential victim some weeks before.[45]

This most peculiar case also had a peculiar ending. A plan originally called for the torso to be placed in a tin container, which would
then be charged with spirits and soldered air-tight prior to burial,
perhaps with an eye to future exhumation. This plan failed, however,
when the tin-plate worker who was engaged to perform the task told

the police that he could not solder the tin vessel without the spirits leaking. The solution was for a 'case, properly constructed' to be made at a cost of 12 shillings. At 2 p.m. on 4 October, the torso was placed inside and the case was soldered down. It was then handed over to the sanitary authorities, who placed it in a black painted wooden box upon which a metal plate was affixed: 'This case contains the body of a woman (unknown) found in Pinchin Street St. Georges-in-the-East 10th Septr./89.' The case was buried at the East London Cemetery on 5 October 1889.[46]

CHAPTER 14

The Fit-Up

Frances Coles (13 February 1891)

Frances Coles has been described as 'perhaps the one true shining diamond in the rough of Victorian Whitechapel'.[1] She was born on 17 September 1859 at 18 Crucifix Lane, Bermondsey,[2] a street of poorly built and dilapidated slum houses, the third of four children born to James William Coles[3] and Mary Ann Carney. Her father hailed from Somerset, probably from the hamlet of Woollard or the slightly larger nearby agricultural village of Pensford on the River Chew, about seven miles south of Bristol.[4] He was a hard-working master boot-and-shoe maker, a craftsman, but his trade came under threat from cheap imports and technology that enabled mass production. As the family's fortunes declined, even Crucifix Lane became unaffordable and they had to move to White Lion Court, a squalid little street of tumbledown, vermin-infested houses, several of which were owned by a wealthy man named Cyrus Legg. Here the family rented a single, horribly over-crowded room at No. 8.

Frances's mother died in 1878,[5] and by 1883 James Coles' health had failed him. Now crippled, he had no alternative but to surrender himself to the workhouse.[6] He would never come out.

Frances had two sisters, Mary Ann (b. 1853) and Selina (b. 1857), and a brother, James (b. 1863), all born in Bermondsey. Despite having four children, it would seem that James and Mary had never married.

At the time of the 1881 Census the eldest daughter, Mary Ann, was a charwoman, unmarried and living at 32 Ware Street, off Kingsland Road in Shoreditch. Frances's other sister, Selina, had a troubled life. In 1877, aged about 20, she had found herself pregnant and had admitted herself to the St Olave's Union Workhouse in Southwark, where she gave birth to a daughter, who died seven weeks later. Selina seems not to have left the workhouse, and the 1881 Census records her there, her occupation given as 'domestic servant'. A newspaper report has her living in 'Kingsland' in 1891,[7] presumably with her sister, although in an interview at the time of Frances Coles' death, Mary Ann said that Selina was working as a laundry maid in a village in Kent, the name of which she could not recall.[8] This may well have been a lie to protect Selina from the press, as her sister's mental health seems to have been unstable: at the time of the 1891 Census, taken on 5 April, she was listed as a lunatic in Leavesden Asylum, Watford.[9] She never came out and died there of tertiary syphilis on 23 April 1897.

The only son, named James after his father, enlisted in the army. The 1881 Census records that he was a private in the 2nd Surrey Militia, stationed at Stoughton Barracks near Guildford. In 1888, a James Coles, aged 24, of no occupation but giving his address as White Lion Court, Bermondsey, was arrested and charged, along with another man, of breaking into a shop in Greenwich and stealing clothing. The fact that he had run off when stopped by a policeman cast a good deal of doubt on his defence that he had found the clothing and was looking for a police station to hand it in! Coles said he had gone to Greenwich to look for work.[10] It is not known whether this was the same James Coles, but the age and address make it likely. Frances's brother died in early 1889 in an accident and an inquest was held.[11]

On leaving school, Frances Coles began work as a trainee in the packing department of Messrs Sinclair, wholesale druggists in the Borough. By 1881, she was living at 192 Union Street, Southwark, and working for Winfield Hora & Co., a wholesale chemist at 58 Minories in the East End. The manager clearly remembered Frances and recalled that she was 'an exceptionally quiet, retiring, well-behaved girl, skilful at the particular branch of labour in which she was engaged, and apparently thoroughly respectable'. So good was she that after she had left the firm, a messenger was sent to see if she would consider returning to it. But the messenger could not find her.[12]

In 1884[13] she moved nearer to her place of work, taking a bed in a common lodging house popularly known as Wilmott's, at 18 Thrawl Street. This was a notorious street – as indeed was almost every street running off Commercial Road. In his *Dottings of a Dosser* (1886), Howard J. Goldsmid offered an outstanding description of Thrawl Street, plucked straight from a Hogarthian nightmare:

This thoroughfare, though short and narrow, contains probably as much destitution and depravity as any that are wider and more pretentious. It leads only from Commercial Street into Brick Lane, and in that short distance are concentrated elements of discord and degradation sufficient to shock even the most callous. The dwelling-houses are all poor and mean; the gutters in the daytime are full of squalling children; and refuse of all sorts is lying about in every direction. When closing-time comes, and the dram-shops and gin-palaces have sent their contingent to re-inforce the representatives of sinning and suffering humanity that crowd the unwholesome street, Thrawl Street is 'a thing to shudder at, not to see.' Women who have reached the lowest depth of degradation to which their sex can sink, are rolling unsteadily along the footpath, or quarrelling in front of the public-houses from which they have just been expelled. Men are fighting, swearing, and hiccoughing out snatches of objectionable songs. Babies, who have been taken in their mothers' arms to the drinking dens which rob them of their food and clothing, are wailing loudly; and the noise of quarrelling, intoxication, and lamentation, are to be heard on every side. It is needless to say, therefore, that it is the happy hunting-ground of 'doss-'ouse keepers,' and that nearly every second house is a common lodging-house.[14]

Wilmott's[15] was a small lodging house for women and was a rather dire place. Visited by the police in June 1890, it was found to be appallingly dirty and a notice was served on the keeper, James Hague, to clean it up. Hague did little or nothing, and on re-inspection the police found the house to be just as filthy, 'the bedding continued to be uncared for and the bedsteads full of vermin'. Finding himself up in court before Montagu Williams, the nemesis of lodging houses, Hague complained that he suffered from heart disease and was too ill to do much, though he did what he could; the house did not pay – he took only about ten shillings a night – and the opening of a Salvation Army shelter in Spitalfields had done much to damage the profitability of lodging houses. Williams listened unsympathetically; he told Hague that his ill health made him unfit to be running a lodging house and said that he was glad to hear about the Army shelters, as anything that caused the lodging houses to close down was good news. Hague was fined five shillings and told to take action, as he could be fined forty shillings for each day he failed to do so.[16]

Frances had begun to call herself 'Coleman', and she also acquired the nickname 'Carroty Nell' (early newspaper reports also suggested she was known as 'Carroty Hannah' and 'Carroty Annie'),[17] though how and why she acquired the nickname is a mystery: she did not have carrot-coloured hair and nor had she one of the Christian names that usually got shortened to 'Nell' (such as Helen or Ellen). She frequently complained that she found her work at Winfield Hora & Co. painful (her father later said that the job hurt her knuckles, which were calloused). Finally she left the job, although she would pretend to her family otherwise, and quickly descended into prostitution. At the time of her death, a man named James Murray, who lived in Bethnal Green, told the police he had known her to be working the streets of Whitechapel, Shoreditch and Bow for eight years – since 1883 – which means that she must have turned to prostitution almost as soon as she left her job, or even while still employed. Though all dates are estimates (and therefore unreliable), it is reasonable to suppose that she turned to prostitution almost as soon as she moved to Thrawl Street.

Murray added one further titbit of interesting information, namely that 'for several years past [Coles had] given way to drunken habits'.[18] This *suggests* that, although Frances had turned to prostitution some eight years previously, it was not until later that she began drinking – imbibing alcohol perhaps being a consequence of her lifestyle rather than the cause of it.

According to James Thomas Sadler, the man with whom she spent her last hours and who would be accused of her murder:

When I first knew her she was a very reserved kind of girl, keeping herself to herself, and never mixing with any other women of her class. When I came home last time, though, I found her very much altered so far as her position went. She had come down in the world like they all do in time, but even then, she hated the women with whom she had to associate. Many a time on that Thursday night when she was murdered, and when we were going from one public house to another, drinking, she would say to me, 'Don't go into that bar, Jim. There's a lot of rough characters there. I don't like them, and if they see me with you they'll want a share of your money.' She was rather weak-minded in that way.[19]

Frances Coles had let herself go; but she was keenly aware of the shame of her lifestyle and avoided the coarse and degraded company of those who had surrendered themselves entirely to their fate. She also tried to keep it a secret from her family, telling her father (whom she visited at the workhouse every Sunday) that she was living at 42 Richard Street, off Commercial Road, with a respectable widowed lady, and that she was still working at Hora's. It was not until his daughter's death that Mr Coles finally discovered the truth. Her sister Mary Ann, whom she last visited on Boxing Day, also thought she was in respectable employment. On that last occasion, Mary Ann had given Frances a dress and an old crape hat, both of which she was wearing the night she died.

Although Frances regularly lived at Wilmott's, she could not take her clients back there, and so she was known at other lodging houses around Whitechapel. It was reported that the Salvation Army had tried to reclaim her and that she frequently slept in the shelter in Whitechapel Road that Mr Hague had complained about.[20] Frances had run up a small debt at Wilmott's and had been sleeping elsewhere, but she had returned to the lodging house and spoken to Mrs Hague: 'Can I come back; I will pay you the trifle I owe you as soon as possible', she had said, to which the landlady had replied, 'Certainly, Frances, that's all right.' Mrs Hague later went to the pub on the corner of Montague Street for her supper beer and saw Frances there with a man who had a fair moustache. (Hannah Hague would later face James Sadler, who was charged with Frances's murder, and state that he was not that man she had seen.) Mrs Hague had offered Frances a half pint as she left, but Frances had declined, saying 'No. He's just given me one', and pointing to her companion.

James Sadler – The Accused

James Sadler was 53 years old, though some said he looked older, and had a distinctive, perhaps rather thuggish appearance. He was

5ft 6in tall and slightly stooped, but contemporary drawings suggest a powerfully built man with close-cropped, receding hair and heavy eyebrows. His chin was covered in a thick, dark-brown beard; he had had side whiskers some years before, but had shaved them off because they were going grey, an act that perhaps hints at a little vanity. His complexion was ruddy from working outside, his voice was deep and was even described as pleasant, and according to one account he looked intelligent. He claimed to have been a hard-working man for thirty-five years, some twenty-five of those spent either at sea or as a docker. He also said that he had put in time digging at one of the Australian gold fields,[21] and one newspaper reported that at some point he had been in the Hong Kong police. He had also worked as a tram driver and conductor in the East End.

Sadler had married sometime around 1876–77. He had met his wife Sarah (he seems to have called her Sally) in the Medway town of Chatham, famous for its bustling dockyard. After a brief court-ship they had married at St John's Church in the town. They subse-quently lived at several addresses in the area of Elephant and Castle in South London. Sadler quit seafaring and took a job as a labourer at Torr's tea warehouse, owned by the London India Dock Company in Cutler Street, Houndsditch. This apparently gave rise to a rumour that Sadler had worked at the London Docks. The police investi-gated but could find no evidence of this, and concluded that the story 'no doubt refers to his employment at the Tea warehouse in Cutler St.'.

Living in the Elephant made getting to work a daily grind, and eventually the couple moved to the East End. Sadler's wife would later say that they had lodged in a house in Buck's Row, the street where Jack the Ripper's alleged first victim, Mary Ann Nichols, was found murdered.

Sadler and his wife moved to Poplar, and Sadler spent a few months working as a tram conductor for the Metropolitan Stage Carriage. It was while they were residing in Poplar that there was an incident involving a knife. It seems that at dinner time one day Sadler and his wife had quarrelled. Mrs Sadler had fled to the room of a Mrs Rose Moriarty, pursued there by Sadler, who threatened her with a 'dagger-shaped knife'. According to Mrs Sadler, however, it was an ordinary pocketknife with some brass on the handle; she had taken the knife from Sadler and hidden it and never saw him with it again. The story was first recounted by his wife after Sadler's arrest and was confirmed by Mrs Moriarty (who was tracked down by the police in 1891 living at a different address in Poplar). It appears to have all been of little more significance than an ordinary domestic incident, but it interested the police.

In 1887 Sadler rented a room at 14 Thomas Street, off Commercial Road, for three shillings per week. He appears to have prospered a little, because he was able to rent a corner shop in Hurley Road, Lower Kennington, where he set up as a greengrocer. The business did not do too well, though, and the couple moved on, this time to Manor Street, Walworth; Sadler returned to working at the tea warehouse in Cutler Street. They next took lodgings with two maiden ladies named Duffield in Colebrooke Terrace (which by 1891 had been renamed Entick Street) in Bethnal Green, where they lived for only four months.

The couple moved from one address to another until 1888, when, at the beginning of August, they quarrelled badly. Sadler left, and when he did not get back in touch, Sarah went to her mother's in Chatham, where she continued to live.

After some seven months' separation, Sadler wrote to his wife suggesting that they meet at Fenchurch Street railway station. They walked about the streets, looking at the shops and stayed together that night in a coffee house opposite Mile End Gate. Sadler claimed to be working in the docks, though his wife did not know whether he meant the London Docks or St Katharine Docks by the Tower. He said he had to work the following day, a Sunday, and asked her to meet him. She waited an hour before he turned up, apparently coming from the direction of a restaurant rather than the dock gates. They went to a pub in Whitechapel, but after Sadler had had some alcohol he became argumentative and began to quarrel with the customers, and so his wife left the pub and went outside. Sadler joined her, still in a bad mood, and began to nag her until she told him that they had better go their separate ways.

They walked together along Whitechapel Road and Sadler suggested that they might visit one of the Ripper murder sites, but Mrs Sadler said it didn't interest her. They continued to quarrel until in the end Mrs Sadler ran away. However, Sadler caught up with her and tried to patch up the quarrel by taking her to an eel-shop for a 'feed'. This seemed to ease the ill-feeling and they returned to the coffee house for the night. Mrs Sadler went back to Chatham on Monday morning, but the outing had done nothing to restore their marriage and the couple continued to live apart, though Sadler would occasionally visit her in Chatham, staying for between a day and a week at a time.

Sadler appears to have continued working at the tea warehouse in Cutler Street, although it is known that he served aboard several vessels from 1887 onwards, and in 1889 had signed on aboard a ship called the *Balboa*, from which he was discharged on 7 July 1889. He probably took lodgings at the Victoria Chambers lodging house, also known as Dann's lodging house, at 40 Upper East Smithfield – the police later established that he was there from 16–20 July 1889. This appears to have been his regular place of abode, the keeper, William Dann, later telling the police that he had known Sadler for between eighteen months and two years. Sadler always paid a week in advance. The police thereby established that Sadler was in London when the murder of Alice McKenzie was committed on 17 July 1889.

On 20 July 1889, he went aboard the SS *Loch Katrine* bound for the Mediterranean. By chance, in 1891 the ship was lying off Fresh Wharf, near London Bridge, and so the police were able to board it and make their inquiries. But the captain and crew had changed completely and there was nobody onboard who had been with the ship when Sadler was. He may have served on her until 1 October 1889, for which date he was able to produce a discharge certificate. He made several sea voyages during 1890, and on 24 December 1890 he joined the SS *Fez* as a fireman. He was friendly with two other firemen, Matthew Curley and Frederick Bowen, both of whom would be questioned by the police.

The *Fez* returned to London from a voyage to Turkey and laid up at St Katharine Dock. James Sadler was discharged at 7 p.m. on 11 February 1891. He made his way to Williams Brothers on the corner of Goulston Street, where he drank a Holland gin; then he went to a superior lodging house in Commercial Street, called the Victoria Home. Opposite was the Princess Alice public house.

* * *

The Victoria Home was an interesting establishment. About 1886, a consortium of gentlemen headed by Lord Radstock had bought a four-storey warehouse and converted it into a model lodging house. They later added the neighbouring premises, to provide a total of 500 beds. There were dormitories (each containing ten or twelve beds) and single rooms, called cabins, with only one bed. The cost was two shillings a week (or 4d a night) for a single bed in a dormitory, or three shillings a week (6d a night) for a cabin. Each bed had two blankets, two sheets and a quilt. Food could be brought in and cooked at the fire in the communal kitchen, or could be bought at the bar. A bowl of soup could be had for 1d, and a dinner with vegetables cost 4d.

Cleanliness was essential, and no known bad characters were admitted. Significantly, no women were admitted; they were thus forced to use more disreputable lodging houses. This also meant that Sadler – evidently a man of good reputation as far as the lodging-house management was concerned – would have to take any lady friend he met to a cheap dosshouse for the night.

* * *

No sooner had James Sadler taken a bed in the Victoria Home on 11 February than he went out. Between 8.30 p.m. and 9 p.m. he crossed the road to the Princess Alice. These days the interior of the pub is a large single room, but in 1891 it was divided into separate, smaller bars. He went into one of these and recognized Frances Coles. He had met her some eighteen months earlier in Whitechapel Road and they had spent the night in a lodging house in nearby Thrawl Street.

He saw that she was alone and beckoned her over, inviting her to have a drink with him. After a while she suggested that they leave the Princess Alice, because other customers would expect him to buy them drinks, too. And so it was that the couple embarked on a pub crawl. About midnight, Sadler and Frances went into the White Swan on Whitechapel High Street (the same establishment that was visited by Martha Tabram on the night she was killed), where he bought half a pint of whisky, which Florence Davis, the landlady, put in a bottle for him.[22] They also went to a pub on the corner of Dorset Street, probably the Britannia (a pub that was demolished long ago but which was evidently used at one time or another by most of the Ripper's victims), though it could have been the Horn of Plenty, at the other end of Dorset Street, on the corner of Crispin Street. Whichever pub it was, Sadler and Frances met a woman named Annie Lawrence there and Frances stopped Sadler from buying her a drink.

The couple then went to a neighbouring street called White's Row and took a room in the lodging house at No. 8 called White's Row Chambers. The nightwatchman, Charles Guiver, saw Frances standing by the office door and Sadler at the bottom of the staircase, and he saw Sadler pay for a double bed. Guiver then showed them up to their room. He thought it was between 10 p.m. and 10.30 p.m., but from other evidence we know that it was a lot later.

The next day, Thursday, 12 February, dawned cloudy and during the morning there was some light rain. Sadler and Frances remained in bed until 9 a.m. and stayed indoors until midday or shortly before, when they ventured out on another pub crawl.

Exactly where they went and when is impossible to determine: Sadler got very drunk and would later get hopelessly confused about the sequence of events and the passage of time. However, from the testimony of other witnesses, we can reconstruct a moderately reliable version of what would become a very messy day. But still the vagaries of timekeeping result in conflicting accounts.

Perhaps requiring some sustenance during their pub crawl, the couple stopped off at Shuttleworth's eating-house at 4 Wentworth Street. The owner, Anne Shuttleworth, recalled Frances coming in alone at about 5 p.m. She said she was waiting for a man and she had some tea. Sadler arrived about twenty minutes later, though it was unclear where he had been. Mrs Shuttleworth did not pay him much attention, but it did not strike her that either Frances or Sadler was drunk. She served them food and they left at about 5.45 p.m., Frances saying as she left that they would return later on. They headed towards Middlesex Street.[23]

William Steer, the head barman in the Bell public house in Middlesex Street, not far from Shuttleworth's, thought Sadler and Coles had come into the pub at about 4.30 p.m. Steer and Sadler had chatted a bit about the Shadwell area. Sadler thought he and Frances spent about two hours in the pub, drinking and laughing. According to Steer, however, the couple actually left after about an hour, at around 5.30 p.m. Steer based this estimate on the fact that another barman had come down for tea at about 5 p.m.[24]

Steer's timings conflict with Anne Shuttleworth's, but what is clear is that Frances and Sadler – regardless of whether they ate before or after drinking in the Bell – were certainly in the area of Petticoat Lane market (Middlesex Street) at around 5 p.m.

Frances had told Sadler about a hat she had begun to buy on instalments about a month earlier. She had apparently paid off a shilling thus far, and Sadler said he would pay for the rest. So, after leaving the Bell, they made their way in the direction of the bonnet shop, though several pubs waylaid them en route. One was the Marlborough Head in Pelham Street (now Woodseer Street), off Brick Lane.

According to the landlady there, Sarah Treadway, they arrived between 6 and 7 p.m. Sadler was known in the pub, having gone there on and off for about a year and having once brought his wife with him. On this occasion, he met up with three men he had seen earlier in the day and, by his own admission, began behaving objectionably, so that Treadway asked him to leave. He did so, arranging to meet Frances later in a public house whose name he could not remember. He went off to meet a man named Nichols in nearby Spital Street.

Curiously, Sarah Treadway did not mention any of this in her testimony at the inquest: according to her, when Sadler came in he seemed to have been drinking, but was not drunk (otherwise she would not have served him). He and Frances, who appeared sober, had three 'quarterns' of gin and peppermint and they left together after about half an hour.[25] One must assume that they then parted, and that once Sadler had concluded his business with Mr Nichols, they rendezvoused in the other pub, as arranged.

The milliner's was at 25 Nottingham Street (today's Vallance Road), not far from Buck's Row. Peter Lorenzo Hawkes was working there that day, the shop being owned by his mother. He recalled Frances and Sadler arriving there between 7 p.m. and 8 p.m. and Sadler giving Frances the 2s 6d needed to conclude the deal. She seems to have lied to Sadler, as she had not been paying for the hat by instalments at all: at the inquest Hawkes said that she had come into the shop and asked to be shown some hats, from which she chose a black crape one costing 1s 11½d. She then went outside and spoke to Sadler, who had been looking in at the window.

According to Sadler, Frances told him that the hat-maker still had some work to do on the hat, and that it would be ready soon. The couple had then gone to a nearby pub to wait. At the appointed hour, Frances left Sadler to fetch the hat. When she returned to the pub, Sadler got her to try it on. Frances already had a hat and Sadler told her to throw the old one away, but she refused and instead he pinned it onto her dress.

Eventually, the couple began wending their way back towards Spitalfields. From this point on, the day began to go horribly wrong. En route they turned into Thrawl Street, off Brick Lane. Sadler would later say that Coles warned him not to walk there because it was full of thieves who would think nothing of robbing him; but Sadler, full of bravado, had told Coles: 'I've travelled nearly all over the world, and in all kinds of company, and I've never yet turned back on anything. I ain't a-going to fence that street.'[26] They had not walked far down the short street when a woman wearing a red shawl appeared and accosted Sadler, hitting him so hard over the head that he fell, stunned, to the pavement, whereupon several men appeared and kicked him as he lay helpless. Quickly they robbed him of his money and his watch, and as quickly as they had appeared they vanished into a nearby lodging house. Coles had stood by and done nothing. As Sadler struggled to his feet, feeling injured as much by Coles' inaction as by the assault, his hurt pride turned to anger at her. Coles protested: 'How could I, Jim? You know if I'd lifted a finger for you I should have been marked by three people, and they'd pay me out when they got the opportunity.' Sadler later acknowledged that Coles had a fair point, but at the time his anger overwhelmed him and he stormed off, leaving Coles at the corner of Thrawl Street.[27]

Timings and sightings are again very confused. Samuel Harris, a fish curer who lived at 8 White's Row, said that he had returned there at 8 p.m. Going into the kitchen, he had seen Frances Coles sitting at a table with her head on her arms, as if asleep; yet Charles Guiver, the nightwatchman at the lodging house, said that Frances had come in at about 10 p.m., and Sarah Fleming, the deputy of the lodging house, said it had been about 10.30 p.m.

At about 11 p.m., James Sadler turned up the lodging house. He asked to be allowed in to see Frances, but he was dishevelled and his face was dirty from his escapade in Thrawl Street, so Sarah Fleming refused to let him in, telling him that strangers were not permitted. Sadler, perhaps remorseful about his treatment of Frances, nevertheless managed to slip into the house and enter the kitchen. He looked around, saw Frances at the kitchen table and went over to join her. Harris, the fish curer, heard Sadler ask if she had any lodging money. Frances lifted her head and looked up at him, but made no reply before resting her head back on her arms. Sadler asked Frances if she could get trust (credit) for a bed for the night until he could get some money owed to him the next day. Frances said she couldn't. Sadler then turned to Harris and asked if he could have a bed on the strength of the money owed to him. Harris told him he was just staying there and was not in charge of the house. At the inquest, Harris said that Sadler appeared to be somewhat excited, was suffering from the effects of drink and looked as though he had been in a scuffle of some sort.

At some point Sadler approached Charles Guiver about getting a bed on credit, but Guiver said it was not a decision he could make. He suggested that Sadler go out into the yard and wash the blood off his face. This he did, but on his return he started a disturbance with the lodgers in the kitchen and Guiver had to turn him out. Sadler approached the lodging house deputy and again asked for a bed on credit, but this was refused and eventually he left the house.

Shortly afterwards, Frances went out, too,[28] and at about 1.30 a.m. walked into Shuttleworth's, where she bought 1½d-worth of mutton and bread, which she ate. She was there for about fifteen minutes before being asked to leave by a waiter, Joseph Haswell, who wanted to shut the shop. Frances, now quarrelsome, rudely told Haswell to mind his own business and refused to leave.

She had to be forcibly ejected. She turned right and headed towards Brick Lane. Haswell, who thought she was tipsy, later claimed to be certain that it was 1.30 a.m., because he had just reset the shop clock, which had a tendency to gain time.

Frances had walked the short distance to the Princess Alice (another account says the White Hart in George Yard)[29] when she met Ellen Callaran,[30] who had known Frances for five years and had seen her drinking with Sadler a couple of times earlier in the day. They walked up Commercial Street together and Frances said she had been turned out of Shuttleworth's where she had been having something to eat. They were then approached by a man whom Callaran described as very short with a dark moustache, shiny boots, blue trousers, and generally with the appearance of a sailor. He propositioned Callaran, but she didn't like the look of him and refused. At this, the man punched her and tore her jacket. Frances had moved three or four yards away and the man went over to speak to her. Callaran said, 'Frances, don't go with that man, I don't like his look.' But Frances had replied, 'I will.' Callaran then said, 'If you are going with that man I will bid you goodnight.' She watched them for a few moments at a distance, then went to Theobald's lodging house in Brick Lane, where she arrived at 2 a.m. A report by Inspector Henry Moore on 3 March 1891[31] indicates that her story was confirmed and that a special report was submitted; but like all too many case papers, this special report is no longer extant.

Running off Mansell Street and connecting that street with Leman Street were two parallel streets separated by a railway line. One was Chamber Street and the other was Royal Mint Street. Formerly known as Rosemary Lane, the latter was infamous for a street market popularly known as Rag Fair, where old and generally very disreputable clothes were sold. Royal Mint Street was where the Great Northern Railway depot was located, and it could be a busy place at night.

William Friday, known as 'Jumbo', had left home about 12.30 a.m. to go to the depot, where he had joined two mates and gone for a walk. However, they had become separated by a crowd of people in Leman Street and Friday went back to Royal Mint Street. He noticed a man and a woman on the opposite side of the road, about five yards from Blue Anchor Yard and forty or fifty yards from Swallow Gardens, where Frances Coles' body would soon be found. They were standing outside No. 42 and appeared to be talking. No. 42 was the home of a young woman named Kate McCarthy, and 'Jumbo' thought the couple were McCarthy and her young man, Thomas Fowles.

He reached the depot about 1.40 a.m., but almost immediately went out again to fetch his horses from the stables in Blue Anchor Yard. As he returned along Royal Mint Street he saw a man and woman standing in the same place. He passed close to them and noticed that the woman was dressed in black and was wearing a crape hat. The man was turned away from him, so he could not see his face, but he was about 5ft 8in, was wearing a hard felt hat with a broad rim, and had on a long, dark-brown overcoat with a velvet collar. 'Jumbo' would later identify the woman he had seen as Frances Coles, but he did so purely on the basis of the crape hat the woman had been wearing. *The Times* on 14 February reported that 'Jumbo' Friday had described the man as 'being above the middle height, and having the appearance of a foreigner, after the style of a ship's fireman'. This description led Detective Inspector Regan of the Thames Division to organize a thorough search of all the vessels lying in the docks and river. The search proved fruitless.

The first couple 'Jumbo' Friday saw was certainly Kate McCarthy and her fiancé Thomas Fowles. She would later tell the inquest that they had been out that evening, and on returning home had stood in the doorway talking for about an hour. She had seen a man named Knapton and another man pass by, and shortly afterwards she had seen 'Jumbo' Friday. Fowles, a doorkeeper at the United Brothers' Club in Commercial Street, confirmed that he had seen 'Jumbo' pass by; he also said that he had set off home no more than five or six minutes later, getting there at 2.15 a.m. From this he estimated that he had left McCarthy at about 2.10 a.m.

Neither McCarthy nor Fowles saw 'Jumbo' pass a second time, so it is likely that the couple he saw on that occasion was different. 'Jumbo' also passed close enough to the couple to be able to recognize them if they had been known to him, and the description he gave of the man's long overcoat suggests that it was not Fowles, who said he had been wearing a short pilot coat. *The Times* would later report that, on close questioning, 'Jumbo' Friday 'varied so materially in his statements that they were found to be of very little value in leading to the identity of either'.[32] This was no doubt true from the perspective of the police, but the possibility nevertheless exists that he did see Frances.

Sadler's movements during these crucial hours are typically confused and confusing. We know he went to a common lodging house he sometimes used – Victoria Chambers, by St Katharine Dock and close to where Frances Coles was found dead. That was at about 1.15 a.m. Sadler asked for a bed, saying he had no money but explaining the events of the night, but John Johnson, the deputy, refused to let him in. Sadler then became argumentative and abusive. He decided to try to get back aboard his ship and returned to the main gate of St Katharine Dock; here he encountered Henry Sutton, a constable employed by the docks company, who initially let Sadler in, but then realized that he was drunk and so turned him out, as he did not think he was in any fit state to go to his ship. Sadler seems to have sat down by the dock gates, which is where he was found when a dock constable named Frederick Session appeared at about 1.20 a.m. and ordered him away.[33]

Sadler did not move (or, if he did, did not go far), because PC William Bogan came across him slumped at the gates. He lifted

Sadler up and Sadler asked to be let into the docks to go aboard his vessel. But Bogan decided Sadler was too drunk to be admitted and told him to go elsewhere. At this point, two dock workers, John Dooley and a man named Harvey, were leaving through the gates. According to PC Bogan one of them offered to pay for Sadler to get a night's lodging. For some reason Sadler refused this charitable act and became abusive. 'I don't want your money, you dock rats', he said. At this the man hit Sadler hard in the ribs, knocking him to the ground. Frederick Session later testified that he had heard Sadler insult the labourers and call them 'rats'. Henry Sutton also saw Sadler scuffling with the two men.

However, one of the labourers, John Dooley, told a slightly different story. He said that he and his mate Harvey had left the docks and joined PC Bogan in telling Sadler to go away. Sadler had become abusive and violent, and had thrown a punch at Harvey. Dooley had gone to his mate's assistance and had also been struck by Sadler. Dooley said he had told Sadler that if the policeman were not present he would 'give him something', whereupon the policeman headed off. Dooley punched Sadler on the left side and knocked him down, Sadler striking his head against the door of a gate as he fell. Dooley and his mate then returned to their lodging house, Melbourne Chambers in East Smithfield, where Dooley made some tea. About ten minutes later there was a knock on the door and Sadler entered the kitchen.

According to Sadler's own account, he was attacked by the dock workers in front of – and possibly with the connivance of – a policeman. So serious was this accusation that the Liberal MP for Aberdeen, Peter Esslemont, raised the matter in parliament on 26 February, asking the home secretary, Henry Matthews, if a man as drunk as Sadler was said to have been was not entitled to police protection? Matthews replied that, according to information received from the commissioner, Sadler's allegation was unsupported by any evidence. The constable who saw him at the dock gate considered

that, although he had been drinking, he was not sufficiently intoxicated as to warrant being taken into custody.[34]

Given that Dooley admitted to having threatened violence to
Sadler in the presence of PC Bogan, it is difficult to escape the
conclusion that the assault on Sadler was achieved with PC Bogan's
connivance and that Henry Matthews' reply was extremely evasive.
PC Bogan may not have been there when the assault occurred, but
he knew it was going to happen and in fact made sure that it did not
occur in his presence. It is perhaps telling that Bogan, an Irishman
from County Cork who had served on the East End's 'H' Division
since December 1881, would be quietly transferred to 'L' Division
the following month and would be dismissed from the police force
in December of that year for being drunk, refusing to pay for some
fried fish, and then striking the lady shopkeeper when she demanded
money.

When Sadler recovered from his beating, he went to Melbourne
Chambers, a lodging house he frequented and where, unbeknownst
to him, Dooley and his mate were staying. Dooley heard Sadler ask
the deputy, George Peakhall, for a bed and Peakhall tell Sadler that
he could have one if he first went to hospital and got his head
dressed. It was now 1.45 a.m. or a little later.

About 2 a.m., Sergeant Wesley Edwards, on duty at the Mint
Pavement, was approached by Sadler, who complained to him that
he had been assaulted by some men at the dock gates. Edwards
asked him how it had occurred and, as the two men walked thirty
yards or so in the direction of the Minories, Sadler gave an account
of events. They were joined by PC Hyde, who, together with
Edwards, examined Sadler's ribs and decided that they were only
bruised. As the Tower clock chimed 2 a.m., PC Bogan joined the
group and Sadler made a hasty departure, saying 'No, I don't think
I'm so much hurt, after all.' Much of this meeting was observed and
confirmed by Frederick Smith, a waiter at an eating-house called
Lockhart's on Tower Hill. He had heard someone groaning and,

looking through the shop window towards the Tower of London, had seen a man about two or three yards away. He saw two policemen go up to him and heard Sadler explain that he had been knocked about. He heard one of the policemen say, 'Let's feel.' The policemen then walked away towards Upper East Smithfield and Sadler went towards the Minories.[35]

At 2 a.m. PC Ernest Thompson was patrolling his beat. It went from the bottom of Chamber Street up to Prescott Street, then along Prescott Street, passing the entrance to Mansell Street, to Leman Street, down a short distance into Chamber Street, along which he went until he reached the charmingly named Swallow Gardens. Rural and rustic though the name was, Swallow Gardens was actually three railway arches that connected Chamber Street with Royal Mint Street. The passage through was about fifty yards long and half of it had been boarded off to create a storeroom used by a builder. What remained was sufficient to allow one cart at a time to pass. There were gas lamps at either end, and together they illuminated about half the passage. In the centre, though, it was very gloomy and was well known as a place used by prostitutes, in spite of police efforts to keep them away; in fact, two women had been arrested for loitering at this spot earlier that night.[36] It took PC Thompson fifteen to twenty minutes to complete a circuit. That night was a particularly nervous time for him: previously a mineworker in the north,[37] he had only joined the police on 29 December and this was the first time he had been alone on his beat. So far, though, he had seen nothing to arouse his interest.

At 2.12 a.m. a man named Solomon Gutteridge, an employee of the Great Northern Railway, passed through Swallow Gardens, neither seeing nor hearing anyone. A couple of minutes later, just before 2.15 a.m., PC Thompson came up Leman Street and glanced at the clock on top of the tower of the Co-operative Store. He then entered Chamber Street, hearing footsteps coming from the direction of Mansell Street. He did not see anyone, however, and

continued along Chamber Street, entering Swallow Gardens. As he
turned into the passage, he saw something on the roadway, roughly
midway under the arch. Walking quickly towards it, he turned on
his lamp and saw that it was the body of a woman.

* * *

One of the most famous policemen in the early years of the twentieth century was Frederick Porter Wensley. In 1891 he was just a
young policeman, but he would rise to become the chief constable
of CID. In his autobiography, he recalled that, as PC Thompson
walked along Chamber Street, 'a man came running out of Swallow
Gardens towards him. As soon as he perceived the officer he turned
tail, made off at speed in the opposite direction, and was in a few
seconds lost to view.' Wensley went on to say:

> It is probable that had Thompson been a little more experienced
> he would have taken up the chase of the fugitive immediately. In
> all likelihood he would have made a capture which might possibly
> have solved a great mystery. But it is understandable that this
> young man was so taken aback by his grim discovery that he did
> not take the obvious steps . . . Whether the murderer was Jack the
> Ripper or not, he escaped. I fancy that the lost opportunity preyed
> on Thompson's mind, for I heard him refer to it in despondent
> terms more than once, and he seemed to regard the incident as
> presaging some evil fate for himself.

This story has been repeated on several occasions,[38] but it is clear
from PC Thompson's testimony given at the inquest that he did not
see anyone, that the footsteps were of someone walking at an ordinary pace, and that there was nothing about them to give rise to any
suspicion. Furthermore, PC Thompson heard them when he was
still some eighty yards from the passageway, so even if he had given
chase it is unlikely that he would have caught anyone.

Nevertheless, Wensley's story could have contained a hint of truth: several foreign newspapers carried what appears to have been an agency story, in which it was reported that 'Constable Thompson is the most unhappy man in London tonight, as he feels he had the most noted criminal of the age within his grasp.'[39] That his inaction preyed on his mind, or that it presaged some evil fate for himself, is probably Wensley adding a touch of melodrama to his story, because a few years later PC Thompson was murdered by a man in what appears to have been a stupid brawl.

* * *

As the constable looked on the face of Frances Coles, he thought she opened and shut one eye. He blew on his whistle three times.

For historians of the Whitechapel murders, one of the many sub-mysteries is who responded to PC Thompson's whistle and who the first policemen were to arrive. The Times[40] maintained that first on the scene was PC Scott. According to the newspaper, he detected a faint pulse – support for PC Thompson's claim that Frances's eyelid moved – and found the body still warm, with blood pouring freely from a wound in the throat.

Benjamin Leeson also claimed to be one of the first policemen on the scene. In his autobiography Lost London, Leeson (who claimed he had done his training with Thompson and had got to know him well) said that when he arrived on the scene he found Thompson with two nightwatchmen, one of them a plain-clothes policeman who had been patrolling the district. Leeson asked Thompson, 'What's up?' and records that Thompson whispered, 'Murder. A Jack the Ripper job.' The plain-clothes policeman was PC George Elliott (275 H),[41] who had been on duty in front of Baron Rothschild's refinery in Royal Mint Street. Shortly after he arrived, he headed off to Leman Street police station, soon returning with Inspector Flanagan. Another policeman early to the scene was PC Frederick Hart (161 H),[42] who examined Frances by the light of his lamp, concluded that she was still alive, and ran off to nearby Dock Street, where Dr Oxley and Dr Allen had a surgery. Oxley was in bed when PC Hart called, but he promised to get dressed and go to Swallow Gardens. Hart returned to Swallow Gardens and searched the area.

Dr Oxley arrived about ten minutes after being summoned and examined the body. Meanwhile other policemen began to arrive, Inspector Flanagan dispatching them on various duties. One was sent to fetch the divisional surgeon, Dr Phillips; another to find Superintendent Thomas Arnold, head of 'H' Division, who immediately ordered telegrams to be sent to the surrounding divisions to apprise them of events and to ask them to make careful inquiries. The chief inspector and the local inspector also arrived, and Robert Anderson, the assistant commissioner, was roused from his sleep. He gave the authorization for Superintendent Arnold to be afforded all the assistance he might require. In a short memo, Anderson later noted: 'The officers engaged in investigating the former Whitechapel murders were early on the spot, & every effort made to trace the criminal. But as in former cases he left nothing, & carried away nothing in the nature of property, to afford a clew.'[43] The officers in question included Chief Inspector Swanson, Superintendent Arnold and the detectives Reid and Thick.

As the search of the area quickly gathered momentum, men were sent to scour the surrounding streets. Inspector Flanagan discovered two shilling-coins, wrapped in a scrap of paper torn from what appeared to be an old copy of the *Daily News* and shoved into a space between a water pipe and some brickwork about eighteen yards from the body. There was nothing to connect the money with the murder, but two shillings was a not inconsiderable sum, and it is difficult to imagine who could have – or would have – hidden the money in such a place and not returned for it.

Dr George Bagster Phillips arrived in a cab and immediately set about examining the body – realizing that Frances was not quite dead, although she was fading fast. Indeed, she expired before the stretcher arrived to take her away.[44] Dr Phillips thought that death had been caused by two cuts to the throat, inflicted with some force. *The Times* reported that one of the cuts:

> ran from right to left, the commencement being upwards of an inch above the ear; while at one point it was three inches in depth. The gash appeared to be somewhat jagged in character, but the great depth clearly showed the amount of physical force that must have been used in inflicting it. The whole of the arteries and tissues were severed, while the spinal column was also injured.[45]

Dr Phillips concluded that Frances Coles had *not* been murdered by the same person as had committed the earlier murders. This conclusion was based on a number of things, such as the nature of the wound, the posture and appearance of the body, and the absence of mutilation.

* * *

The following day Dr Phillips would conduct a more detailed post-mortem, reporting that Frances's throat had in fact been cut three times, the first cut going from left to right, the second from right to left, and the third from left to right again. Some abrasions above and below the incisions looked to have been made by fingernails, and some contused wounds on the back of the head had probably been made when Frances's head had hit the paving stones. From his examination of the body, Dr Phillips was able to build up a grim picture of Frances's last minutes. She had been violently thrown to the ground and had struck her head on the pavement so hard that she had probably been concussed and insensible. She therefore offered no resistance as the murderer knelt on her right side and, with his right hand, lifted up her chin to expose her throat, which he sliced with a knife held in his left hand. The body had been tilted to the left, whether by accident or design, and this meant that the murderer would not have been saturated with blood. Phillips also concluded that the murder had not been done by a skilful person, and from the post-mortem appearance he did not believe that Frances had been drunk when killed.

* * *

As soon as Dr Phillips had pronounced Frances dead, her body was removed to the Whitechapel mortuary and stripped. Her clothes were old and shabby, the heels of her boots almost worn away, and her worldly possessions in her pockets amounted to an old comb and a few pieces of cloth or rags. Her old hat was found pinned to the folds of her dress, the new one bought by Sadler lying on the pavement close to her body.

A name was also starting to emerge (although certain identification was some time off): a number of people, including several policemen, recognized her as a known or suspected prostitute who was frequently to be seen loitering around Tower Hill and in Leman Street and who was known variously as Frances Hawkins, Frances Coleman, or 'Carroty Nell'.[46]

Shortly before 5 a.m., Chief Inspector Swanson arrived at Swallow Gardens, accompanied by Inspector Moore. They appear to have been particularly interested in any writing on the walls, but they found none. Some blood from the small pool that had formed as it flowed from Frances's neck was preserved for analysis; then Swanson ordered the murder scene to be washed and the archway opened to traffic. Another police chief who turned up at Swallow Gardens about the same time as Swanson was Melville Macnaghten, assistant chief constable CID, who had gone to Leman Street police station as soon as he had been informed of the murder. After a brief discussion with Superintendent Arnold,[47] he had gone with Arnold to the murder scene.[48]

* * *

After speaking to Sergeant Edwards (and beating a hasty retreat when PC Bogan arrived), Sadler had gone back to White's Row Chambers and had seen Charles Guiver, the nightwatchman, who was sweeping the floor by the open front door. It was about 3 a.m., and this time Guiver was certain because he had just looked at the clock (he was responsible for waking one of the lodgers for work). Sadler asked Guiver if he could use the kitchen, explaining that he had been knocked about again and felt faint. Guiver could see that blood was still trickling down his face. The nightwatchman was sympathetic, but said he did not have the authority to let him in. The lodging house deputy, Sarah Fleming, then opened the office window and Sadler repeated his request, again complaining of feeling faint. The deputy said he could not be admitted and Guiver, heading down to the kitchen, told Sadler to go to the London Hospital and get his head seen to. Sadler instead walked over to the deputy's office and asked if Frances was in. Fleming said she wasn't and that she hadn't seen her since she went out at about midnight. Sadler then asked to be allowed into the kitchen. He explained that he had been knocked down and kicked about and robbed of his money and his watch. When Sadler called her a hard-hearted woman and drew her attention to a cut on his right cheek and another under his left eye, she pointed out that it was precisely because of his injuries that she couldn't let him stop in the house – people might think they had been caused there. Sadler went to the front door and loitered there for a few moments, only walking away when Fleming was about to call Guiver to eject him.

The next sighting of Sadler was at 3.30 a.m. PC Arthur Sharp was on duty opposite the London Hospital in Whitechapel Road. News of Frances's murder had reached him, and when he saw the blood on Sadler's face he stopped and questioned him. Sadler said, 'I have fallen down. I was drunk and I knocked my nose on the pavement and also hurt my ribs.' PC Sharp thought that Sadler was sobering up and believed the story, but took the precaution of

searching Sadler for a weapon. He failed to find one – something
that would be of immense importance to Sadler in the coming days.

According to PC Sharp, Sadler said he was going to the London
Hospital and he crossed the road in that direction. Either Sharp's
times were wrong or Sadler did not go straight to the hospital, because
Joseph Richards, the manager of a coffee shop at 19 Whitechapel
Road, said that Sadler had turned up at his shop about 4.05 a.m. and
asked for a cup of coffee. He said he had no money, as he had been
robbed of his watch and chain and purse. From his hat he took a
paper, an account for wages that was stained with blood, and showed
it to Richards. But the manager was unwilling to give him coffee on
the strength of his word, so Sadler produced some tobacco and tried
to sell it to Richards, who refused to buy it and turned him out of the
shop. By now it was about 4.15 a.m., he thought.

It was 4.45 a.m. or thereabouts when Sadler turned up at the
London Hospital. The night porter, a man named William Fewell,
was reluctant to let Sadler in, but Sadler started arguing and was
finally allowed into the accident ward. According to Fewell, Sadler
had a lacerated scalp and a small cut over one eye. Fewell trimmed
the hair from the scalp wound, which was on the right side, washed
Sadler's face and dressed the wounds. While this was going on,
Fewell asked him a few questions, to which Sadler replied, saying
that he had been with a woman and that she had done for him, that
he had been robbed of seven or eight shillings and a watch, and that
it was not so much the robbery that bothered him as the fact that his
assailants had knocked him about.

Sadler was by now trembling with cold. When Fewell learned
that he had no lodgings, he let Sadler lie on a sofa, where he went
to sleep. The night porter estimated that Sadler slept for about an
hour and a half before Fewell had to wake him when he went off
duty. Fewell gave Sadler a penny and the grateful Sadler went away.

Sadler said that he left the hospital and went straight to
the Victoria Chambers lodging house in Smithfield, where he

unsuccessfully begged for some money. At about 6.30 a.m. he went to a coffee shop at 73 Whitechapel Road and a waiter named Charles Littlewood served him a cup of cocoa, presumably paid for with the penny given him by Fewell. Littlewood noticed some blood on Sadler's left wrist and Sadler complained that his ribs hurt. The waiter thought Sadler smelt as if he had been treated by a doctor. But when Sadler asked for a second cup, Littlewood thought he was drunk and refused to serve him. However, he did not eject Sadler, who stayed at the coffee shop reading a newspaper until Stephen Longhurst, the manager of the shop, came down the stairs. Longhurst exchanged a few words with Sadler, but allowed him to stay. He eventually left the shop at 8.30 a.m., by which time Littlewood thought he had sobered up.

About 10.30 a.m., James Sadler went to the Tower Hill shipping office and saw Edward Gerard Delaforce,[49] the deputy superintendent. He produced a document showing that he was entitled to wages of £4 15s 1d. There was some blood on the back of the paper, and Sadler explained that he had been knocked about by some hags in Thrawl Street and robbed of a watch valued at £2 10s. Sadler was in the office for about twenty minutes and was then paid.

At some point that morning he went to the White Swan on Whitechapel High Street, where he had gone the day before with Frances, and was again seen by the landlady, Florence Davis.

* * *

The police issued a formal description of Frances Coles: she was aged about 25, 5ft tall with brown hair and eyes and a pale complexion. She had on a black jacket, black dress, satin bodice with white underlinen and button boots. There was a black ribbon round her neck and she wore black vulcanite earrings and a black crape hat. The lobe of one of her ears had been torn away, but that had evidently happened a considerable time earlier.[50]

News of the murder drew large crowds to Swallow Gardens, to the mortuary where Coles' body lay, and to Leman Street police station, and journalists tried to piece together the complicated story of what had happened for the evening editions. It was not easy. As one journalist reported, officers at Leman Street were claiming that the reality had been greatly exaggerated by rumour and that a woman had been murdered but had not been mutilated. Nevertheless, one newspaper began, 'Horror thrilled the community of Whitechapel early this morning', and reported that Jack the Ripper had reappeared in the East End.[51]

A source of much speculation was Frances's possession of two hats. Soon a story was doing the rounds that the police thought the murderer was a woman, or a man who disguised himself as a woman.[52] One newspaper attributed this theory to 'one of the most experienced local police officers',[53] and another identified the policeman as Chief Inspector Swanson, adding that it had long been theorized that the murderer dressed as a woman; Swanson supposedly thought the hat found beside the body had been dropped by the murderer and forgotten in the rush to flee the scene.[54] It is uncertain if there is any truth to this story.

At 6 p.m., Sadler returned to Victoria Chambers and apologized to the deputy, John Johnson, for his earlier behaviour. Johnson noticed that Sadler had hurt his head and asked him about it, Sadler explaining that he had had it dressed at the London Hospital. He then went up to Room 36 and stayed there for the rest of the day and overnight, venturing no farther than a nearby public house called the Phoenix.[55]

Meanwhile the police received their first piece of reliable information: Samuel Harris, who had been in the kitchen of the common lodging house in White's Row when Sadler had come in and spoken to Frances, had heard of the murder. His suspicions raised, he went with the lodging house doorkeeper and the deputy to the police station, and from there to the mortuary, where they immediately identified the body as that of 'Frances Coleman'. Harris also gave a description of James Sadler.

The next morning, Saturday, 14 February, the police began a search of all the lodging houses, public houses, beer-houses, and other places Sadler was likely to have gone, and shortly before noon Detective Sergeant John Don and Detective Gill arrived at the Phoenix. They had Harris in tow and he went into the pub, emerging a few moments later to tell the officers that Sadler was inside. Gill went in and brought Sadler out. Don told him that they wanted him to return with them to Leman Street police station to answer some questions about his movements the night before.

Sadler, who must by now have heard about the murder of Coles, said, 'I expected this.' On the way to the police station, he complained:

> I am a married man and this will part me and my wife. You know what sailors are, I used her for my purpose for I have known Frances for some years. I admit I was with her, but I have a clean bill of health and can account for my time. I have not disguised myself in any way, and if you could not find me the detectives in London are no damned good. I bought the hat she was wearing and she pinned the old one under her dress. I had a row with her because she saw me knocked about and I think it was through her.[56]

At the police station, Sadler was handed over to Chief Inspector Swanson for questioning. Sadler asked, 'Am I arrested for it?' and Swanson replied, 'No, certainly not, but it is necessary to take a statement from you to help us to throw some light upon the matter.' Sadler then gave his story. News of the arrest soon became public knowledge and the police station where Sadler was confined was surrounded by an immense crowd of people, mostly women, who yelled wild threats to lynch him. Later that evening, when Sadler was taken to the court, a large number of police were required to guard him.[57]

A sizeable crowd was also gathered outside the handsome frontage of the Working Lads' Institute on Whitechapel Road when the coroner arrived at 4.30 p.m. on Saturday, 14 February, to open the inquest. Nearly an hour was spent sorting out problems with the jury: five of those summoned had sent substitutes to act on their behalf, and a couple had not turned up at all. At first the coroner, Wynne Baxter, said the inquiry was too important to allow any juryman to be absent, and on this occasion he must decline to accept substitutes. However, after some discussion and with assurances that the substitutes were respectable local residents, Baxter relented and allowed three to serve. But he refused to accept two of them – one a shameless self-publicist and self-proclaimed chairman of the disbanded Whitechapel Vigilance Committee, Albert Bachert. He had already managed to get his name in the newspapers by claiming to have seen Frances Coles twice on the night she was murdered, and had also declared that he had been chosen to serve on the inquest jury. Bachert was unhappy with the rejection and sat fuming on a nearby bench, while Baxter instructed a court officer to find suitable replacements for the two excluded men. When Baxter had finished issuing his instructions, Bachert rose from the bench:

> Mr Coroner, why won't you let me serve on the jury? I came here as the representative of someone who was summoned, and you are letting other representatives serve. You ought to accept me, but I know why you don't. It's because I am the chairman of the Vigilance Committee, and you know I'm going to investigate this case.

'You are not a representative like those I have accepted', retorted Baxter.

'Why?'

'I decline to give you a reason', said Baxter. 'Why are you so anxious to serve? I decline to accept you.'

'Yes, because you know I shall inquire into the case', said Bachert.

'You have already been told I shall decline to accept you.'

Bachert turned and walked to the back of the court, where he threatened, 'You will hear more of this.'

The moment of excitement passed as the coroner's officer returned and a jury now satisfactory to Wynne Baxter was sworn in and taken to see the body of Frances Coles. On their return, Bachert again questioned Baxter, at which point Baxter replied, 'You be quiet, sir; if you are not I shall have you ejected.' This was evidently more than satisfactory to one juryman, who seems to have had no illusions about Bachert or his purpose. 'That settles his little game', he said.[58]

There was a curious little snippet reported in one newspaper, to the effect that Wynne Baxter had been sent a letter which read:

Honoured sir, the enclosed is Mr. Backert's [*sic*] letter to the *Daily Chronicle*. You can see what he says, and what he intends to do. He's to the front again in this case. May I suggest that he is a little more truthful than he was in the last 'Ripper' scare, I being the woman he so cruelly belied, and had got the whole neighbourhood in alarm. Signed, THE WOMAN HE SO CRUELLY BELIED.

The letter did not contain any enclosure,[59] although it was presumably supposed to have been the letter Bachert had written claiming to have twice seen Frances shortly before she was murdered. While the identity of the writer is not known for sure, she is probably the woman who featured in a story Bachert had earlier used to get some press coverage.[60]

PCs Ernest Thompson, Frederick Hart and George Elliott all gave testimony; then Baxter adjourned the inquest.

That night Detective Sergeants Record and Kuhrt tracked down Coles' father, James William Coles, in Bermondsey Workhouse, where he had been living for eight years. The old man was very feeble and was taken in a cab to the mortuary, where he immediately identified his daughter. The policemen also located Mary Ann Coles, Frances's sister, and she, too, identified the body.[61]

* * *

By now one of the great oddities of the case had taken place. A man named Duncan Campbell turned up at Leman Street police station with a story that carried some weight with the police and that was almost enough to send Sadler to the gallows.

Campbell was lodging at the Sailors' Home in Well Street. Between 10.15 a.m. and 10.30 a.m. on Friday, 13 February he had come down from his room and was standing by the communal fire in the gloomy hall. A man wearing a hat with a cloth peak came in and sat down by the fire to warm himself. After a while, he went over to Campbell. 'Mate,' he said, 'I am nearly dead. I have been out all night and I got robbed. I am dying for a drink.' He took a large clasp knife from his right-hand pocket: 'Will you buy it?' Campbell took the knife and examined it. On opening the large blade, he observed that it was not an English knife. 'No,' said the man, 'I bought it abroad. In America.' Campbell paid a shilling and some tobacco for the knife and put it in his pocket. The man hurried out into Leman Street. One Thomas Johnson, a seaman serving aboard the *Mandolar*, had been standing by the fire. He saw the man leave, and although he claimed not to have paid him much attention, he noticed that he had a mark on his cheek and was wearing a cap with a shiny peak and, he thought, a striped coat.

About half an hour later, Campbell heard about the Swallow Gardens murder and re-examined the knife he had just bought. The blade was blunt and there was no trace of blood on it, but when he washed it in a basin of clean water he noticed that the water turned

slightly salmon coloured. He dismissed it as rust and thought
nothing more of it. He put the knife back in his pocket and went to
bed, sleeping until 3.30 p.m.

The following day, Saturday, Campbell pawned the knife for 6d
at Thomas Robinson's marine store at 4 Dock Street. Robinson,
who later sharpened the knife on a whetstone and used it to cut his
bread and meat, observed to him, 'It looks like Jack the Ripper's
knife.' It was a casual, throwaway remark, but it set Campbell
thinking, and on Sunday, after talking to some sailors in the home
and telling them about his purchase, he went to Leman Street police
station and recounted his story to two sergeants. They immediately
escorted him to Robinson's shop and Sergeant Ward took possession of the knife.

* * *

Back at Leman Street police station, Sergeant Ward told Sadler that
he fitted the description of a man who had sold a clasp knife to a
sailor at the Sailors' Home. Sadler immediately denied this. 'I never
had a knife to sell', he protested. 'The only one I had was an old one,
worth about 2d, that I used to cut tin with years ago.' Sadler was
then taken to a dimly-lit cellar room, where he took his place in a
semicircle of fifteen or sixteen sailors. Campbell was brought in, and
in the flickering, yellow gaslight he walked along the row of men.
He picked out James Sadler, whom he claimed to have recognized
because of the scar over his left eye.

Curiously, among the men in the line-up in the basement of
Leman Street police station was Thomas Johnson, the man who had
been by the fire in the hall when Campbell bought the knife. When
the stranger left, Johnson had noticed little more than that the man
had a mark on his cheek, was wearing a cap with a shiny peak and
possibly had on a striped coat. Johnson was later (on 24 February)
asked to identify the man he had seen and he picked out Sadler,
recognizing him principally by his beard and moustache, and by the

mark on his cheek. How reliable this identification was is open to question: he identified Sadler by a mark on his cheek (which Campbell did not mention) and thought the peak of the man's cap was shiny (whereas Campbell said he was certain it was of cloth). Also the man's beard was far from distinctive: Campbell himself said it was 'a very common one amongst seamen. It is the American style.'[62] Finally, Johnson had already seen Sadler picked out of the line-up by Campbell *before* he was asked to identify the man. As the unhappily named Mr Lawless, who was acting on Sadler's behalf at the inquest, succinctly put it, 'Then you were not asked to identify the man until somebody else had done so in your presence?' Pressed on the point by Mr Lawless – who went on, 'You also recognised him as the man you had seen picked out at Leman-street?' – Johnson could only answer 'Yes'.[63]

One can only wonder whether the police were aware that Thomas Johnson had participated in the line-up and had seen Duncan Campbell pick out James Sadler. If they were, how much store could they have thought to set by his identification? But his recollection of the man did not match Campbell's, and his identification ultimately rested on the scar on Sadler's cheek. In light of this, it is difficult not to have some sympathy for Sadler's later claim that the police had aided and abetted Campbell, and even that they had paid him for his evidence!

Sadler maintained that Campbell had twice gone along the line of men and had not picked anyone out – even though Sadler was wearing a cap covered in clotted blood and his eyes were swollen and bruised. It was only when a policeman stood opposite Sadler and fixedly stared at him, at the same time asking Campbell, 'Can't you recognize him?', that Campbell, even now seemingly uncertain, walked along the line-up lifting the men's hats one by one, until he reached Sadler. On lifting his hat and seeing the scar, he said, 'That's the man.'

A journalist asked Sadler why he had not complained about the irregularity of the identification process, and Sadler claimed that at the time he had had no opportunity to do so, but had afterwards told Inspector Moore that he was going to prosecute Campbell for perjury. According to Sadler, Moore had said, 'Oh, you'd better not. You weren't taken to the Central Criminal Court. If you were, and Campbell had repeated his evidence there, you might have had ground, but I don't think you'd better take proceedings now.'[64]

All in all, Campbell's testimony at the inquest was not so different from Sadler's. The cellar was gloomy, Campbell's eyesight was poor and he did not recognize Sadler until he saw the scar on his forehead. It was all very unsatisfactory. Yet Sergeant Ward would testify that Campbell had said to Sadler, 'I could pick you out of a hundred.' Neither Campbell's nor Sadler's testimony would seem to support this.

Quite apart from that, ultimately, the knife sold to Campbell could not have been used to kill Frances Coles. It was blunt and Dr Oxley, who had examined the body of Frances, was of the opinion when he was shown the knife on the Sunday that it could hardly have produced so large and clean a cut.

Nevertheless, that Sunday evening Inspector Henry Moore went to Leman Street police station and, at about 11.45 p.m., charged Sadler with 'wilfully causing the death of Frances Coles'. Sadler quietly replied, 'Yes, yes' and Moore told him to pay attention. 'I don't see the reason', said Sadler. 'I know the charge, and I suppose I shall have to go through the routine.' Moore searched Sadler (rather late in the day, given the length of time he had been in custody) and found on him a purse containing £2 17s 4d, thirty-six seaman's discharge papers, a wages account, eight lottery tickets, a quantity of loose tobacco, and a postal order for £2. As this was going on, Sadler said, 'The old man has made a mistake about the knife; he never saw me before.' As he was moved off to the cells he said, 'Make it as light as you can, gentlemen.' But before too long it would become clear that he was in peril of losing his life.[65]

It was presumably on Sunday, 15 February (or perhaps on the Monday) that James Sadler was confronted with 'Joseph Lavender'. According to the *Daily Telegraph*:

> Further, it is certain that the police are not neglecting the facts which came to light in connection with the previous murders. Probably the only trustworthy description of the assassin was that given by a gentleman who, on the night of the Mitre-square murder [Catherine Eddowes], noticed in Duke-street, Aldgate, a couple standing under the lamp at the corner of the passage leading into Mitre-square. The woman was identified as one victim of that night, Sept. 30, the other having been killed half an hour previously in Berner-street. The man was described as 'aged from thirty to thirty-five; height 5ft 7in, with brown hair and big moustache; dressed respectably. Wore pea jacket, muffler, and a cloth cap with a peak of the same material.' The witness has confronted Sadler and has failed to identify him.[66]

The gentleman referred to is unquestionably Joseph Lawende, a commercial traveller in the cigarette trade. By the time of his wedding in 1873, he had anglicized his name to 'Lavender' and had moved to Islington, where he lived for the next decade or more, albeit at various addresses. Back in 1888, on the evening of 29 September, Lavender had gone to the Imperial Club in Duke's Place. He left at about 1.30 a.m. the following morning with two men, Joseph Hyam Levy and Harry Harris.[67] They had walked down the road and past a short passage leading into Mitre Square. On the corner, Lavender had seen a man and a woman talking. A short time later a policeman had found the mutilated corpse of Catherine Eddowes in Mitre Square, and Lavender later identified Eddowes by her clothes as the woman he had seen. However,

Lavender repeatedly stated that he would not be able to identify the man he had seen in her company.[68]

It seems quite clear from the use of Lavender that the police did think for a while that Sadler was Jack the Ripper – or at least the murderer of Catherine Eddowes.

On Monday, 16 February, Dr Houchin visited the Arbour Square police station and treated Sadler for a broken rib.[69] In the afternoon, he was taken before Frederick Mead, the magistrate at the Thames Police Court. Superintendent Arnold asked that only evidence of the arrest be heard that day, but Mead insisted that some evidence connecting Sadler with the charge had to be heard. Samuel Harris was then called to the witness box. *The Times* reported that Sadler, who seemed still to be suffering from the effects of drink, listened attentively to the witness testimony and frequently interrupted, at one point warning both Harris and Fewell to 'Be careful about what you are saying.'

Another newspaper reported that Sadler appeared composed, his hands in his pockets and glancing around 'as if he was a disinterested spectator of the proceedings'. Later, when asked if he had any questions for a witness, Sadler said:

There are two or three little things, but I am not in good trim to cross-examine. I am thoroughly hungry and cold. I have had nothing since tea-time last night, and I don't feel fit to take an interest in the proceedings. I have been shifted from one cold cell to another, and my clothes have been taken off me at the will and option of the police and doctors. I have not anything to ask now. I am not fit to do it. There are one or two things wrong in what he says, but I can't ask anything now. I am really too hungry.

Mr Mead shortly thereafter remanded Sadler in custody for a week.[70]

Sadler would later claim that he had been put into a draughty, cold anteroom at Leman Street police station, and throughout Saturday and Sunday had been called for several identity parades. He had had to dress in various clothes, he said, some of them damp and others positively wet. On top of that, he said, he had been taken from one place to another in a draughty 'Black Maria', and on the Saturday night had had to sleep on a plank.

According to Sadler, at 7 a.m. on the Monday he had breakfasted on a couple of slices of bread and butter, but had been given no further food, and so was getting very hungry by the time he appeared in the magistrates' court at 2 p.m. He was also still suffering from the knocking-about he had received on the night of the murder. On top of everything, he was worried because he felt the police were against him and he did not know whether he would have anybody to defend him. He realized that he ought to do all he could to keep his wits about him. After the hearing he was provided with food.

According to Sadler, pressure was put on him to confess: '. . . the police, and everybody in their employ, were dead against me, and meant to have me if they possibly could. They tried to get me to incriminate myself in any way they knew how to.'[71] While being held in Holloway, he was visited by the governor and the chaplain, along with half a dozen other people. The governor tried to get Sadler to admit that he could have murdered Frances when he was drunk and did not know what he was doing. When asked about Campbell's positive identification, Sadler said he firmly believed that Campbell was in the pay of the police.

The inquest resumed at the Working Lads' Institute, Whitechapel, on Tuesday, 17 February. Opening the proceedings, Wynne Baxter said that, in view of the fact that James Sadler was in custody and charged with the murder, it was necessary to take a much broader approach than he had at first deemed necessary. They would have to trace not only the movements of the deceased woman, but also those of Sadler. The first witness called was James William Coles. He was followed by Mary Ann Coles, Peter Lorenzo Hawkes, Charles Guiver and Samuel Harris. The inquest was then adjourned until 10 a.m. on Friday, 20 February.

On 18 February, James Sadler wrote from Holloway Prison to Mr Wildgoode, an official of the Seamen's Union:[72]

Mr. Wildgoose [sic] – from T. Sadler, a stoker, and member of your union, Burntisland Branch, No. 311. (my last payment was made at Tower Hill last Friday, 13.) Wishing prosperity to the union. I must apply to you to act as my friend, as I have no claim on any one else in particular. My wife was always a doubtful friend. My mother is too old. I have no brother or sister or public-house palls [sic] worth a damn. I should like a reporter connected with the *Seafaring* or the *Star* to watch over me. Police will hurry my case on to suit their own ends, and anything turning up in my favour will be squashed. All the money and sense of Scotland Yard will be used to hurry me to a finish. What a Godsend my case will be to them if they can only conduct me, innocent as I am, to the bitter end. The whole detective force of Scotland Yard will be whitewashed in the sight of the whole world. Money presents will roll in to them. But, on the other hand, if I have any true friend in a reporter, to see that I am not talked down or sat upon entirely by the police and Courts, I hope to walk out as I deserve to go. The knife business is false. I have neither bought nor sold any knife. I had one knife and fork only – a pair given to me by my old mother a few months ago. J.T. Sadler.[73]

Sadler's somewhat rambling letter conveys his distrust of the police, who (he clearly thought) were determined to have him convicted of the murder of Frances – and probably of being Jack the Ripper. But there can be no doubt that it was a genuine appeal for help to the fledgling union, and consequently the Bow Street solicitors Wilson & Harris were appointed by the union to act on Sadler's behalf.

They in turn instructed the barrister Henry Hamilton Lawless to appear for Sadler when the inquest resumed and at any further appearances in the police court.[74]

Meanwhile, the public mood against Sadler gradually began to soften, and an exaggerated interview given by Sadler's wife gained him some sympathy. The newspaper reported her as saying that her husband had an 'ungovernable temper' and was prone to irrational and violent outbursts; that he was acquainted with every nook and corner of London, and especially of Whitechapel; and that he had had a strange-looking clasp knife with a long, dagger-like blade. Mrs Sadler objected vehemently, claiming that she had said none of those things, and that the journalist had sensationalized what she had said.[75]

Chief Inspector Swanson travelled to Chatham on 19 February. After a meeting with Superintendent Coppinger of the local police, he went on to 3 Skinner Street, where Mrs Sadler lived. There he questioned her, but found it very difficult to get a coherent story out of her. He persevered, and during their time together they were interrupted no fewer than three times by reporters.[76] George R. Sims, in his column in the *Referee*, attacked his fellow journalists, accusing them of 'trying to hang Sadler for the crimes of Jack the Ripper, without trial, and on the unsworn and inadmissible evidence of his wife'.[77] In the House of Commons, a Mr Howarth asked if the newspapers were not seriously prejudicing the case against Sadler, and wondered if it did not amount to contempt of court. The home secretary, Henry Matthews, chastised the press for publishing material prejudicial to Sadler, but claimed not to have seen the articles and therefore to be unable to say whether they amounted to contempt. The reply was received with cheers.[78]

As the public mood began to swing in favour of Sadler, Wynne Baxter resumed the inquest at the Working Lads' Institute on Friday, 20 February. Now Sadler was represented by the able Mr Lawless. Testimony was heard from Anne Shuttleworth, William Steer, Sarah Treadway, Sarah Fleming, PC William

Bogan, Frederick Session, Henry Sutton, John Dooley, Sergeant
Wesley Edwards, Inspector James Flanagan, PC Arthur Sharp,
Joseph Richards and William Fewell. Apart from a brief interval
for lunch, the inquiry lasted from 10 a.m. until 5.15 p.m., at which
time Baxter adjourned for the weekend. The hearing resumed on
24 February.

On Wednesday, 25 February, a witness died. Charles Guiver,
who had already given evidence at the inquest, passed away aged 34
at 8 White's Row. Dr Dukes of Brick Lane was summoned, but
could not determine the cause of death, and so Dr Roderick
MacDonald, the coroner for North East Middlesex, ordered a post-
mortem. Apparently viewing the corpse of Frances Coles had
affected Guiver both physically and mentally. Dr Dukes said his
post-mortem examination suggested that the nightwatchman had
died of apoplexy, accelerated by excitement and shock.[79]

The following day, Frances Coles was buried at the East London
Cemetery, Plaistow. An open hearse containing a handsome polished
elm coffin studded with white nails left the mortuary yard and
turned into Whitechapel Road at 2.15 p.m. A little to the west of
the entrance to the mortuary yard were three funeral coaches
containing the dead woman's father and sister and a group of representatives from the Common Lodging House Mission, which had
paid for the funeral. As the hearse passed by, the coaches fell in
behind. A crowd estimated to be 2,000 strong had gathered outside
and along the road, many following as the cortège travelled up Mile
End Road, Burdett Road, East India Dock Road, Barking Road and
Hermit Road to the cemetery, where the gates were closed and
several hundred people were denied admission. The grave was situated on rising ground, close to a young poplar tree, and for some
considerable distance in all directions were gathered several thou-
sand people, who listened attentively to the moving service and
watched as the flower-laden coffin was lowered into the grave. One
newspaper complained that people stood on the rails and stonework

of the neighbouring graves, and apparently many people were indignant when, during the service, a number of men passed to and fro hawking memorial cards at a penny apiece.[80]

The British press did not report widely (if at all) that the crowd was ill-disposed towards to the police, which people seemed to hold responsible for the murder (albeit only as a consequence of not having caught Jack the Ripper). But it was only with difficulty that the police prevented a serious demonstration of popular anger.[81]

On 26 February Sadler again appeared at the Thames Police Court. He looked a lot better than he had on previous occasions, and his conspicuous black eye had healed. The court agreed that he should remain on remand until the coroner's investigation was completed.

This took place the following day, Baxter summing up at length. In large part his able summation contributed to Sadler's eventual release. Sadler's story bore all the hallmarks of truth, he said, and as far as possible it had been corroborated by witnesses. The blood on his face and hands was accounted for by the 'cowardly assault upon him at the dock gates'; Duncan Campbell's story was damaging, but the knife was anyway blunt and could not have inflicted the wounds on Frances, it had no blood on it, and no knife had been found on Sadler when he was searched at 3.30 a.m. in Whitechapel Road by PC Sharp.

As for Sadler's movements that night, in Baxter's view they were inconsistent with guilt. To begin with, he had very little time to get to Swallow Gardens. There was also no suggestion that he had arranged to meet Frances there, and it would have been extremely fortuitous if he had gone and simply found her at that place. All his movements after leaving Frances in White's Row suggested that he was trying to get a night's rest either at the docks or at a lodging house close by.

Baxter finally observed that it was doubtful whether Sadler, beaten up, with a broken rib and suffering from a hangover, was physically capable of committing the crime.

The jury retired at 2.50 p.m. and took exactly thirteen minutes to reach an open verdict of 'wilful murder against some person or persons unknown'. The jury expressed its opinion that the police had done their duty in detaining Sadler – which undoubtedly they had, although it might be wondered why they persisted so doggedly in trying to prove Sadler's guilt when the evidence so strongly indicated his innocence.

Sadler's ordeal came to an end on Wednesday, 4 March 1891, when he appeared at the Thames Police Court. The prosecutor, Charles Matthews, formally and long-windedly threw in the towel:

> Having had the advantage of a consultation with the learned Attorney-General, who has carefully considered the evidence given in the course of the inquiry before the coroner, as well as the most able summing up to the jury impanelled before him, and having regard to the verdict returned by that jury, after a patient and exhaustive inquiry, I do not propose, on the materials at present in our possession, to proceed further with this prosecution, and, Sir, if it should meet with your approval, it will have the sanction both of the learned Attorney-General and of the Treasury authorities, that no further evidence should now be offered against the accused.

Mr Lawless replied on behalf of Sadler in his Irish brogue: 'I need hardly say, on behalf of the prisoner, that I have no objection to that course.' And so it was that Sergeant Baker, the gaoler, turned to Sadler and said simply, 'Go away.'[82]

Sadler left the dock, but was not immediately allowed to leave the court. He was detained, together with his solicitor and a reporter for *The Star*, the newspaper that had taken up his case, in the gaoler's room, because it was feared that his appearance outside could incite the crowd that had gathered. Eventually a cab was drawn up in the courtroom yard and Sadler, his solicitor and journalist got in. When the crowd saw it, there was a cheer; and as it moved off down the street the crowd ran after it. Sadler put his head out of the cab window and waved his hat.[83]

That night James Sadler celebrated in the East End.

After the trial, Sadler fell ill and, for a time, took to a bed in a cheap and dirty coffee house in Shadwell, where he was visited in a small and dingy room by a reporter for the *East End Observer*. Sadler was barely visible by the light of a candle, but he was tossing and turning beneath the bedclothes. 'He's feverish, mate', explained a docker who shared the room. 'Better not disturb him much.' Told that he had a visitor, Sadler sat up in bed, but the movement brought on a painful fit of coughing. He is reported as saying:

> The police have just about done for me over this affair. Up to that Saturday morning when I was taken in charge at Leman-street, I had always enjoyed good health ... but the time I spent in the cells and gaols of this civilised country over this murder business has just about finished me up.[84]

The previous evening he had been to see Dr Kay in Commercial Road, who had diagnosed bronchitis. On examining Sadler's ribs, the doctor said he thought he ought to go immediately into hospital. Sadler refused.

James Sadler brought legal proceedings for heavy damages against the *Standard* and the *Daily Telegraph* for libel and against others for false imprisonment. He won his cases against the newspapers, and with the money in May 1891 he bought a chandler's shop at 121 Danbrook Road, Lower Streatham – a relatively comfortable, low-cost and mainly residential development completed some thirty years earlier. He devoted himself to the business, rarely leaving the shop and then only to visit his mother, who was at that time living in Newington Butts.

The business prospered, his shop doing a steady ready-money trade, taking about £2 10s per day.[85] He took up with his wife again, but Mrs Sadler would visit the police on 11 December with a lodger, James Moffatt, an elderly former sailor, to make a complaint against Sadler. He had assaulted her, treated her cruelly and had repeatedly threatened to kill her, she said. Moffatt supported her, saying that in all his years at sea he had never heard such horrible language as that directed by Sadler to his wife. He was obliged to lock his bedroom door every night, for in his opinion Sadler was a treacherous and cowardly man.[86]

Sadler received a warning from the police and for a while behaved himself. But in May 1892 he was hauled up before the magistrate at the Lambeth Police Court on a charge of threatening to murder his wife. He was bound over to keep the peace for six months at a personal cost of £10.[87] But the relationship could not last, and in January 1893 the couple separated. Sadler took lodgings at 108 Faraday Street, Camberwell.

And so it was that James Thomas Sadler walked out of the history books. Frances Coles' murderer was never identified and never caught.

CHAPTER 15

American Swansong?

Carrie Brown (24 April 1891)

I will say unhesitatingly that the people who have charge
of the police in London, with the great powers allowed them,
ought by this time to be enabled to effect the arrest of the
murderers.

Such was the opinion of Chief Inspector Thomas Byrnes of the
New York Municipal Police Detective Bureau, in an interview
published in October 1888.[1] A former gas fitter, fireman and Union
Army soldier who had fought at the Battle of Bull Run,[2] Byrnes had
been mustered out of the army in 1863, after which he joined the
New York Metropolitan Police. Steady promotion followed, and
from 1870 to 1878 he commanded various precincts and the
Broadway squad. He solved the great Metropolitan Bank robbery
case and secured the conviction of several major gang members.
Byrnes stood out at a time when the police were notoriously failing
to solve major crimes, and in 1880 he was promoted to inspector and
placed in charge of the Detective Bureau. His career was not without
controversy, however, peppered as it was with accusations of corruption and police brutality. His uncompromising methods of questioning suspects popularized the term 'the third degree', a phrase
apparently coined by Byrnes.

Byrnes was happy to expound on the subject of Jack the Ripper and was highly critical of the London police's failed attempts to apprehend the murderer. He felt his approach would succeed, if only his opposite numbers at Scotland Yard would listen:

With the great power of the London police I should have manu-factured victims for this murder. I would have taken fifty of the female habitués of Whitechapel and covered the ground with them. Even if one fell a victim I would get the murderer. My men, ununiformed, would be scattered over the whole district, so nothing that happened could escape them.[3]

Byrnes' readiness to sacrifice another woman in order to catch the murderer shows his 'unconventional' detection methods, and the perceived inactivity of the London police obviously exasper-ated him.

Three years after the original Whitechapel murders had begun, and a mere eight weeks after the death of Frances Coles, Inspector Byrnes and the New York police were put in the unexpected posi-tion of having to deal with their own Jack the Ripper – a situation that must have sparked keen interest (and perhaps not a little gloating) among their British counterparts.

* * *

The Lower East Side of New York City, situated on the north bank of the East River in Manhattan, was one of the oldest parts of that great metropolis, and its location made it predominantly a working-class and immigrant community. As early as 1816, the neighbour-hood around Corlears Hook, a point of land jutting out into the river, was notorious for prostitutes,[4] being described as 'a resort for the lewd and abandoned of both sexes', and by 1821 its streets were populated every night with 'preconcerted groups of thieves and prostitutes'.[5] In effect, with its overcrowding, poverty, immigrant communities and proximity to the river, the Lower East Side was New York's 'East End'.

One of the roughest areas was the slum district of the Fourth Ward, exemplified by Water Street. Indeed, by the beginning of the 1890s, it was said that there was 'no other part of New York that resembles the Whitechapel district of London as Water Street does. The hovels here are filthy, low places whose income is derived entirely from drunken sailors.'[6]

On the corner of Water Street and Catherine Slip stood the East River Hotel, known by some as the Fourth Ward Hotel,[7] a large and grandiose building that was effectively an 'extended stay' hostel, more in keeping with a common lodging house. It was known by the residents of the Fourth Ward as the 'House of All Drinks', from the big sign it displayed advertising 'the many kinds of vile beverages that are on draught there'.[8] It was situated in a singularly disreputable neighbourhood of slums, and was considered 'perhaps one of the worst of its class'.[9] A notorious haunt for prostitutes, it was said that 'the women who lure sailors into the dive are wretched creatures. The only men other than drunken sailors who go to these places are pert thieves who help the women rob sailors.'[10]

At 11 p.m. on 23 April 1891, a man and a woman checked into the East River Hotel. The man, who appeared to be about 32 years old – roughly half the age of the woman – and shabbily dressed, signed the guest book 'Knickloi and wife',[11] and the couple was led by Mary Miniter to Room 31 on the top floor. No more was heard from them for the rest of the night. At 9 a.m. the following morning, Eddie Fitzgerald, the bellboy, knocked on the door of Room 31. He was doing the cleaning rounds and needed to check whether the occupants were still inside. There was no reply, and so Fitzgerald let himself in with the skeleton key. A woman was lying naked on the bed, her body shockingly cut and mutilated. A deep gash extended from the lower part of the abdomen upward to the breast, so that the woman was completely disembowelled. The entrails had apparently been torn from the body and were scattered over the bed. There were also two deep cuts crossing each other on the back in the form of an exact cross. Lying in a pool of blood by the bed was a broken four-inch table knife.

Fitzgerald raised the alarm and a messenger was hastily sent to the police station. Captain O'Connor lost no time in notifying police headquarters and the coroner's office of what had happened. He raced over to Water Street with three detectives, and they were soon joined by Coroner Schultz, more detectives and a small posse of press reporters who had made a habit of camping outside the Mulberry Street police station on the look-out for breaking news. With the reporters in tow, the detectives checked the other rooms on the floor. Curiously, they found a wash bowl containing blood-stained water in Room 32. In the meantime, Coroner Schultz undertook his initial examination of the body.

The East River Hotel was immediately cordoned off on all sides, and nobody was permitted to venture near the upper floors. The news spread rapidly through the area. The first assumption was, of course, that Jack the Ripper had crossed the Atlantic to recommence his fiendish work. On the evening after the murder, the *Brooklyn Daily Eagle* posed the question: 'Is Jack here?'[12] The following day it announced that 'there is an apparent similarity of motive, and the attendant circumstances are so strikingly identical that those inclined to believe that "Jack the Ripper" is really here may very readily be pardoned'.[13] One newspaper recalled the sexual mutilations of the Ripper crimes: 'Whether by chance or skill, the cut was made so as to effect the object aimed at by the London Jack the Ripper, namely, the removal of the uterus.'[14] In fact, the uterus had not been removed, but some organs had been taken out of the abdominal cavity.

The woman had been struck on the side of the head, strangled, and had some of her undergarments wrapped around her neck and head. Strangulation was the probable cause of death, with the mutilations following, although there was also the opinion that death may have been caused by a combination of strangulation *and* haemorrhaging.[15] The throat had not been cut, but the body had been mutilated with cuts to the lower abdomen, the intestines protruding from a deep gash on the left side. There was a series of cuts that ran from the lower abdomen back between the woman's legs, to end just above and to the right of the coccyx. The majority of wounds consisted of light scratches and abrasions to the legs and buttocks. On the bed were found two pieces of intestine and the left ovary.

It is no wonder that thoughts immediately turned to Whitechapel.

Inspector Byrnes' words about the methods of the British police now came back to haunt him. One editorial stated that 'there has been a general expression of confidence in our superior detective skill, and this has led to the belief that the perpetrator of the London horrors could not escape detection on this side of the ocean. Here, then, is a superb opportunity for the vindication of that sentiment.'[16]

The woman was soon identified by a number of people as 56-year-old Carrie Brown.[17] It was said that she had first appeared in New York about fifteen years earlier, when she had been considered a good-looking woman of middle age, quite refined and very intelligent. This last quality had led her to be known as 'Shakespeare'. Mary Miniter, the housekeeper at the East River Hotel, also knew her as 'Jeff Davis',[18] though no one seemed to know how she had come by that nickname. She became very popular among those with whom she associated because of her kindness and her keen intelligence. She had plenty of money, but was heavily addicted to alcohol, and when drunk she would spend freely or even give her money away. Her life declined rapidly, and she would often disappear for long stretches of time before returning to her friends in the low dives of the Lower East Side.[19]

Curiously, claims about her life before her arrival in New York appear somewhat romantic, as this piece from the *Trenton Times* clearly demonstrates:

Jack the Ripper's American victim is still remembered in Salem. Her story is one of the saddest ever penned. She was born in Liverpool, England in 1832. As a girl she was known as Caroline Montgomery. She landed with her parents at New York and settled with them when still a child in Brooklyn, N.Y., where she grew into a pretty girl. Then she met Captain James Brown, of this city. He was but eighteen years old when he married her. Her husband brought her to Salem. After a happy married life of five years a little girl was born to them, and subsequently another child, also a girl, and later a son. Mrs. Brown had been married some ten years when she began to manifest an unfortunate desire for intoxicating liquor. In spite of all that her husband and friends could say or do, her appetite increased so rapidly that her whole character was changed and debased. Captain Brown entered the navy and served his country faithfully. While in command of the brig *Elizabeth* on the Gold Coast he was stricken down with African fever and died. By his will he left his wife a dollar and the balance of his estate to his two daughters.

Captain Brown had made a complete separation from his wife some years before. Nearly fifteen years ago she came back to Salem and entered the service of a retired sea captain as a domestic. At that time strong hopes were entertained of her redemption from a life of sin. At one time it was thought that she had rallied, but she suddenly fell.[20]

It became clear quite early on that Mary Miniter, who had escorted the couple to Room 31, was the only person who had seen the man Carrie had been with prior to her death.[21] The police also learned that Carrie lived most of the time at 49 Oliver Street, a basement lodging house operated by Mary Harrington. She was able to offer some valuable information and to fill in some of the blanks surrounding the circumstances on the night before the murder.

According to Harrington, Brown had been at the lodging house in Oliver Street when, at about 7 p.m., two men entered the premises. One was a man known as 'Frenchy', but Harrington did not know the other one. They enquired after another occupant of the lodging house, a prostitute named Mary Ann Lopez. Lopez was not there at the time and so the two men waited for her. In the meantime, they struck up a conversation with Carrie, and eventually all three left the lodging house and made their way to John Speekmann's saloon at the corner of Oliver Street and Oak Street.

'Frenchy' was apparently known to the staff of the East River Hotel and was of great interest to the police, because 'everybody seemed to fear him and he was said to be a fellow who would use a knife'.[22] The police now had an interesting lead, made more significant when it was discovered that 'Frenchy' had been staying with Mary Ann Lopez at the East River Hotel on the night of the murder. Even more importantly, they had been in Room 33, directly across the hall from the crime scene. Four men were taken into custody, including a 'Frenchy', apprehended on Water Street between 9 p.m. and 9.30 p.m. on 24 April.

According to a statement read out by Inspector McLaughlin on 25 April, this particular 'Frenchy' was not believed to be the murderer. Rather he was the cousin of the murderer, was called George François and bore the same nickname as the murderer. François refused to give any information regarding the missing man, who was apparently a native of Syria and spoke with an Arab–French accent.

François was arrested for biting Mary Ann Lopez, his companion in Room 33 that night. She was also being held as a witness, along with a number of other women.[23] Various newspapers made mention of a pair of blood-spotted trousers that were now in the possession of the police,[24] but that was as much as the police were willing to divulge at that stage.

The following day, confusion reigned as Inspector Byrnes announced that the murderer had not been caught: 'I did not say I knew who the man was nor that Frenchy was the man, I said he was suspected of being the man. As soon as the newspapers get through discovering the murderer I can do better work on this case.'[25]

The police were keeping matters under wraps, which no doubt led to even more speculation by the press and public. Perhaps to make things a little clearer, the press dubbed the man in custody 'Frenchy No. 1', and the cousin, the potential murderer still at large, 'Frenchy No. 2'. The men were apparently similar in appearance and both were described as 'the most vicious creatures in the quarter . . . They had a mania for vice in its lowest form.'[26]

Days went by and, despite scores of arrests, 'Frenchy No. 2' eluded what the press called 'a dragnet sweeping New York's slums'.[27] Mary Miniter was shown all the likely suspects being held in custody, but failed to identify any of them as the man she had seen in the hotel with Carrie Brown. Descriptions of 'Frenchy No. 2' were supplied by the local prostitutes, but rather derisively Byrnes announced to the papers that 'the police were no longer confining themselves to the description generally accepted . . . the people depended upon to give it were a drunken lot without enough intelligence to remember how the man looked'.[28]

On 28 April, the press reported a bombshell – a total repudiation by Byrnes of all that had been said previously: 'I wish to deny emphatically that we believe that Frenchy No. 2 . . . is suspected of the murder. I never thought so or said so.'

'The Inspector undoubtedly had some deep reason for making such strange denials,' commented the *Morning Journal*, 'but what he meant by them even his oldest detectives cannot fathom. Later in the day the Inspector when again questioned in regard to his denials, refused to either deny or confirm his original denials.'[29]

It was nothing short of farce, and it was noted that the authorities in Britain, who had been sniffed at for so long by Byrnes and his associates, were 'watching his movements with eager interest and perhaps restraining with difficulty a disposition to smile'.[30]

But Inspector Byrnes was working on a case against 'Frenchy No. 1', whose real name was Ameer Ben Ali. This man, an Algerian who had been honourably discharged from the French army after eight years of service, had been in America for a year and spoke little English.[31]

Mary Miniter insisted that Ali was not the man she had seen with Carrie Brown; however the police worked around this problem by suggesting that 'Frenchy No. 2' (the man seen with Carrie) had left the hotel unseen, leaving Ali ('Frenchy No. 1') with the opportunity to enter Room 31 and commit the murder.

Miniter was soon discredited as a witness by Byrnes. Then, as if by magic, new evidence emerged: a blood trail leading from Room 31 to Room 33 across the hallway. What was peculiar about this new evidence was that none of the press reporters who had been on the scene immediately after the discovery of Carrie Brown's body had noticed any blood in the hallway.

One detective claimed at the inquest that he had seen blood at the scene of the crime the day after the initial inspection. This was all highly dubious: immediately before the detective made his statement, another witness – the detective who had actually handled the clean-up operation – testified that all traces of blood had been removed on the day of the initial inspection.

Further evidence was produced in the form of material from beneath Ali's fingernails, said to contain traces of blood. However, it should be pointed out that in those days blood could only be identified as mammalian, with no distinction as to whether it was human or otherwise.[32] The evidence was shaky indeed.

The hunt for the man who checked in with Carrie Brown ('Frenchy No. 2') had used up huge amounts of manpower and time and now appeared to be have been a fruitless and pointless exercise.

It all smacked of a desperate fit-up, with the police 'gunning for' Ameer Ben Ali, anxious to prove that they could capture and convict a killer – who may have been Jack the Ripper – in a high-profile murder case.

Ali's trial was set for 3 July 1891. The French government, upon hearing of his situation and in light of his good-service record in the army, sent the French consul, Count D'Alzac, to protect his interests, but to no avail: Ali was convicted of the murder of Carrie Brown.[33] His lawyer, Frederick House, moved for a fresh trial, citing errors in the admission of evidence and the fact that the verdict was contrary to the evidence. Recorder Smythe rejected the proposal and sentenced Ali to life imprisonment, commenting on the 'low order of humanity to which the prisoner belonged'. Ali was led away.[34]

It seems that nobody was happy with the verdict. Even Inspector Byrnes and his men must have felt short-changed as Ali was convicted of second degree (unpremeditated) murder, which carried a life sentence, rather than the death sentence for first degree murder. One British newspaper declared that 'Everybody is glad that the Frenchy trial is over.'[35] One regrettable consequence of the long-drawn-out events was that Carrie Brown was not buried until August.

It appears that the police in New York did what the Metropolitan Police in London tried to do with James Sadler, following the murder of Frances Coles. But they succeeded where the Metropolitan Police had failed. It seems almost as if, by 1891, the exasperated authorities would try anything to make it appear that they had caught Jack the Ripper.

As Ameer Ben Ali languished in gaol, others worked on his behalf to have him exonerated of the crime:

The movement looking to the securing of a pardon for Ameer Ben Ali, better known as 'Frenchy', who was recently convicted of the murder of a lewd woman in the slums, and sentenced to imprisonment for life, has gained strength since the latest ripper's crime in London which demonstrated that 'Frenchy' is not, as had been claimed by the police, the original 'Jack the Ripper.' 'Frenchy' is now employed in the brush making department of the Auburn penitentiary. He has found it pretty hard to learn the trade, but is very attentive to his work. The prison officials have no trouble with him, and warden Durston says that he is as honest as a kitten. The keepers who are brought into contact with him every day say that they believe him entirely innocent of the crime for which he has been convicted.[36]

Eleven years later, the campaign was successful and Ameer Ben Ali was pardoned and released. He supposedly returned to Algeria and was never heard of again.

Carrie Brown's killer – whether it was 'Frenchy No. 2' or somebody else – was never apprehended.

Elizabeth Senior (31 January 1892)

The following year, there was another murder in North America that bore the hallmarks of the Ripper's knife. On 31 January 1892, the body of 73-year-old Elizabeth Senior was found in the candy store she ran with her husband in the small town of Millburn, New Jersey. She had been strangled, her throat had been cut and she had been stabbed in the breast and sides eleven times. In a manner reminiscent of the murders of Estina Crawford in Jamaica and Carrie Brown, the woman's face had been covered, this time with her shawl. The murder weapon, a blunt case knife (table knife), was found on the counter, covered in blood. The evidence suggested that the killer, obviously in no hurry, had washed his hands and then proceeded to ransack the house before escaping into obscurity. Robbery was obviously the motive, as $45 had been taken from a secure hiding place.[37]

August Lentz, a violent robber, was originally accused of Elizabeth Senior's murder. However there was no evidence at all to link him to the crime and he was allowed to go free. Thus this most appalling murder remained unsolved.[38] The robbery motive notwithstanding, the brutal throat-cutting and stabbing of Mrs Senior did have a whiff of the Ripper's work. However, it was not until over a century later, in works by R. Michael Gordon and Trevor Marriott, that any suggestion was made that she could have been another victim of the Whitechapel murderer, now settled in America.[39]

Afterword

O<small>N</small> 28 A<small>UGUST</small> 2013, <small>THE</small> *E<small>AST</small> L<small>ONDON</small> A<small>DVERTISER</small>*, <small>THE</small> sole survivor of the East End's local press from 1888, produced a twelve-page supplement on Jack the Ripper to mark the 125th anniversary of the Whitechapel killings. Subtitled 'Murders that shocked the world', it mined the newspaper's archives to provide an overview of the crimes. Meanwhile the paper's website offered a day-by-day update on the events in 1888 Whitechapel. Since the infamous series of murders had been the newspaper's biggest ever 'story', it was probably inevitable that there would be some form of 'review' of the East End's darkest days.

It was not a new idea. Back in 1988 – the centenary year of the Ripper murders – the *Advertiser* had published a twelve-part series on the crimes, researched by Mark Gould.[1] This had covered not just the murders, but also the police investigation and wider social issues, and it had looked at several suspects. It also included mortuary photographs of some of the victims – photographs that had been discovered and returned to Scotland Yard only the previous month.[2] For this, the *Advertiser* (and other newspapers that published them) came under fire from groups that had formed to protest against what they felt was increasing violence by men against women:

By printing the mortuary photograph of Polly Nichols and recounting explicit details of the mutilation she suffered, you are using the sexual murder of women to entertain and titillate your readership . . . when will journalists realise that they are contributing to the mass industry of glamorising a murderer?[3]

In 2013, the same issues were again raised. Indeed, a week after the supplement appeared, the *Advertiser* felt compelled to print a special debate entitled 'Does publicising the Jack the Ripper murders glorify violence against women?' Sarah Jackson of the East London Suffragettes was certainly of the opinion that it did, echoing the sentiments of the activists in 1988:

> I love a bit of gory local history, but I'm getting fed up with Jack the Ripper. I can't help but feel that by always putting 'Jack' in the spotlight, we're showing that we don't take violence against women seriously.
>
> There is endless speculation about his identity, his knowledge of anatomy and even admiration for his ability to evade capture. In contrast, the women he murdered are generally reduced to objects for study or evidence to be analysed. We hear very little about their lives but can't escape the intimate details of their deaths.[4]

This point of view ignores entirely the work of many responsible authors and researchers over the past century and focuses on the lowest common denominator – those who gawp at the Ripper-themed exhibits in the London Dungeon or the Chamber of Horrors at Madame Tussauds.

Ripper researcher Edward Stow attempted to set matters straight:

> Jack the Ripper was one of the first known serial killers. He was particularly brutal, but was never caught. He was given a horrifying name, possibly by an enterprising journalist, that immediately captured the popular imagination. Pretty much everything about him is based on conjecture.

It is disputed by some that he was a serial killer. The murders could have been committed by different people. Others argue that the motive behind them was a sinister conspiracy.

That is why there is a fascination with the case. It is a 'whodunit'. It is not based on glorification of the culprit, nor of his vile deeds. Establishing who may have 'dunit' is the best restitution for his victims. Should these poor women be forgotten? Should their lives be erased? . . .

Obviously, the subject has to be handled sensitively. Real people were killed.

Anybody who has read a reputable book on the Whitechapel murders will know exactly what Stow was talking about. The study of these crimes has enabled those women – women who would certainly have been forgotten if they had been murdered by anybody else – to be remembered, and not just as victims.

The host of unknown variables in the Jack the Ripper mystery means it is all too easy to create obfuscation and play around with facts, or even to invent new 'facts' to make a point. The raw materials available – witness statements, police reports and press coverage – can sometimes be used very selectively, drawn upon only when they support a preconceived notion. One casualty of this arbitrariness can be the victims. Their status – whether they are 'in' or 'out' – depends on the whim of the theorist.

The full publication in 1965[5] of Melville Macnaghten's memorandum naming five victims 'and five victims only' set a precedent for this: neither Martha Tabram nor Emma Smith was counted as a true Ripper victim. Up until then, Tabram had almost always been 'in'.

Theories about the Ripper's identity can influence both the length and the content of the victim list: if a writer insists that his Ripper suspect was in no position to murder a particular victim, that victim can simply vanish from the list . . .

The case of Montague Druitt offers a good example of this. He was the barrister whom Melville Macnaghten suspected of being the Whitechapel murderer, and who was found dead in the Thames on the last day of 1888. While the theory that he went insane and drowned himself after murdering Mary Kelly is not unreasonable, it does mean that logically neither Alice McKenzie nor Frances Coles can be a true Ripper victim.

Elizabeth Stride has always been the most tentative of the 'canonical five', owing to the obvious lack of abdominal mutilations and the suggestion that the weapon used to cut her throat was different from that used in the other murders: Walter Dew had doubts about her inclusion in the canon, and in 1937 author Edwin Woodhall was certain that she was not one of the Ripper's tally.[6] More recently, Donald Rumbelow has confidently discounted Stride.[7]

The choice of Ripper suspect can also serve to *increase* the number of victims: M. J. Trow's theory that Whitechapel mortuary attendant Robert Mann was Jack the Ripper places Martha Tabram squarely at the head of the victim list and Alice McKenzie at the end.[8] Trow maintains that although Tabram was killed by her soldier companion, the large wound to the breastbone was the only one he inflicted. It was Robert Mann, having somehow come across her body, who frenziedly inflicted the remaining thirty-eight wounds with a small clasp knife, thereby obtaining some form of gratification. He may not have committed the actual murder, but he did inflict most of the wounds: his discovery of Martha Tabram's corpse thus becomes the catalyst. By the time Alice McKenzie was murdered, Mann was terminally ill and could not work with the same ferocity, which explains the superficiality of her wounds.

Severin Klosowski, alias George Chapman, was hanged in 1903 for poisoning his three wives. At the time, Frederick Abberline, prominent in the police during the period that the Whitechapel murders were committed, noted that Klosowski had spent some time in America after the London murders and suggested that there could be several cases in the USA that would repay scrutiny.[9] Abberline probably never really believed that Klosowski was the Ripper, but the notion was taken up by R. Michael Gordon.[10] His book expands the number of Ripper attacks to include various unsolved American crimes, including the murder of Carrie Brown in April 1891 and the death of Elizabeth Senior in New Jersey (the obvious motive of robbery coinciding with a period of straitened circumstances for Klosowski). The author likewise includes Hannah Robinson, a servant girl who was strangled on Long Island in August 1891. In her case, he notes the similarity to the death of Catherine Mylett. Closer to home, the author also ascribes to the Ripper the torso murders at Rainham, Whitehall and Pinchin Street, and the death of Elizabeth Jackson (clearly a change in *modus operandi* for the versatile Klosowski).

Finally, former British detective Trevor Marriott embraced the concept of the Ripper as a truly global killer when he discovered that convicted murderer Carl Feigenbaum, a German seaman, had confessed to his lawyer that he was Jack the Ripper. This led Marriott to consider a welter of Ripper-like murders that had taken place in London, America and Germany between 1863 and 1894, one, some or all of which could be attributed to Feigenbaum. These included the deaths of Carrie Brown, Elizabeth Senior and, strangely, the women supposedly murdered in Jamaica and Nicaragua (of whom only one, Estina Crawford, is actually known to have been killed).[11]

* * *

Regarded thus, the women victims do become mere 'benchmarks', to be analysed and 'reduced to objects for study'. In a sense, then, Sarah Jackson's argument in response to the *East London Advertiser*'s 125th anniversary supplement is right. But it is also wrong. A huge amount of work has gone into uncovering the background stories of those women whose lives were following a tragic path long before they were put to death in the East End slums.

Sensitive research has allowed descendants of the victims to learn of – and come to terms with – their ancestors' fates, and so better understand their own lineage. Not unnaturally, some descendants are reluctant to speak publicly about this, but others have embraced their new knowledge, have visited the crime scenes and the graves of their murdered forebears and have achieved 'closure' of long-standing family rumours.

But by and large this is true only of those victims with a high profile – Nichols, Chapman, Stride, Eddowes and Kelly. Their graves are regularly adorned with floral tributes, usually peaking around the anniversaries of their deaths. And each year small groups of 'pilgrims' pay their respects on the appropriate dates. But the fact is that their graves are marked, whereas those of Emma Smith, Alice McKenzie and the others are not . . .

Heartfelt signs of respect are often posted on internet message boards and on Facebook by people who have nothing to do with the murdered women, beyond an abiding interest in the events that led to and surrounded their deaths. Those women have a strange power to touch people's lives. Is it genuine sympathy, or is it a by-product of a sense of guilt – an apology for being so fascinated by a subject that only exists because of their awful demises? It is hard to say, but it is not easy to find parallels in other murder cases.

It is just possible that you may have heard of Kathleen Maloney, Rita Nelson or Hectorina MacLennan. But it is less likely that you would know which cemetery to visit in order to pay your respects. Yet these are just some of the women murdered by John Christie at 10 Rillington Place, London, between 1943 and 1953. The names Brenda Baker, Susan Raincourt, Roberta Parks and Georgeann Hawkins may not ring any bells, but they were all victims of American serial killer Ted Bundy. In both cases, the murderer is well known, but the victims less so. In the case of Jack the Ripper, his true identity remains a mystery, yet some of his victims – specifically the 'canonical five' – are remembered across the world.

For many years, the Whitechapel Society 1888 has been pushing for a permanent memorial in the East End to the victims of the Whitechapel murders.[12] This is obviously a noble gesture, but there is one enduring problem: just who are the victims? Is the idea to remember the 'canonical five', or does the remit cover Smith, Tabram, McKenzie and Coles? Should it extend to the unidentified torsos and Elizabeth Jackson? And what about Kitty Ronan and Mary Ann Austin, both of whom met their deaths in the squalid dosshouses of Dorset Street?[13] Should it perhaps commemorate all Whitechapel unfortunates who were murdered by killers known or unknown? Who is more deserving and where should it stop?

It is impossible to say who really was killed by Jack the Ripper – assuming there was a single murderer. But if one man was responsible for these infamous crimes, the power of legend and the media (plus a sort of 'Ripperological' *status quo*) has seen to it that a small number of victims have etched themselves into the public consciousness like martyrs.

The rest, the 'forgotten victims', remain just out of reach. For now, at least.

Notes

Introduction

1. Mary Burridge's story received limited coverage in the newspapers – the *Pall Mall Gazette* and *The Star* both reported it (13 September 1888). It later crossed the Atlantic to be reported in the *Boston Daily Globe* (10 November 1888) and was recalled years later (see *Sunday Globe* (Minnesota), 3 April 1892, for example). The woman's age is taken from her death certificate.
2. Named 'Mrs Sodeaux' in all newspaper reports: *The Echo* and the *Evening News* (11 October 1888), *Morning Advertiser* (12 October 1888) and others. The spelling 'Sodo' comes from census returns and death records.
3. *Brooklyn Daily Eagle* (New York), 15 June 1889.
4. Charles Fort, *Lo!*, Claude Kendall, New York, 1931. Fort's importance as a collector of mysteries from all over the world led to the coining of the phrase 'Forteana' and his legacy continues in magazines like *Fortean Times*, established in 1973. It has been known to publish articles on Jack the Ripper.

Chapter 1: The Whitechapel Murders

1. Winston Churchill, *Lord Randolph Churchill*, Macmillan, London, 1906.
2. Edward Carpenter, *My Days of Dreams: Being autobiographical notes*, Allen and Unwin, London, 1916.
3. The 'Gilded Age' was a term coined by Mark Twain and Charles Dudley Warner as a satirical title for an era when great growth, particularly in the railroad, mining and manufacturing industries, hid serious social problems, the poverty being covered with a thin veneer of prosperity.
4. Significantly, in 1884, Chicago was witness to the first of what would initially be a uniquely American phenomenon, when the ten-storey Home Insurance Building was erected, the first steel-framed building and, importantly, the first 'skyscraper', a potent symbol of power and buoyancy.
5. As suggested in 1886 by the economist Alfred Marshall, in an address to a royal commission, that it was a downturn in profits and interest which did not really affect productivity. See Peter Mathias, *The First Industrial Nation: Economic history of Britain, 1700–1914*, Routledge, London, 1983.
6. The average life expectancy in London in 1800 was 40 years. By the 1880s it had risen to almost 50. Infant mortality rates were still high, however.
7. Interestingly, the 1880s had also seen an upsurge in the importance of leisure. With the middle classes having what was effectively spare cash, holidays and excursions became popular, and this decade saw an increase in activities such as lawn tennis, cycling and

football. The year 1888 would be a pivotal one: the Lawn Tennis Association and the English Football League were formed, and on 27 July parliament passed an Act permitting bicycles to be ridden on roads.

8. Churchill, *Lord Randolph Churchill*.

9. The 'Great Wen' was a disparaging nickname for London coined in the 1820s by William Cobbett, the radical pamphleteer and champion of rural England, who saw the rapidly growing city as a carbuncle on the face of the nation: 'But, what is to be the fate of the great wen of all? The monster, called, by the silly coxcombs of the press, "the metropolis of the empire?"' William Cobbett, *Rural Rides in the Counties*, Dent, London, 1830.

10. *The Times*, 9 February 1886.

11. Henderson had been chief commissioner since 1869, only the second person to fill the post. As with many in his position, he was popular to begin with, fulfilling the need for a commissioner with both military and civilian backgrounds. But he faced growing difficulties in the 1870s: reduced pensions led to the first police strike in 1872, and evidence of police corruption was exposed in 1877. He began to lose his hold on the force at this time and failed to recognize inadequacies in the staffing of the higher echelons of the police. When Fenian bombing campaigns began in London in 1883, he was content to leave the handling of this worrying development to his assistants, who included James Monro (later commissioner himself) and Robert Anderson (later assistant commissioner CID).

12. *Hansard*, 3 March 1887, Vol. 311, cc1069–70.

13. *The Times*, 20 March 1886.

14. *Pall Mall Gazette*, 13 March 1886.

15. Sir Robert Ensor, *England 1870–1914*, Oxford University Press, Oxford, 1936.

16. John Henry Mackay, *The Anarchists: A picture of civilization at the close of the nineteenth century*, Benj. R. Tucker, Boston, 1891.

17. Henry Mayhew, *London Labour and the London Poor*, 1861; Dover, New York, 4 vols, 1968–83.

18. As can be seen in Gustave Doré and William Blanchard Jerrold, *London: A pilgrimage*, Grant & Co., London, 1872; Anthem Press, 2005.

19. William J. Fishman, *East End 1888*, Duckworth, London, 1988; Five Leaves, Nottingham, 2005.

20. *East London Observer*, 27 October 1888. If green spaces were not included in the calculations, the Bell Lane area had 800 people per acre.

21. Fishman, *East End 1888*.

22. Henrietta Barnett, *Canon Barnett: His life, works and friends*, Vol. 1, Houghton Mifflin, London, 1919.

23. Commonly known as the 'Cross Act' after Richard Cross, Disraeli's home secretary and the Act's instigator. It was considered one of the most significant Acts of the Disraeli administration; however only ten out of eighty-seven boroughs in England and Wales chose to exploit it. The most use of it was made in Birmingham.

24. New developments in George Yard resulted in the construction of George Yard Buildings *c*. 1875 and St George's house in 1880.

25. This was specifically an area bounded by Thrawl Street, Flower and Dean Street and George Street; demolition was not complete until 1883 and a further three years passed before Charlotte de Rothschild Dwellings and Lolesworth Buildings were constructed and opened in 1887.

26. Letter from 'A Ratepayer', *Daily Telegraph*, 21 September 1888.

27. On 1 March 1881, Tsar Alexander II of Russia was assassinated, provoking a wave of persecution against Jews in Eastern Europe; anti-Jewish 'pogroms' prompted huge migration, as thousands attempted to flee dire poverty and unremitting maltreatment. For many, the only way to escape the relentless hardship and enforced transience was to go overseas.

28. Charles Booth (1840–1916) was a philanthropist and social researcher, most famed for his innovative work on documenting working-class life in London at the end of the nineteenth century. Through detailed explorations and observations of the streets and homes of the city, he created his famed 'Poverty Maps', the first of which was published in 1889.
29. Booth's estimate was presented in 'The Inhabitants of Tower Hamlets', read before the Royal Statistical Society on 17 March 1887.
30. Charles Booth, *Life and Labour of the People of London*, Vol. 1: *East London*, Macmillan, London, 1892.
31. Alan Palmer, *The East End*, J. Murray, London, 1989.
32. Todd E. Endleman, *The Jews of Britain 1656–2000*, University of California Press, Berkeley, 2002.
33. The journalist Arnold White told the House of Commons Immigration Committee on 5 June 1888 that, with a weekly sale of 1,700 copies, *Der Arbeter Fraint* was surely a widespread malevolent influence. Jewish MP Samuel Montagu countered that not only was the weekly sale more in the region of 200 copies, but also that in the previous week there had been no publication owing to lack of funds.
34. *Der Arbeter Fraint*, 28 December 1888.
35. It must be borne in mind that not the whole of the East End was quite so desperate. Many occupants of the main thoroughfares were businessmen and their families, respectable and, in some ways, middle class themselves. Areas such as Bow and parts of Mile End appeared unaffected by the hardships. It was to the concealed side-streets and overcrowded alleys and courts that one had to look to find the terrible conditions spoken of so fearfully.
36. 'Slumming' was a particular hobby of the more privileged classes and found popularity in the 1880s. It became fashionable to venture into the East End to experience the *frisson* of a down-at-heel neighbourhood, to drink in the busy pubs, enjoy the smoky music halls and, if one was so disposed, to partake of the services of the many prostitutes who plied their trade there.
37. At the London Dungeon gift shop, the visitor can even buy key-rings, mugs, coasters, fridge magnets and T-shirts emblazoned with Jack's iconic image.
38. Although people had been visiting the murder sites since the times of the crimes themselves, the first really official organized tours were started in the late 1960s. Their popularity remains undiminished and, without exaggeration, at peak times the streets of Spitalfields are awash with guided walks.
39. Police report dated 25 October 1888; MEPO 3/141, ff. 158–63 (National Archives).
40. By 1888, telegraphy was an important means of communication and international telegraphy had been in existence since the 1860s. The telephone, though still in its infancy, was in use by larger businesses and important institutions, including newspaper agencies and the police.
41. Founded in 1865, the *Pall Mall Gazette* began as a paper for the 'higher circles of society', written 'by gentlemen for gentlemen'. By the time of William Thomas Stead's editorship (1883–89), the paper had metamorphosed into a radical, free-thinking journal. Stead was not afraid to get his hands dirty in exposing a wrong or championing a cause, and in 1885 himself penned a series of hard-hitting articles, 'The Maiden Tribute of Modern Babylon', exposing the scandalous trade of 'buying' children for the purposes of prostitution. Stead's willingness to go all the way to prove his point earned him a three-month prison sentence for 'buying' a young girl for immoral purposes. The result of Stead's campaign was a rise in the age of consent for girls from 12 to 16 that same year. It is an excellent example of the influence that journalism was gaining.
42. *The Star*, an evening newspaper founded in 1788 by John Murray, was the newspaper that garnered the greatest notoriety and popularity on the back of the Whitechapel

murders. In 1888, its newly appointed editor was Thomas Power 'T. P.' O'Connor, considered today a leading light of the 'new journalism'. He described his paper's style of reporting as one which was intended to 'hit the reader right between the eyes'.

43. Fingerprinting was offered to the Metropolitan Police as a detection method by Dr Henry Faulds in 1886, but it was rejected. Even into the early twentieth century, the concept of killing for pleasure, without any sense of guilt or empathy for the victim, was an alien one to many authorities, who felt that only a motive would hold the key to an unsolved murder. However, in the world of medicine, 'moral insanity' was deemed by some to be a genuine condition, the closest the Victorians came to what we now call 'psychopathy'.

44. On 29 September 1888, the satirical magazine *Punch* published a poem entitled 'The Nemesis of Neglect', a lengthy verse which exposed the wrongs of the slums and how failure to right such wrongs had resulted in the visitation of awful crime. The poem was accompanied by a most evocative illustration depicting a translucent phantom floating through a slum alley, large knife drawn, staring out like some form of supernatural predator, its eyes piercing and its jaw hanging loose in a horrifying gape. The left hand was extended, with the bony fingers forming a claw. On its forehead was the word 'CRIME'. This illustration was, without doubt, the most striking image from those times.

45. Such as Lewis Carroll, Lord Randolph Churchill, Walter Sickert, William Gladstone, Dr Thomas Barnardo, William Booth, Vincent Van Gogh, Robert Louis Stevenson and the 'Elephant Man', to name but a few.

46. Dated 25 September 1888 and commonly known as the 'Dear Boss' letter. It was followed a few days later by a postcard bearing the same signature. Subsequently, the letter was imitated by literally thousands of writers. Around 250 (those that survive) are currently kept in the National Archives and the London Metropolitan Archives. It is impossible to say whether any were sent by the murderer himself, but undoubtedly they were a phenomenon in their own right.

47. A term coined by author and researcher Martin Fido in 1987.

48. This list is currently in the possession of the Swanson family.

49. HO 144/221/A49301C, ff. 220–3 (National Archives).

50. This report is widely accepted as being an early (or even the first) example of what has become known today as 'offender profiling', a fact first pointed out by Professor David Canter in *Criminal Shadows*, Harper Collins, London, 1994.

51. MEPO 3/140, ff. 259–62 (National Archives).

52. *Cassell's Saturday Journal*, 28 May 1892.

53. *Cassell's Saturday Journal*, 11 June 1892.

54. Sir Robert Anderson, *The Lighter Side of My Official Life*, Hodder and Stoughton, London, 1910, p. 135.

55. *Eastern Post and City Chronicle*, 3 February 1893.

56. MEPO 3/140, ff. 177–83 (National Archives).

57. These three suspects, widely discussed since the discovery of the memorandum in 1959, were Montague John Druitt, Michael Ostrog and 'Kozminski'.

58. Dr George Bagster Phillips died in 1897.

59. *Morning Advertiser*, 23 April 1910.

60. A good example is that of Peter Sutcliffe, the 'Yorkshire Ripper', who murdered thirteen women in the north of England between 1975 and 1980. A further seven women survived his attacks (the earliest in 1969), and on some occasions this was because he was interrupted. Several of the survivors were able to give the police a description of the assailant, and several of the photofit images bore a good likeness to Sutcliffe. Nonetheless, he was still interviewed numerous times by the police before eventually being taken into custody by chance in January 1981, whereupon he confessed to being the Ripper.

Chapter 2: The East End was a Dangerous Place

1. In *The London of Jack the Ripper: Then and now* (Breedon Publishing, Derby, 2009), Robert Clack and Philip Hutchinson suggest that Annie Millwood was really named Fanny Millwood, who, according to the 1871 and 1881 Censuses, was living with her husband Richard in St Pancras. Neither is to be found in the 1891 Census, which could support the identification with Annie Millwood, as both she and her husband would be dead by that time. However, census records can be an unreliable indicator of death, as a person may be missing from the register for a number of reasons. Also, Fanny Millwood would have been 47 at the time of the attack, whereas Annie Millwood was 38. Either age could be wrong; again, this is something that is not uncommon. Fanny Millwood had three children, two of whom died in infancy: Richard (d. 1874), George Richard (d. 1878) and George (b. 1880). Taking a different tack, a contributor to the 'Casebook: Jack the Ripper' message boards named Mark Ripper looked at different spellings of the surname and discovered a Richard and Annie Milward. They were married at the parish church of St Luke's, Chelsea, in 1872. Richard's age was given as 38 and his occupation as soldier. His father, deceased at the time of the wedding, was a farmer named Thomas Milward. Annie East Perry was 25 years old (which would make her three years older than Annie Millwood) and the daughter of Thomas Perry, a solicitor.
2. Responsibility was transferred to London County Council in 1894.
3. *Daily Telegraph*, 3 October 1888, names her as Ann Mason.
4. Several newspapers reported the story, notably the *Evening News*, 3 October 1888. The lodging house in question was in George Yard and was owned by Mrs Wilmot, a baker who lived in Brick Lane. It provided beds for sixty to seventy people every night. Wilmot also owned a lodging house at 18 Thrawl Street, where Ripper victim Mary Ann Nichols occasionally resided.
5. As reported by the *Evening News*, 23 November 1888.
6. Alice McKenzie stayed at 'Crossingham's in White's Row' (according to the inquest testimony of Elizabeth Ryder, *The Times*, 18 August 1889) and Crossingham's brother-in-law was watchman at 8 White's Row in 1901 (*The Times*, 20 June 1901).
7. *Daily Telegraph*, 13 November 1888.
8. *Eastern Post and City Chronicle*, 31 March 1888.
9. *Lloyd's Weekly Newspaper*, 1 April 1888.
10. The inquest is briefly mentioned in the *East London Advertiser* and the *Eastern Post and City Chronicle*, 7 April 1888.
11. Tom Cullen, *When London Walked in Terror*, Houghton Mifflin, Boston, 1965.
12. *The Times*, 11 December 1886.
13. *London Standard*, 30 December 1886.
14. *The Times*, 14 December 1886.
15. *East London Press*, 18 December 1886.
16. Ibid.
17. Report by Inspector Abberline, 1 November 1888; MEPO 3/140/221/A49301C, ff. 204–6 (National Archives).
18. *Chicago Tribune*, 7 October 1888.
19. In 1886 and 1887, a brilliant gynaecologist at Kensington Episcopal Hospital outside Philadelphia named Howard Atwood Kelly (1858–1943) visited Britain and Germany with other eminent hospital surgeons. He is not known to have been writing any monograph for which he might need a specimen of a uterus, although the reason why the doctor may have wanted the organ could have become garbled by the time it reached Baxter, and there is no reason beyond his eminence and the fact that he was from Philadelphia to suppose that he was the doctor in question. Curiously, however, he did write a letter to the *Medical News* (13 October 1888) in which he suggested that the murderer was a sexual sadist who needed to hurt a woman in order to obtain

gratification. 'Instances of this kind are not rare in literature,' he wrote, 'and the instinct to victimize the object of the passion is shown in a scale of progressive crime, from the simpler forms in which the sexual pervert finds it necessary to bite, or scratch, or stick pins into the woman to excite his desire, or to cut or injure in such a way as to draw blood, all the way up to those frightful cases of fiendish barbarity, in which the life of the victim is demanded as a sacrifice to secure the full enjoyment of the sexual act.'

20. Douglas G. Browne, *The Rise of Scotland Yard: A history of the Metropolitan Police*, George G. Harrap, London, 1956.

Chapter 3: The Gangs of Whitechapel

1. According to the testimony of Mary Russell, *Walthamstow and Leyton Guardian*, 14 April 1888.
2. Walter Dew, *I Caught Crippen: Memoirs of ex-Chief Inspector Walter Dew CID*, Blackie and Son, London, 1938, p. 83.
3. Ibid.
4. At least two hours elapsed between the estimated time of the assault and Emma Smith managing to reach her lodgings, and it is commonly assumed that she was either unconscious somewhere or in great pain and struggling to walk home. However, we know so little about the attack that it is entirely possible that she was found unconscious by a man who assisted her back to her lodgings. Some newspapers – the *Daily News*, the *Morning Post* (6 April 1888) and the *Eastern Post and City Chronicle* (7 April 1888) – support Dew, reporting that Emma Smith 'was taken home, and subsequently conveyed to the hospital'. The *Daily News* report was headlined 'Another fatal outrage in Whitechapel'. What did it mean by 'another'?
5. The *East London Advertiser*, 14 April 1888, and other newspapers claimed that she was a widow, but the London Hospital admission registers state that she was married and gave her occupation as charwoman. London Hospital, Patient Admission Register, 1888, RLHAM.
6. Originally formed as the Earl of Donegall's Regiment of Foot in 1701, in 1881 it was united with the 107th Regiment of Foot (Bengal Light Infantry) to form the Royal Sussex Regiment. A piece of paper found at the scene of a Ripper murder (that of Annie Chapman) bore the crest of the Royal Sussex Regiment. Annie Chapman was also seen to wrap some pills in a piece of paper she found on the floor in the kitchen of her lodging house. It bore the crest of the Royal Sussex Regiment, the letter 'M' in a man's handwriting and a postmark: 'London, 28 August, 1888'.
7. Edmund Reid's report is now missing, but its contents were recorded in notes taken by Ian Sharp for the BBC in preparation for its six-part series *Jack the Ripper*, broadcast in 1973.
8. Sir Frederick Treves, *The Elephant Man and Other Reminiscences*, Cassell, London, 1923, pp. 54–5 (reprinted by Star Books in 1980).
9. He is called Mr George Haslip in Inspector Reid's report, Dr Hellier in *Lloyd's Weekly Newspaper*, 8 April 1888, and Dr G. H. Hillier in the *Morning Advertiser*, 9 April 1888.
10. *Daily Telegraph*, 1 September 1888.
11. *The Times*, 19 January 1888. A correspondent calling himself 'A Board Master' mentioned both gangs in a letter in which he agreed with current concerns that lax punishment by the magistrates was encouraging the proliferation of such gangs and their disregard for the law.
12. *The Times*, 16 August 1898. Members of the gang appeared at the Thames Police Court charged with general rowdyism and pushing people from the pavement, threatening violence to anyone who complained. When the magistrate asked if anyone had come forward to make a complaint, a policeman explained 'people were afraid to come up'.

13. Arthur Harding, *East End Underworld: Chapters in the life of Arthur Harding*, Routledge and Kegan Paul, London, 1981.
14. Donald McCormick, *The Identity of Jack the Ripper*, Jarrold, London, 1959; Arrow Books, London, 1970.
15. *Daily News, Daily Telegraph, Morning Advertiser*, 1 October 1888 (my emphasis).
16. Anonymous, *The Whitechapel Murders, or The Mysteries of The East End*, G. Purkiss, London, 1888.
17. In 1886, a Liverpool newspaper – the *Daily Courier* – carried an article claiming that members of the gang had yelled 'High Rip', but the article is factually highly inaccurate. The *Liverpool Citizen* on 16 May 1888 said that the execution of the murderers was 'one of the heaviest blows' dealt to the High Rip, but the article actually illustrates how the name had become an almost generic term for gangs.
18. *Liverpool Echo*, 18 February 1885.
19. *The Times*, 21 December 1897.
20. Sir John William Nott-Bower, *Fifty-two Years a Policeman*, Edward Arnold & Co., London, 1926, p. 148. Born on 20 March 1849 and educated at Cheltenham and Sandhurst, he had served in the army and the Royal Irish Constabulary. He was chief constable of Leeds (at the time Charlie Peace was tried there), before being appointed the head constable of Liverpool in 1881 (Liverpool at that time having the largest city police force in the country; among the cases coming under his jurisdiction was that of Florence Maybrick). In March 1902, Captain John William Nott-Bower was elected commissioner of the City of London Police, successor to Major Smith, who was assistant commissioner at the time of the Ripper murders. He won the election by a mere five votes over Assistant Commissioner Major E. F. Wodehouse. One of his sons, J. Nott-Bower, would become deputy commissioner of the Metropolitan Police.
21. Day's son wrote a letter to *The Times* (Monday, 22 February 1932) correcting a previous correspondent's suggestion that Justice Day had suppressed garrotting, writing 'what he is said to have put down with the cat was the High Rip gang in Liverpool'. Day is certainly on record as having passed some stiff sentences, notably on two 19-year-olds charged with stabbing a member of a rival Liverpool gang, the Logwood Gang, whom he sentenced to fifteen years apiece (*Daily Telegraph*, 15 November 1886).

Chapter 4: Soldiers

1. It was described as 'that monstrous Victorian greenhouse' in the *Evening News*, 1 July 1913, and was a phrase quoted in *The Times* the following day.
2. See *The Times*, 30 June, 1, 2 and 13 July 1892.
3. 'Professor Baldwin' – who was paid £100 for his balloon ascents at Alexandra Palace (*Pall Mall Gazette*, 27 August 1888) – was not really a professor at all, but a former circus performer named Thomas Scott Baldwin (1854–1923) who would become one of the more significant pioneering aviators. After a stint in his youth as a brakeman on the Illinois railroad, he joined the circus as an acrobat. In 1875 he ascended in a hot air balloon, and for the next ten years, at shows and fairs across the United States, he developed an act in which he performed acrobatics on a trapeze suspended below the balloon. On 30 January 1885, he made one of the first parachute jumps from a balloon. He went on to make parachute descents around the world to audiences numbering in the hundreds of thousands. Between 1900 and 1908, he built a number of non-rigid airships, and in 1905 founded the Baldwin Airship Company, which in 1907 was commissioned by the US Army Signal Corps to build it an airship. In 1909, he designed an aeroplane and in 1910 began to tour with a flying exhibition. During the First World War he was commissioned as a captain in the Aviation Section of the Signal Corps, being promoted to major. At the end of the war he became a designer and manufacturer of airships for the Goodyear Tire and Rubber Company in Akron, Ohio. He died at the age of 68 and was buried with full military honours in Arlington

National Cemetery. He was mentioned in passing by the noted journalist George R. Sims, who implied that a seemingly semi-mythical Ripper suspect nicknamed 'Leather Apron' was at the time more newsworthy than a whole host of extraordinary news items, including Professor Baldwin, who 'could go up into the sky attached to a half-penny kite, and cut its tail off, and come down after attaining an altitude of a hundred miles' (*The Referee*, 16 September 1888).

4. *Evening Standard*, 8 August 1888.
5. *The Echo*, 23 August 1888.
6. Lawrence H. Officer, 'Purchasing power of British pounds from 1264 to 2007', MeasuringWorth.com, 2008.
7. *East London Advertiser*, 24 August 1888.
8. Inquest testimony, *East London Observer*, 25 August 1888.
9. MEPO 3/140, ff. 49–51 (National Archives), 24 August 1888.
10. In 1891, its name was changed to Planet Street, and in due course it was demolished.
11. *East London Advertiser*, 25 August 1888.
12. Tom Cullen, *Autumn of Terror*, Bodley Head, London, 1965. The chain no longer exists, so far as one can tell.
13. *Morning Advertiser*, 24 August 1888.
14. The nickname 'Mogg', which is usually spelt with a single 'g' and is a shortened version of Margaret, is applied to Connelly in only one newspaper, *The Echo* (10 August 1888).
15. There has been some discussion on internet message boards suggesting that Connelly was a transvestite, the grounds being her masculine appearance, husky voice, and apparently exaggerated female actions at the identity parades, but masculine women were not especially rare, and a policeman named Benjamin Leeson, in his autobiography (*Lost London*, Stanley Paul, London, 1934) refers to a notorious character known as 'Mog the Man', who, when in drink, was a brawler of notoriety and distinction. Honest, cheery, intelligent and religious (insofar as praying at a public bar can be described as religious) when sober, when drunk: 'Stripped bare to the waist, I have seen her fight the worst Amazons of Spitalfields and Whitechapel, and despite their inborn knowledge, nearly beat the life out of them, after which she would resist the united efforts of several policemen to remove her to the station, which they were never able to do until they had strapped her on to an ambulance.' Leeson met her again some years later in Kensington Gardens, when she had managed to start a new life as a nurse for 'a name respected and esteemed', which Leeson promised not to reveal.
16. *East London Observer*, 18 August 1888.
17. See *The Star*, 24 August 1888, for Ann Morris's statement that she saw Tabram standing alone on the kerb.
18. In 1890, Toynbee Hall took over the building and renamed it Balliol House in honour of the Oxford University settlement volunteers who came to lodge there. It was demolished in the early 1970s.
19. *East London Observer*, 11 August 1888.
20. *Eastern Post and City Chronicle*, 18 August 1888.
21. *East London Observer*, 18 August 1888.
22. Alfred George Crow, inquest testimony. Variously reported, but see *East London Advertiser* and *East London Observer*, 11 August 1888. The physical description was given in the latter.
23. *The Echo*, 17 August 1888.
24. *East London Advertiser*, 11 August 1888.
25. *East London Observer*, 11 August 1888.
26. *Weekly Herald*, 17 August 1888.
27. MEPO 3/140, f. 34 (National Archives).
28. *The Echo*, 10 August 1888.
29. *East London Observer*, 11 August 1888.

30. *East London Advertiser*, 18 August 1888.
31. Inspector Reid's report is contained in MEPO 3/140, f. 40 (National Archives).
32. The Canbury Arms still exists. With an unpromising back-street location, since being bought from the pub company Enterprise Inns, the Canbury Arms has been transformed into a successful and award-winning community pub.
33. Frederick Porter Wensley, *Detective Days*, Cassell, London, 1931, p. 13.
34. MEPO 3/140, f. 54 (National Archives).
35. Variously reported, but see *East London Observer*, 18 August 1888.
36. MEPO 3/140, f. 42 (National Archives).
37. Dew, *I Caught Crippen*, p. 103.
38. *Weekly Herald*, 17 August 1888.
39. *East London Observer*, 11 August 1888.
40. Ibid.
41. Ibid.
42. *Eastern Post and City Chronicle*, 25 August 1888.
43. Dew, *I Caught Crippen*, pp. 101, 103.
44. *East London Advertiser*, 11 August 1888.
45. Dew, *I Caught Crippen*, p. 103.
46. *The Echo*, 20 September 1888.
47. *Pall Mall Gazette*, 24 March 1903; Anderson, *The Lighter Side of My Official Life*, p. 135; Dew, *I Caught Crippen*, p. 97.

Chapter 5: Jack Strikes

1. As stated in the 'Macnaghten Memorandum'.
2. The known locations of the 'canonical' victims' graves are:
   Mary Ann Nichols – City of London Cemetery (Little Ilford), Manor Park (public grave 210752).
   Annie Chapman – Manor Park Cemetery (exact location unknown).
   Elizabeth Stride – East London Cemetery, Plaistow.
   Catherine Eddowes – City of London Cemetery (Little Ilford), Manor Park (public grave 49336, square 318).
   Mary Jane Kelly – St Patrick's Roman Catholic Cemetery, Leytonstone (grave 66, row 66, plot 10).
3. Cross was actually born Charles Allen Lechmere. The surname 'Cross' comes from his stepfather after his mother remarried, but curiously the only time he used this name is during his association with the Nichols murder. We have chosen to use that name as it is what appeared in the official files.
4. *Daily Telegraph*, 3 September 1888.
5. In mid-April 1888, Mary Ann began working as a domestic for Samuel and Sarah Cowdrey in Wandsworth; three months later she left, taking with her clothing to the value of £3 10s.
6. *The Star*, 31 August 1888.
7. *The Star*, 1 September 1888.
8. Report by acting Superintendent W. Davis, 7 September 1888; MEPO 3/140, f. 238 (National Archives).
9. John Chapman died of cirrhosis of the liver and dropsy on Christmas Day 1886.
10. Annie Georgina (b. 1873) and John Alfred (b. 1880). A third child, the eldest, Miriam Ruth (b. 1870), died of meningitis in 1882.
11. The details of Chapman's injuries were published in *The Lancet*, 29 September 1888.
12. *East London Observer*, 15 September 1888.
13. Persistent pleas to the home secretary, Henry Matthews, were unsuccessful, with the reply stating that 'such offers of reward tended to produce more harm than good, and the Secretary of State is satisfied that there is nothing in the circumstances of the

present case to justify a departure from this rule' (*East London Advertiser*, 22 September 1888).

14. Missing for many years, this infamous letter was returned to Scotland Yard anonymously, with other documents relating to the case, in 1987. It is currently held at the National Archives: MEPO 3/3183, ff. 2–4.

15. Elizabeth appears in police records as a professional prostitute in 1865, the year she gave birth to a stillborn daughter.

16. At No. 55, known as Cooney's. Elizabeth Stride was a regular inhabitant of 32 Flower and Dean Street, and Mary Ann Nichols was believed to have used the dosshouse at 56 Flower and Dean Street.

17. The three men were Joseph Lawende, Harry Harris and Joseph Hyam Levy, who were leaving the Imperial Club on Duke Street at about 1.30 a.m.

18. Even though there was nothing to stop officers from either force stepping over their respective boundaries, they would not have jurisdiction outside their own districts. This was the case until the Police Act 1964, which allowed the freedom to operate in either area.

19. This is the version found in the files of the Metropolitan Police. City Police accounts phrase it as 'The Juwes are not the men that will be blamed for nothing.'

20. Contrary to popular myth, Warren did not resign over his inability to handle the Ripper case. He did so after protracted conflicts with Home Secretary Matthews, which came to a head when Warren was chastised by Matthews for writing a critical article about the police in *Murray's Magazine*. It was the final straw for the unpopular Warren, who had actually tendered his resignation before. On this occasion, it was accepted.

21. Sir Melville Macnaghten, *Days of My Years*, Arnold, London, 1914.

22. *Evening News*, 12 November 1888.

23. *Western Mail*, 12 November 1888.

24. Dr Thomas Bond's extensive post-mortem report: MEPO 3/3153, ff. 10–18 (National Archives).

25. *The Globe* (Canada), 13 November 1888.

Chapter 6: 'He's Gone to Gateshead'

1. *Daily News*, 27 September 1888.

2. Jane's character appears to have come under scrutiny and to have been maligned, *The Echo* reporting that 'She had not a stainless reputation, having had two illegitimate children.' What the basis for the apparently unfounded slur was is not known.

3. He spelled his name 'Waddell', but on official documents and in most newspapers it was spelled 'Waddle'. I have followed Waddell's own spelling.

4. *The Times*, *Evening News*, 26 September 1888.

5. James Falloon, who was born in Kildress, Cookstown, Co. Tyrone in Ireland in 1858, had served in India and in what is now known as the Second Afghan War (1879–80), for which he received the Afghan War Medal. Promoted to corporal in October 1885, he reverted to private at his own request in 1887, because he felt 'unequal to the performance of the duties of the position'. He returned to England in November 1887, being discharged in June 1889.

6. Information from James Falloon and William Kibbens was reported in the *North-Eastern Daily Gazette*, 27 September 1888.

7. *Pall Mall Gazette*, 27 September 1888.

8. *The Times*, 27 September 1888.

9. Low Fell, a suburb of Gateshead, was the terminus for trams from Newcastle and remained so until the 1950s.

10. *Daily Telegraph*, 25 September 1888.

11. *The Star*, 24 September 1888.

12. *Daily Telegraph*, 25 September 1888.

13. *Daily News*, 24 September 1888.

14. *Morning Advertiser*, 24 September 1888.
15. *The Star, The Times*, 26 September 1888.
16. *Irish Times* and *Freeman's Journal and Daily Commercial Advertiser*, both 27 September 1888.
17. *The Star*, 1 October 1888.
18. *Daily Telegraph*, 26 September 1888.
19. *The Times*, 26 September 1888; *Daily Telegraph, The Star, The Times*, 27 September 1888.
20. Yetholm is, in fact, two small villages – Kirk Yetholm and Town Yetholm – which straddle Bowmont Water and are connected by a three-arched stone bridge built in the early 1800s. It is famous as the home of the Faa family, who for a long time were the acknowledged kings of the Scottish gypsies.
21. *Weekly Herald*, 5 October 1888.
22. *The Echo*, 17 December 1888.
23. *Newcastle Weekly Courant*, 22 December 1888.
24. *Thomson's Weekly News*, 12 February 1927.
25. *The Times*, 14 December 1888.
26. *The Times*, 18 December 1888.
27. *The Times*, 19 December 1888; Berry's account is in *The Post*, 10 January 1914.
28. *Newcastle Weekly Courant*, 22 December 1888.

Chapter 7: Bits of Body Turning Up Here and There

1. It seems likely that this was the same man as – or was the son of – one Edward Henry Hughes, a waterman of Gravesend, who, in 1842, was discovered carrying away the greater part of a bine from one of the poles at a hop farm in Ifield, Kent (bines being popular purchases among sightseers in Gravesend). He briefly escaped from custody, but when overtaken had drawn a knife and threatened to stab anyone who came near. Eventually he was overpowered and sent for trial in Maidstone, where he stood to receive imprisonment for three years or transportation for an astonishing ten to fifteen years (*The Times*, 1 September 1846). He was almost certainly the same Edward Henry Hughes, waterman of Gravesend, who had given witness testimony at the inquiry into the sinking of the steamer *Duchess of Kent* in the Thames in 1852, and who described himself as having been connected with the river for twenty-eight years (see *The Times*, 12 August 1852).
2. *The Times*, 13 June 1887.
3. *The Times*, 30 July 1887.
4. *Penny Illustrated Paper*, 14 June 1887.
5. *Daily News*, 9 October 1888.
6. Fairly consistently called Hibbert in the press.
7. *The Times*, 12 September 1888.
8. *Irish Times*, 9 October 1888.
9. *The Times*, 14 and 15 September 1888.
10. *The Echo*, 12 September 1888.
11. *The Star*, 29 September 1888.
12. *The Star*, 28 September 1888.
13. *Daily Telegraph*, 3 October 1888.
14. J. H. M. Mapleson, *The Mapleson Memoirs 1848–1888* (2 vols), Remington & Co., London, 1888. Also J. H. M. Mapleson, *The Mapleson Memoirs: The career of an operatic impresario 1858–1888*, ed. Harold Rosenthal, Appleton-Century, New York, 1966.
15. *The Star*, 9 October 1888.
16. *Daily Telegraph*, 9 October 1888. Although no mention was made of it at the inquest, the *Pall Mall Gazette*, 6 October 1888, reported that the dressmaker who had made the skirt had been traced to the West End and that it was hoped that her records might identify the torso. Unfortunately, the newspaper reports of this event were as wild as they were often inaccurate and contradictory. If this story was true, then it is to be supposed that the lead petered out.

17. Inquest reports, *Daily News, Daily Telegraph, The Star*, 9 October 1888.
18. Condy's fluid was a disinfectant that, if applied to the skin, made it turn brown. Fans of E. Nesbit's timeless classic *The Wouldbegoods* may recall that: 'HO painted his legs and hands with Condy's fluid to make them brown so that he might play Mowgli . . .' It was developed and patented by Henry Bollmann Condy and manufactured at his works in Bermondsey. It was very widely used to prevent smells and, diluted in water, was used for cleaning, washing, and to treat internal and external ailments. It was widely used in stables, kennels and aviaries. It was instrumental in increasing public awareness of disinfection, and a bottle was to be found in almost every home. Interestingly, in the 1880s men used a dilute solution to prevent venereal disease, and some prostitutes offered disinfectant to their clients.
19. In 1886, Adelaide Bartlett stood trial at the Old Bailey for the murder of her husband, Thomas Edwin Bartlett. In August 1885, the couple had taken furnished rooms at 85 Claverton Street, Pimlico, and on 1 January 1886 Thomas Bartlett was found dead, the cause being ingestion of liquid chloroform. The beautiful Adelaide, who had previously bought a quantity of chloroform, was accused of having poisoned James, but very little positive evidence was produced and she was acquitted, leaving unresolved one of the most intriguing poisoning cases of the nineteenth century. The problem was that liquid chloroform burns the skin, but while there was chloroform in the stomach, neither the mouth nor the throat showed signs of its having been swallowed. After the acquittal, Sir James Paget of St Bartholomew's Hospital is alleged to have said that Adelaide 'should tell us in the interests of science how she did it'. When discovered, Edwin had within his reach a wine glass three-quarters full of what a doctor thought was brandy and something that smelt like ether; on a tray near the table was a tumbler half filled with Condy's fluid. The latter could have been used by Edwin Bartlett for several purposes: he may have used it as a disinfectant in the treatment of a venereal disease he thought he had; he may have used it to lessen the horribly noxious smell of his breath caused by rotten teeth; or he may have used it as a mouthwash to soothe and lessen infection following some recent dental treatment.
20. *Daily Telegraph*, 3 October 1888.
21. *The Star*, 3 October 1888.
22. *Daily Telegraph*, 9 October 1888.
23. *Pall Mall Gazette*, 5 October 1888.
24. *Illustrated Police News*, 6 October 1888.
25. *Daily Telegraph*, 3 October 1888.
26. *Daily Telegraph*, 4 October 1888.
27. *The Star*, 4 October 1888.
28. *The Star*, 5 October 1888.
29. *The Star*, 6 October 1888.
30. *The Star*, 11 October 1888.
31. *The Times*, 20 October 1888.
32. *The Times*, 19, 23 October 1888.

Chapter 8: 'What a Cow!'

1. *Daily News*, 20 November 1888.
2. *East London Advertiser*, 24 November 1888.
3. That is until 1986, when a gravestone was erected by John Morrison, a Leytonstone man who had been researching the murders for several years and who had attracted interest in the local press over his fight to have Mary Kelly's reputation rehabilitated. This gravestone was later damaged and removed, but was replaced by another which still stands. The grave is not confirmed as being in exactly the correct location, as that section of the cemetery was reclaimed in 1947; however it receives many visitors and the gravestone is often decked with tributes and gifts.

4. Based at 5 New Bridge Street, London, the Central News Agency became a significant player during the Whitechapel murders. Formed in 1863 as the Central Press, and renamed in 1871, it immediately tried to outdo its two main rivals, Reuters and the Press Association. Its tendency to find and distribute sensational stories gave it a reputation that was often sneered at by more responsible journalists. Its notoriety was ensured during the Ripper crimes, with its receipt of the 'Dear Boss' letter that launched the name 'Jack the Ripper'. Its methods came under scrutiny many years later, when *The Times* made a comparison of telegrams received by the agency and the subsequent reports that were issued by it based on those communications. This analysis revealed a great deal of 'fleshing-out' with unreliable information.

5. *Evening News*, 21 November 1888.

6. *Aitchison Daily Globe* (Kansas), 21 November 1888.

7. *Evening Star* (Washington, DC), 21 November 1888.

8. *Evening News*, 21 November 1888.

9. First opened in 1868 by Patrick Sullivan, the house was taken over by John Satchell in June the following year; he remained the owner until the premises were closed down in 1891. In 1888, Satchell also owned 20 George Street (where he lived), as well as premises at 6, 7, 8, 31, 32 and 33 Flower and Dean Street; 32 Flower and Dean Street was the preferred lodging house of Elizabeth Stride.

10. *Daily Telegraph*, 22 November 1888.

11. Hearsay of another potential Whitechapel murder even led to a brief mention in the House of Commons on the morning of 21 November (*Morning Advertiser*, 22 November 1888).

12. This could be the same Ellen Marks, a young woman of Duke Street, Spitalfields, who appeared at Worship Street magistrates' court in 1886 as a plaintiff after she was stabbed by her former partner, George Squibb (*News of the World*, 19 September 1886). An Ellen Marks, aged 22, was also charged at the same court in December 1888 with wilful damage to a piano organ (*Morning Advertiser*, 17 December 1888).

13. *The Star*, 21 November 1888. Various reports speak of different exclamations – the *Daily Telegraph* has the man using a 'common expression' (swearing) and saying 'look at what she has done!'

14. Ruffell told the *Daily Telegraph* (22 November 1888) that he had lost sight of the man near the Frying Pan pub on the corner with Brick Lane. If Bennett did see the man disappear down a court, it would have been Mission Hall Court, the only possible exit on Thrawl Street between George Street and Brick Lane – but it was a dead end. However, Sarah Turner was standing outside her home at 27 Thrawl Street and saw the man run past and into Brick Lane (*Evening News*, 21 November 1888).

15. Eyewitness reports of Ruffell, Harris, Sullivan and Bennett from the *Morning Advertiser*, 22 November 1888.

16. *East London Advertiser*, 24 November 1888.

17. *Manchester Guardian*, 22 November 1888; *St James Gazette*, 21 November 1888; *The Star*, 21 November 1888; and many others.

18. *Daily Telegraph*, 22 November 1888.

19. *The Star*, 21 November 1888.

20. *East London Advertiser*, 24 November 1888; *Daily Telegraph*, 22 November 1888.

21. *Daily Telegraph*, 22 November 1888.

22. *The Times*, 21 November 1888.

23. *Morning Advertiser*, 22 November 1888.

24. *Evening News*, 21 November 1888.

25. Ibid.

26. *The Times*, 23 November 1888.

27. *St James Gazette*, 21 November 1888.

28. *Evening News*, 26 November 1888.

29. *East Anglian Daily Times*, 26 November 1888.

30. *Trenton Times* (New Jersey), *Lima Daily Times* (Ohio), *Chicago Tribune*, all 23 July 1889.
31. Francis Ruffell was born in Spitalfields in 1860, one of many children born to John and Mary Ann. In the 1891 Census, he is listed as living at Quaker Street Buildings with his wife and first child and is described as a carman.
32. *The Star*, 21 November 1888.
33. At about 11.45 p.m. on 8 November 1888, Mrs Cox walked into Dorset Street from Commercial Street and saw Kelly walking in front of her with a man. They turned into Miller's Court and went into No. 13, at which point Mrs Cox bade Kelly goodnight. Mary Kelly was apparently very drunk and could barely answer, but managed to say goodnight in return. The man Mrs Cox saw was described as about 36 years old, 5ft 5in tall with a fresh complexion and blotches on his face. He had small side-whiskers, a thick, carroty moustache and was dressed in shabby dark clothes, dark overcoat and a black felt hat. He was holding a quart can of beer.

Chapter 9: Murder by Natural Causes

1. Ada Wilson was attacked at her home at 19 Maidman Street on 28 March 1888.
2. *Daily News*, 28 December 1888.
3. *The Times*, 26 December 1888.
4. *Daily News*, 22 December 1888.
5. Ibid.
6. It is worth reiterating that 18 George Street was the lodging house where Emma Smith had been living when attacked by a gang earlier in the year. Next door was Satchell's lodging house where Martha Tabram had lived and where Annie Farmer was assaulted nearly a month earlier. Mary Kelly, the last canonical victim of Jack the Ripper, had also lived in George Street. Kelly lived with Joseph Barnett, who said that when they decided to live together they had taken lodgings in George Street where he, Barnett, was known.
7. *Morning Advertiser*, 26 December 1888.
8. *Daily News*, 26 December 1888; *The Times*, 3 January 1889.
9. *The Times*, 10 January 1889.
10. *The Times*, 3 January 1889.
11. Ibid.
12. Inquest testimony reported in *The Times*, 10 January 1889, but in earlier sources her address is given as Simpson's Row off Poplar High Street, about thirty or forty yards from Clarke's Yard: *Daily News*, 24 December 1888.
13. *Daily News*, 26 December 1888; *The Times*, 3 January 1889.
14. *Daily Chronicle*, 28, 29 December 1888.
15. *Daily News*, *The Times*, 22 December 1888.
16. Newspaper accounts vary. *The Times*, 10 January 1889, said 1.45 a.m.; *Daily News* and *The Times*, 24 December 1888, gave 2.30 a.m.
17. *Daily News*, *The Times*, 24 December 1888.
18. *East End News*, 21 December 1888.
19. *Lloyd's Weekly Newspaper*, 13 January 1889.
20. *The Times*, 10 January 1889.
21. Poplar mortuary was in Queen Street (later Bickmore Street), which ran south off Poplar High Street. It was just next to Poplar Workhouse. The mortuary was built in 1871 by Hodge & Robinson of Bisterne Place, Blackwall, to designs by A. & C. Harston, at a cost of £261. By the early 1890s it was thought to be both inadequate and below the standards required by London County Council. It was replaced by a new mortuary erected in Cottage Street in 1910–11. From *Survey of London*: Vols 43 and 44: *Poplar, Blackwall and Isle of Dogs* (1994).
22. *The Times*, *Daily News*, 22 December 1888; *The Times*, 3 January 1889.

23. *The Times*, 10 January 1889.
24. Report by James Monro to the Home Office, 23 December 1888. HO 144/221/A49301H, ff. 7–14 (National Archives).
25. *The Star*, 24 December 1888.
26. Ibid.
27. The medical evidence is given in several newspapers: *Daily News*, *The Times*, 22 December 1888; *The Star*, 24 December 1888; *The Times*, 10 January 1889.
28. *Daily News*, 22 December 1888.
29. *The Times*, 22 December 1888.
30. HO 144/221/A49301H, ff. 7–14.
31. *The Star*, 24 December 1888.
32. HO 144/221/A49301H, ff. 7–14 (emphasis in original).
33. HO 144/221/A49301H, ff. 7–14.
34. *The Times*, 3 January 1889.
35. *The Times*, 10 January 1889.
36. Report by Robert Anderson to James Monro, 11 January 1889; MEPO 3/143, ff. E–J (National Archives).
37. Stewart P. Evans and Donald Rumbelow, *Jack the Ripper: Scotland Yard investigates*, Sutton Publishing, Stroud, Gloucester, 2006.
38. Letter from Dr Brownfield; MEPO 3/143, f. O (National Archives).
39. MEPO 3/143, f. O (National Archives).
40. Letter from Alexander MacKellar to James Monro, 14 February 1889; MEPO 3/143, ff. P–Q (National Archives).
41. Anderson, *The Lighter Side of My Official Life*.

Chapter 10: The Ripper That Never Was

1. *Tri-weekly Budget*, 29 December 1888.
2. *Daily Gleaner* (Jamaica), 14 January 1889, although the same paper of 11 January 1889 puts the time of discovery at 5.50 a.m.
3. *Tri-weekly Budget*, 29 December 1889.
4. *Daily Gleaner*, 11 January 1889.
5. *Daily Gleaner*, 16 January 1889.
6. *Daily Gleaner*, 14 January 1889.
7. *Daily Gleaner*, 11 January 1889.
8. Her name is given as Letitia Crawford in the *Daily Gleaner*, 1 January, 24 January and 5 February 1889.
9. *Daily Gleaner*, 14 January 1889.
10. *Daily Gleaner*, 16 January 1889.
11. *Daily Gleaner*, 11 January 1889.
12. *Daily Gleaner*, 11 January 1889.
13. *Daily Gleaner*, 14 January 1889.
14. *Daily Gleaner*, 16 January 1889.
15. Ibid.
16. Ibid.
17. *Daily Gleaner*, 24 January 1889.
18. *Mitchell Daily Republican* (South Dakota), 23 January 1889.
19. *Daily Gleaner*, 5 February 1889.
20. *Brooklyn Daily Eagle*, 6 February 1889.
21. *Atchison Daily Globe* (Kansas), 7 February 1889.
22. *The Times*, 18 February 1889; *Penny Illustrated Paper*, *Croydon Advertiser*, 23 February 1889.
23. *Penny Illustrated Paper*, 23 February 1889.
24. *Mitchell Daily Republican*, 13 February 1889.

Chapter 11: A Gruesome Jigsaw

1. The name Shad Thames appears as early as John Rocque's 1747 map of London, and is possibly a corruption of 'St John-at-Thames', a reference to the nearby church of St John's Horsleydown, designed by Nicholas Hawksmoor and completed in 1733. The church was damaged by enemy bombs during the Second World War and was eventually demolished in 1974.
2. *Nottingham Evening Post*, 5 June 1889.
3. *The Times*, 4 July 1889.
4. *London Standard*, 17 June 1889.
5. Allan McLane Hamilton and Edwin Godkin, *A System of Legal Medicine*, E. B. Treat, New York, 1894.
6. *Sheffield Independent*, 5 June 1889.
7. *Dundee Courier*, 6 June 1889.
8. *Morning Post*, 6 June 1889.
9. *Newark Daily Advocate* (Ohio), 5 June 1889.
10. *Daily Gazette for Middlesbrough*, 6 June 1889.
11. *Morning Post*, 6 June 1889.
12. *London Standard*, 7 June 1889.
13. Ibid.
14. *Aberdeen Journal*, 7 June 1889.
15. *London Daily News*, 7 June 1889.
16. *Lloyd's Weekly Newspaper*, 8 June 1889.
17. *Bury and Norwich Post*, 11 June 1889.
18. *Nottingham Evening Post, Dundee Courier, Sheffield Independent*, 7 June 1889; *Portsmouth Evening News, Yorkshire Gazette*, 8 June 1889.
19. *Dundee Courier*, 8 June 1889.
20. *Lloyd's Weekly Newspaper*, 16 June 1889. In English law, Lammas Lands were lands or meadows held in severalty (or exclusive ownership) during the crop-raising period but subject to common rights at other times (such as for pasturage). There are several locations which still hold this name, including Bengeo Lammas Land in Hertfordshire and Lammas Road near Well Street Common in Hackney, London.
21. *London Standard*, 8 June 1889.
22. The Royal Humane Society – then called the Society for the Recovery of Persons Apparently Drowned – was founded in London in 1774 by two doctors, William Hawes (1736–1808) and Thomas Cogan (1736–1818). They were concerned at the number of people wrongly taken for dead – and, in some cases, buried alive. Both men wanted to promote the new medical technique of resuscitation and offered money to anyone rescuing someone from the brink of death, particularly from drowning. Today the aim of the Society is to recognize the bravery of men, women and children who have saved, or tried to save, someone else's life.
23. *Nottingham Evening Post*, 8 June 1889.
24. *London Standard*, 10 June 1889.
25. *Daily Gazette for Middlesbrough*, 8 June 1889.
26. *Lloyd's Weekly Newspaper*, 9 June 1889.
27. Ibid.
28. *Lloyd's Weekly Newspaper*, 16 June 1889.
29. *Portsmouth Evening News*, 12 June 1889.
30. *Huddersfield Chronicle, Gloucester Citizen, York Herald*, 13 June 1889.
31. *Evening Star* (Washington, DC), 4 June 1889.
32. *Newark Daily Advocate* (Ohio), 5 June 1889 (early edition).
33. *Gloucester Citizen*, 7 June 1889; *Dundee Courier, Manchester Times, Grantham Journal*, 8 June 1889.
34. *Nottingham Evening Post*, 13 June 1889.

35. *Lloyd's Weekly Newspaper*, 16 June 1889.
36. *Dundee Courier, Nottingham Evening Post, Shields Daily Gazette*, 17 June 1889.
37. Isaac Brett, aged 15, gave testimony about the first Battersea discovery and 11-year-old Patrick McCarthy spoke of the remains found at Horsleydown (*London Standard*, 17 June 1889).
38. *Birmingham Daily Post, Dundee Courier*, 17 June 1889; *Lancaster Gazette*, 19 June 1889; *Nottinghamshire Guardian, Worcester Journal*, 22 June 1889.
39. *Shields Daily Gazette, Belfast News Letter, Freeman's Journal*, 26 June 1889.
40. *London Daily News*, 2 July 1889.
41. *London Daily News*, 26 June 1889.
42. *London Daily News*, 2 July 1889.
43. *The Times*, 26 June 1889.
44. *London Daily News*, 2 July 1889.
45. The *Western Daily Press* said it was 10 Turk's Row.
46. *Illustrated Police News*, 13 July 1889.
47. *Western Daily Press*, 27 June 1889.
48. *Illustrated Police News*, 13 July 1889.
49. The Albert Palace was located in Battersea Park, where it faced, and formed a backdrop, to the lake there. It was an iron and glass building, not unlike the Crystal Palace, which had partly housed the Dublin International Exhibition of 1865. In 1882 it was dismantled and returned to Dublin.
50. *Western Daily Press*, 27 June 1889; *Aberdeen Journal*, 28 June 1889.
51. Reports vary. *The Times* of 2 July and 26 July 1889 called him 'Faircloth', as did the *Western Gazette* and *Hartlepool Mail*, 9 July, among others. Many other reports use the name 'Fairclough'.
52. *The Times*, 5 July 1889.
53. *The Times*, 9 July 1889.
54. *Portsmouth Evening News*, 8 July 1889.
55. Inquest report in *The Times*, 9 July 1889.
56. *The Times*, 26 July 1889.
57. Ibid.

Chapter 12: Jack the Ripper or Not?

1. *Morning Chronicle*, 5 July 1823.
2. *The Times*, 31 August 1849.
3. *The Times*, 16 November 1864.
4. *The Times*, 4 February 1863.
5. *The Times*, 28 August 1875.
6. *Daily Gleaner* (Jamaica), 26 July 1889.
7. *Alderley and Wilmslow Advertiser*, 19 July 1889.
8. *Illustrated Police News*, 27 July 1889.
9. Variously described as being at No. 52 or No. 54, it was in fact a large establishment that consisted of four adjoining properties, Nos. 50, 51, 52 and 53. No. 50 was first registered in July 1854, No. 51 in February 1879 and Nos. 52 and 53 in April 1880. The collective houses were licensed for a total of 198 residents. The owner was actually Thomas Tempany, a Cambridgeshire lodging house keeper. His name has also been spelt 'Tenpany' and 'Tampany'.
10. *The Times*, 18 July 1889.
11. Ibid.
12. Also known as the Cambridge Music Hall, the theatre opened in 1864. It was destroyed by fire in 1896 but quickly rebuilt. The theatre was demolished in 1936 to make way for extensions to a tobacco factory, which still stands.

13. Report by Sergeant McCarthy, 24 July 1889; HO 3/140, f. 278 (National Archives).
14. Other pubs close by which may have been the venue for this incident include the Commercial Tavern, a few doors along Commercial Street, and the White Hart in Little Pearl Street.
15. Report by Sergeant McCarthy, 27 July 1889; HO 3/140, f. 277 (National Archives).
16. *The Times*, 19 July 1889.
17. Ibid.
18. *East End News*, 19 July 1889.
19. *The Times*, 18 July 1889.
20. 'Classified Advertising', *The Times*, 26 July 1847.
21. *The Times*, 18 July 1889.
22. Often wrongly transcribed in the contemporary press reports as 'Edmund Berry' or 'Bougham', Sergeant Badham transported the body of earlier victim Annie Chapman from the backyard of 29 Hanbury Street to the mortuary on an ambulance.
23. *The Times*, 18 July 1889.
24. Undoubtedly one of the chandler's shops owned by John McCarthy at 27 or 34 Dorset Street. McCarthy, it may be remembered, was Mary Kelly's landlord.
25. *Walthamstow and Leyton Guardian*, 20 July 1889.
26. *Evening Star* (Washington, DC), 18 July 1889.
27. *Daily Gleaner* (Jamaica), 26 July 1889.
28. *Trenton Times* (New Jersey), 18 July 1889.
29. *The Times*, 19 July 1889.
30. Report by Dr Bond; MEPO 3/140, ff. 259–262 (National Archives).
31. Report by Dr George Bagster Phillips, 22 July 1889; MEPO 3/140, ff. 263–71 (National Archives).
32. Report by Dr Thomas Bond, 17 July 1889; MEPO 3/140, ff. 259–62 (National Archives).
33. Letter from James Monro, 17 July 1889; HO 144/221/A49301I, ff. 5–6 (National Archives).
34. Anderson, *The Lighter Side of My Official Life*.
35. Letter from Home Office to Scotland Yard, 23 August 1889; MEPO 3/141, f. 12 (National Archives).
36. *Sheffield Evening Telegraph*, 22 July 1889.
37. *Lloyd's Weekly Newspaper*, 28 July 1889.
38. *The Times*, 15 August 1889.
39. *Pall Mall Budget*, 9 October 1890.
40. *Kimberley Advertiser* (South Africa), 29 June 1889.
41. *The Times*, 2 August 1889.
42. *Lloyd's Weekly Newspaper*, 18 August 1889.

Chapter 13: The Body from Elsewhere

1. *East London Observer*, 14 September 1889.
2. *The Times*, 25 September 1889.
3. Following the destruction of the Royal Berwick Theatre, Rev. George Smith of the Methodist Mariners Church on Dock Street decided to build a hostel for sailors on the site. It was opened in 1835, with accommodation for 100 sailors, later expanded to 500. The London Nautical School opened there in 1893. In 1955 it was modernized and renamed the Red Ensign Club. Well Street was renamed Ensign Street in honour of the hostel. Following the decline of the British Merchant Fleet, the club closed in 1974. Author Joseph Conrad lived in the Sailors' Home aged 21 and returned several times throughout his life (John Stape, *The Several Lives of Joseph Conrad*, Pantheon, New York, 2007).
4. *The Times*, 12 September 1889.

5. *The Times*, 25 September 1889.
6. *Evening Star* (Washington, DC), 11 September 1889.
7. *East London Observer*, 14 September 1889.
8. *The Times*, 12 September 1889.
9. *The Times*, 25 September 1889.
10. Sometimes reported as 'Another Whitechapel!' According to the *Burnley Express*, 14 September 1889, ' "Whitechapel Again!" has become the telegraphic code signal of the metropolitan police, and now only needs to be sounded to bring to bear on Whitechapel the scrutiny of the whole force. Yet in spite of the most elaborate system, the most careful organisation, and the most rigorous surveillance, another of those terrible crimes which have shocked the whole country has been coolly perpetrated, almost within a stone's throw of the city boundary.' The City Police had a similar code, both forces bringing the system into force in July 1889 following the death of Alice McKenzie.
11. *Eastern Post and City Chronicle*, 14 September 1889.
12. *The Times*, 25 September 1889.
13. *Shields Daily Gazette*, 11 September 1889.
14. *Trenton Times* (New Jersey), 12 September 1889.
15. *The Times*, 25 September 1889.
16. *East London Observer*, 28 September 1889.
17. *The Times*, 11 September 1889.
18. *Nottingham Evening Post*, 12 September 1889.
19. *Liverpool Echo*, 11 September 1889.
20. *Pall Mall Gazette*, 10 September 1889.
21. *Shields Daily Gazette*, 10 September 1889.
22. *Trenton Times* (New Jersey), 10 September 1889.
23. *Evening Star* (Washington, DC), 11 September 1889.
24. *The Times*, 11 September 1889.
25. *The Times*, 12 September 1889.
26. Stuart C. Cumberland, *Thought-Reader's Thoughts*, S. Low, Marston, Searle & Rivington Ltd, London, 1888.
27. *The Times*, 3 March 1922.
28. *Evening News*, 10 November 1888.
29. *Illustrated Mirror*, 29 July 1889.
30. *Trewman's Exeter Flying Post or Plymouth and Cornish Advertiser*, 24 August 1889.
31. *Birmingham Daily Post*, 13 September 1889.
32. *Birmingham Daily Post*, 1 September 1889.
33. Dr Lyttleton Forbes Winslow grew up in the private asylums owned by his father Forbes Benignus Winslow. He would later join his father in practice, and on his father's death took over the running of the asylums. He came to believe that he knew the identity of Jack the Ripper, and believed that, if given a team of six constables, he could catch the murderer. His suspect was G. Wentworth Smith, a Canadian who lodged with a Mr and Mrs Callaghan at 27 Sun Street, Finsbury Square. Smith came under suspicion from Mr Callaghan when he was heard saying that all prostitutes should be drowned. Callaghan took his suspicions to Winslow, who in turn contacted the police. His theory was fully investigated and shown to be without foundation, but this did not stop Winslow, who for many years pestered the authorities with his ideas at every opportunity. Winslow, through his persistence, caused the police to briefly suspect him, and to check on his movements at the time of the Ripper murders.
34. *Trewman's Exeter Flying Post or Plymouth and Cornish Advertiser*, 24 September 1889.
35. *East London Advertiser*, 14 September 1889.
36. *Morning Post*, 11 September 1889.
37. *New York Herald* (London Edition), 11 September 1889.
38. Statement by John Arnold; MEPO 3/140, ff. 162–4 (National Archives).

39. Report by Donald Swanson; MEPO 3/140, ff. 153–7 (National Archives).
40. *Edinburgh Evening News*, 11 September 1889.
41. *New York Herald* (London Edition), 11 September 1889.
42. *Liverpool Mercury*, 25 September 1889.
43. *The Times*, 25 September 1889.
44. *El Tiempo* (Mexico), 30 October 1889.
45. *Penny Illustrated Paper*, 5 October 1889.
46. Report by Inspector Henry Moore, 5 October 1889; MEPO 3/140, ff. 178–80 (National Archives).

Chapter 14: The Fit-Up

1. Casebook: Jack the Ripper (http://www.casebook.org/victims/coles.html).
2. Birth certificate and address given in *Daily News*, 17 February 1891.
3. The surname is given as Cole in the 1861 Census and as Coles in that for 1871.
4. *Bristol Mercury and Daily Post*, 18 February 1891.
5. Register of Deaths, parish of St Olave, September 1878, Vol. 1d, p. 182.
6. *East London Advertiser*, 21 February 1891, reported that James Coles had been living in Bermondsey Workhouse for eight years.
7. *East London Advertiser*, 21 February 1891.
8. *Western Mail*, 17 February 1891.
9. By a strange coincidence a leading Jack the Ripper suspect, Aaron Kosminski, was committed to Leavesden in 1891.
10. *Morning Post*, 25 May 1888.
11. Mrs Hannah Hague, Coles' landlady at 18 Thrawl Street, in a statement to a journalist on 15 February said that that morning she had found beneath the mattress of Coles' bed a bundle of letters from her father and sister and 'a Coroner's order for the old man's attendance at an inquest held on his son, George [*sic*] Coles in 1889, the latter being killed by an accident.' Assuming that George Coles was not a son we do not know about, this was presumably James.
12. *Daily News*, 17 February 1891.
13. Mrs Hague said Coles had been there some seven years.
14. Howard J. Goldsmid, *Dottings of a Dosser: Being revelations of the inner life of low London lodging-houses*, T. Fisher Unwin, London, 1886.
15. First registered on 12 May 1852 and then owned by Patrick Henley, it was taken over in November 1863 by George Wilmott, who owned other lodging houses in Thrawl Street. By 1888 it was owned by Alfred Wood (Register of Common Lodging Houses, London Metropolitan Archives). Mary Ann Nichols had lodged there. It no longer exists.
16. *The Standard*, 20 October 1890.
17. *Daily News*, 14 February 1891, and *East London Observer*, 14 February 1891, respectively. Both are probably mishearings.
18. Report by Sergeant F. Kuhrt concerning the identification of Frances Coles dated 15 February 1891; MEPO 3/140, ff. 119–21 (National Archives).
19. *East London Observer*, 28 March 1891.
20. *Dundee Courier and Argus*, 14 February 1891. She was also said to frequent another lodging house for single women called Sherry's at 5 Thrawl Street (*Daily News*, 14 February 1891).
21. Interview with Sadler, *East London Observer*, 28 March 1891.
22. *The Times*, 28 February 1891.
23. *The Times*, 21 February 1891.
24. Ibid.
25. Ibid.
26. *East London Observer*, 28 March 1891.
27. Ibid.

28. *The Times*, 16 and 17 February 1891.
29. *The Times*, 14 February 1891.
30. Also called Ellen Callana, Colanna and Calman.
31. MEPO 3/140, ff. 86–8 (National Archives), 3 March 1891.
32. *The Times*, 16 February 1891.
33. *The Times*, 21 February 1891.
34. *The Times*, 27 February 1891.
35. According to Sadler, Edwards' account was accurate, although he wasn't sure in which direction he had gone: 'I was so drunk I did not know which way I turned. I thought I turned Leman Street way towards the London hospital, but if he says I turned towards the Minories I would not contradict him' (*Berrow's Worcester Journal*, 21 February 1891).
36. *Eastern Post and City Chronicle*, 14 February 1891.
37. *The Times*, 14 February 1891.
38. For example, Hereward Carrington, 'The Inside Story of "Jack the Ripper" ', *Fate Magazine*, May 1949.
39. *San Francisco Chronicle*, *Manitoba Daily Free Press* (Canada), 14 February 1891.
40. *The Times*, 14 February 1891.
41. For some reason, identified as PC Hinton, 275 H, in a report by Superintendent Thomas Arnold dated 13 February 1891 (MEPO 3/140, ff. 112–14, National Archives).
42. Given as PC Frederick Hyde, 161 H, in a report by Superintendent Thomas Arnold dated 13 February 1891 (MEPO 3/140, ff. 112–14, National Archives).
43. MEPO 3/140, f. 116 (National Archives), 13 February 1891.
44. *East London Advertiser*, 14 February 1891.
45. *The Times*, 14 February 1891.
46. In Colin Wilson and Patricia Pitman, *Encyclopedia of Murder*, Arthur Barker, London, 1961 (p. 303), Colin Wilson misremembered an article in a magazine called *Tit-Bits*, in which General Booth, founder of the Salvation Army, had supposedly theorized that his secretary was Jack the Ripper, on the grounds that the young man was troubled by 'dreams of blood' and had one day told Booth 'Carroty Nell will be the next one to go'. The article, which appeared in *Tit-Bits* on 23 September 1939, was in fact the memoir of a Salvation Army commissioner named David C. Lamb, who recalled that the remark had been made by a visiting sign-writer.
47. *Eastern Post and City Chronicle*, 14 February 1891.
48. *The Times*, 14 February 1891.
49. Some sources give the name as Edward Delaforce Gray.
50. *The Times*, 14 February 1891.
51. *Woodford Times*, 13 February 1891.
52. *Brooklyn Daily Eagle* (New York), 13 February 1891.
53. *Bristol Times and Mirror*, 14 February 1891.
54. *San Francisco Chronicle*, 14 February 1891.
55. *The Times*, 28 February 1891.
56. Report by Sergeant Don about finding James Thomas Sadler, 16 February 1891; MEPO 3/140, ff. 117–18 (National Archives).
57. *Daily Northwestern* (Wisconsin), 16 February 1891.
58. *Lloyd's Weekly Newspaper*, 22 February 1891.
59. Ibid.
60. Bachert did not allow the perceived slight to pass. On Monday, 16 February, by chance he was called to serve on an inquest jury investigating the death of a man named James Evans. Through the day he persisted in badgering Wynne Baxter (*Lloyd's Weekly Newspaper*, 22 February 1891).
61. *East London Advertiser*, 21 February 1891. Report by Sergeant F. Kuhrt concerning the identification of Frances Coles dated 15 February 1891; MEPO 3/140, ff. 119–21 (National Archives).
62. *The Times*, 24 February 1891.

63. *The Times*, 28 February 1891.

64. *East London Observer*, 28 February 1891.

65. *The Times*, 28 February 1891.

66. *Daily Telegraph*, 18 February 1891.

67. See Chapter 5.

68. Reported at Catherine Eddowes' inquest and in reports by Inspector James McWilliam and Chief Inspector Donald Swanson.

69. *The Times*, 17 February 1891.

70. *The Times, Bangor Daily Whig and Courier*, 17 February 1891.

71. *East London Observer*, 28 March 1891.

72. The National Amalgamated Sailors' and Firemen's Union of Great Britain and Ireland was founded in Sunderland in 1887 by Joseph Havelock Wilson. In 1893 it became the National Sailors' and Firemen's Union.

73. *Dundee Courier*, 20 February 1891.

74. *Glasgow Herald*, 20 February 1891.

75. Ibid.

76. Report by Chief Inspector Swanson giving the 'History of Sadler' dated 21 February 1891; MEPO 3/140, ff. 65–74 (National Archives).

77. *The Referee*, 1 March 1891.

78. *Dundee Courier and Argus*, 20 February 1891.

79. *The Times*, 3 March 1891.

80. *East London Observer*, 28 February 1891.

81. *Decatur Daily Republican* (Illinois), 26 February 1891.

82. *The Times*, 4 March 1891.

83. Report by Inspector Henry Moore dated 3 March 1891; MEPO 3/140 ff. 86–8 (National Archives); *The Times*, 4 March 1891.

84. *East London Observer*, 28 March 1891.

85. Report dated 1 January 1892 by Sergeant Boswell about Sadler and his wife; MEPO 3/140, ff. 94–5 (National Archives).

86. Report by Chief Inspector Donald S. Swanson dated 11 December 1891 concerning an assault by Sadler on his wife; MEPO 3/140, ff. 89–90 (National Archives).

87. Report by Sergeant Boswell dated 16 May 1892; MEPO 3/140, f. 110 (National Archives).

Chapter 15: American Swansong?

1. *Daily Northwestern* (Wisconsin), 3 October 1888.

2. The Battle of Bull Run was the first major Civil War land-battle of the armies in Virginia, in 1861.

3. *The Star*, 4 October 1888.

4. The prostitutes of Corlears Hook were later referred to as 'hookers'.

5. Edwin Francis Hatfield and Samuel Hanson Cox, *Patient Continuance in Well-doing: A memoir of Elihu W. Baldwin*, J. Leavitt, New York, 1843.

6. *Brooklyn Daily Eagle* (New York), 25 April 1891.

7. *Stevens Point Daily Journal* (Wisconsin), 2 May 1891.

8. *Brooklyn Daily Eagle* (New York), 25 April 1891.

9. *Qu'Appelle Vidette* (Canada), 7 May 1891.

10. *Brooklyn Daily Eagle* (New York), 25 April 1891.

11. *Decatur Daily Republican* (Illinois), 25 April 1891. Called 'C. Nicholi' in the *Stevens Point Daily Journal* (Wisconsin), 2 May 1891.

12. *Brooklyn Daily Eagle* (New York), 24 April 1891.

13. *Brooklyn Daily Eagle* (New York), 25 April 1891.

14. *Arizona Republican*, 25 April 1891.

15. As stated on the death certificate.

16. *Brooklyn Daily Eagle* (USA), 25 April 1891.
17. The age is given as written on the death certificate. However, as there is no date or place of birth on the certificate, it is impossible to state whether this age is accurate or not.
18. *Manitoba Daily Free Press* (Canada), 27 April 1891.
19. *Brooklyn Daily Eagle* (New York), 26 April 1891.
20. *Trenton Times* (New Jersey), 27 April 1891.
21. While searching the hotel, the detectives came upon Mary Healey, who had been seen drinking with Carrie Brown shortly before she was killed. Healey was found in Room 12 and was so drunk that she was not able to make any kind of statement.
22. *New York World*, 25 April 1891.
23. *Brooklyn Daily Eagle* (New York), 26 April 1891.
24. *Arizona Republican*, 26 April 1891.
25. *Brooklyn Daily Eagle* (New York), 27 April 1891.
26. *Chicago Tribune*, 25 April 1891.
27. *Manitoba Daily Free Press* (Canada), 27 April 1891.
28. *New York Herald*, 27 April 1891.
29. *Fort Wayne Morning Journal* (Indiana), 28 April 1891.
30. *Fort Wayne Morning Journal*, 28 April 1891.
31. *Portsmouth Evening News*, 3 July 1891.
32. This point was picked up a few years later in an article entitled 'Cannot Disguise It': 'In microscopy Mr. Ewell hangs firmly to the theory that it is impossible to decide between the blood stains made with fluid from warm blooded animals. The microscopes can always tell whether or not suspected stains are blood, but there is no way of determining whether or not the blood once flowed through a human's veins. Mr. Ewell firmly holds to the belief that the Syrian who was convicted as Jack the Ripper in New York some years ago was the victim of improper expert testimony, one Philadelphia physician swearing that the blood found beneath the finger nails of the suspect was human. He offered his services to the attorneys for the defense after the fellow was convicted, but they would not move for an appeal' (*Trenton Times*, 12 September 1894).
33. *Portsmouth Evening News*, 3 July 1891.
34. *Daily Gazette and Bulletin* (Pennsylvania), 11 July 1891.
35. *Sheffield Independent*, 6 July 1891.
36. *Arizona Republican*, 19 August 1891.
37. *Middletown Daily Times* (New York), 1 February 1892.
38. Lentz was eventually arrested in Summit, New Jersey, in 1909 after a brutal attack on a friend. Lentz smashed his friend in the head three times with a shovel, threw him down a flight of stairs, hit him again in the head with a club and finally stabbed him. The friend survived and Lentz was arrested. This assault was an attempted robbery and strongly indicated the type of violence he was capable of when robbing his victims.
39. R. Michael Gordon, *The American Murders of Jack the Ripper*, Praeger, New York, 2003; Trevor Marriott, *Jack the Ripper: The 21st-century investigation*, John Blake, London, 2005.

Afterword

1. *East London Advertiser*, 2–18 September 1988.
2. These photographs, once the property of an unnamed former police officer, were the mortuary photographs of Mary Ann Nichols, Annie Chapman, Elizabeth Stride and a second crime-scene photo of Mary Kelly. Their return sparked considerable press attention at the time.
3. *East London Advertiser*, 23 September 1988.
4. *East London Advertiser*, 4 September 2013.

5. Although partly published in Tom Cullen's *Autumn of Terror*, it first appeared in its entirety in Robin Odell, *Jack the Ripper in Fact and Fiction*, Harrap, London, 1965; Mayflower-Dell, London, 1966; Mandrake, London, 2008.

6. Edwin T. Woodhall, *Jack the Ripper: Or when London walked in terror*, Mellifont Press, London, 1937; P & D Riley, Runcorn, 1997.

7. Donald Rumbelow, *The Complete Jack the Ripper*, Virgin Books, London, 2013 (originally published in 1975 by W. H. Allen).

8. M. J. Trow, *Jack the Ripper: Quest for a killer*, Pen and Sword, London, 2009.

9. Interview in the *Pall Mall Gazette*, 24 March 1903.

10. Gordon, *The American Murders of Jack the Ripper*.

11. Marriott, *Jack the Ripper: The 21st-century investigation*.

12. The Whitechapel Society 1888 is an organization that promotes the study of Jack the Ripper and the social impact of the Whitechapel murders on the East End.

13. Mary Ann Austin died on 26 May 1901 from stab wounds received while staying at Crossingham's lodging house at 35 Dorset Street; Kitty Ronan was found with her throat cut in Room 20, Miller's Court on 2 July 1909. Neither murder has been linked to Jack the Ripper.

List of Illustrations

Acknowledgements

AUTHORS FREQUENTLY GIVE THANKS TO THEIR EDITOR, AND NO doubt it is often deserved; but it is never more merited than in the case of our editor, Heather McCallum, whose good humour, understanding and unending patience during the long development of this book must surely be unsurpassable.

Other people we would like to thank are: Debra Arif, Neil Bell, Robert Clack, Michael Conlon, Patricia Cornwell, Martin Fido, Christopher T. George, the late Wilf Gregg, Loretta Lay, Clive Liddiard, Donald Rumbelow, Chris Scott, Keith Skinner, Adam Wood, Eduardo Zinna, and all the researchers who share the fruits of their labours on the various Jack the Ripper internet message boards.

Index